# The
# EVERYTHING.
# Low-Cholesterol Cookbook

Dear Reader,

My father has had high blood pressure all of his adult life, and he had angio-plasty surgery years ago. So I grew up learning to leave salt out of recipes and making an effort to cook with lower-fat, lower-sodium foods. I read labels and try to include as many whole grains, fruits, and vegetables in my cooking as possible.

There is a lot of controversy about which fats are healthy and which are bad for us. There is consensus on only one issue: Trans fats should be avoided whenever possible. These artificial fats raise LDL cholesterol, lower HDL cholesterol, and change cell function. The standard recommendation is to reduce saturated fats along with overall fat content, and that is what this book advises. Some researchers think saturated fats aren't as bad for you as once thought, but that controversy is explained in another book, *The Everything® No Trans Fat Cookbook*.

If your doctor has informed you that you have high cholesterol and a poor HDL/LDL ratio, this book will help you get back on track. The recipes are all developed with low sodium, lower fat, healthier fats, nutrient density, and fiber in mind. It's not easy to make a change in your dietary habits, but it's more possible when the foods you eat are still delicious and satisfying.

I hope that you enjoy the recipes in this book and that the changes you make in your diet and lifestyle make you a healthier, happier person.

*Linda Larsen*

# Welcome to the EVERYTHING Series!

These handy, accessible books give you all you need to tackle a difficult project, gain a new hobby, comprehend a fascinating topic, prepare for an exam, or even brush up on something you learned back in school but have since forgotten.

You can read an *Everything*® book from cover to cover or just pick out the information you want from our four useful boxes: e-questions, e-facts, e-alerts, e-ssentials. We give you everything you need to know on the subject, but throw in a lot of fun stuff along the way, too.

We now have more than 400 *Everything*® books in print, spanning such wide-ranging categories as weddings, pregnancy, cooking, music instruction, foreign language, crafts, pets, New Age, and so much more. When you're done reading them all, you can finally say you know *Everything*®!

**QUESTIONS?**

Answers to
common questions

**FACTS**

Important snippets
of information

**ALERTS!**

Urgent
warnings

**ESSENTIALS**

Quick
handy tips

## Editorial

Director of Innovation: Paula Munier

Editorial Director: Laura M. Daly

Executive Editor, Series Books: Brielle K. Matson

Associate Copy Chief: Sheila Zwiebel

Acquisitions Editor: Kerry Smith

Development Editor: Brett Palana-Shanahan

Production Editor: Casey Ebert

## Production

Director of Manufacturing: Susan Beale

Production Project Manager: Michelle Roy Kelly

Prepress: Erick DaCosta, Matt LeBlanc

Design Manager: Heather Blank

Senior Book Designer: Colleen Cunningham

Interior Layout: Heather Barrett, Brewster Brownville

*Visit the entire Everything® series at* www.everything.com

# THE
# EVERYTHING®
# LOW-CHOLESTEROL
# COOKBOOK

Lower your LDL with these
delicious, low-fat meals
your whole family will love!

Linda Larsen
The About.com Guide for Busy Cooks

Avon, Massachusetts

To the memory of my grandfathers,
Stanley T. Johnson and Louis Mork.

An Everything® Series Book.
Everything® and everything.com® are registered trademarks of F+W Publications, Inc.

Published by Adams Media, an F+W Publications Company
57 Littlefield Street, Avon, MA 02322. U.S.A.
*www.adamsmedia.com*

ISBN 10: 1-59869-401-4
ISBN 13: 978-1-59869-401-7
Printed in the United States of America.

J  I  H  G  F  E  D  C  B  A

**Library of Congress Cataloging-in-Publication Data**
available from the publisher.

This publication is designed to provide accurate and authoritative information with regard to the subject matter covered. It is sold with the understanding that the publisher is not engaged in rendering legal, accounting, or other professional advice. If legal advice or other expert assistance is required, the services of a competent professional person should be sought.
> —From a *Declaration of Principles* jointly adopted by a Committee of the American Bar Association and a Committee of Publishers and Associations

Many of the designations used by manufacturers and sellers to distinguish their products are claimed as trademarks. Where those designations appear in this book and Adams Media was aware of a trademark claim, the designations have been printed with initial capital letters.

*The Everything® Low-Cholesterol Cookbook* is intended as a reference volume only, not as a medical manual. In light of the complex, individual, and specific nature of health problems, this book is not intended to replace professional medical advice. The ideas, procedures, and suggestions in this book are intended to supplement, not replace, the advice of a trained medical professional. Consult your physician before adopting the suggestions in this book, as well as about any condition that may require diagnosis or medical attention. The author and publisher disclaim any liability arising directly or indirectly from the use of this book.

*This book is available at quantity discounts for bulk purchases.*
*For information, please call 1-800-289-0963.*

# Contents

# Acknowledgments

Thanks to my parents, Duane and Marlene, for insisting that I learn to cook healthy foods and for giving me free rein in the kitchen. I'd like to thank my agent, Barb Doyen, for her unwavering support, and my editor, Kerry Smith, for her encouragement. And, as always, thanks to Doug, my dear husband, for his strength and love.

# Introduction

Cholesterol and its effect on your body, especially your heart, is a complicated topic. This book breaks it down into easily understandable sections, explains the different components and variables, and then tells you what you can do to reduce cholesterol levels and improve your health.

The foods you eat and the way you move your body have a huge impact on your health. Cholesterol blood levels can be reduced quite easily with some basic changes. And the best part is that the foods that reduce cholesterol and triglycerides are delicious and easy to cook.

Believe it or not, diets can be too low in fat. Your body needs fat to transport nutrients around the body, to maintain a consistent body temperature, to protect your organs, and to provide quick energy. If you aren't eating enough fat, you may be more tired, develop more infections and illnesses, and become deficient in vitamins and minerals.

Eating the right kind of fat, in the right quantities, is essential. If a recipe is slightly higher in fat than you'd like, look at the type of fat used. If it comes from extra-virgin olive oil, nuts, seeds, or vegetables, don't be afraid of that extra bit of fat. These monounsaturated fats are very healthy and actually raise HDL cholesterol levels.

Read labels carefully. For a food to be labeled "cholesterol free," it must have less than 2 mg of cholesterol per serving. A "low cholesterol" food has less than 20 mg per serving. A "sodium free" food has less than 5 mg of sodium per serving, and a "low sodium" food has less than 140 mg per serving. A "high fiber" food has 5 grams of fiber or more per serving. A food labeled "low saturated fat" must have 1 gram or less of saturated fat per serving. And a "low fat" food has 3 grams or less of fat per serving.

All of the recipes in this book have less than 100 mg of cholesterol per serving. Most have much less than that, and many have none at all. You have the option of using butter or plant sterol margarines in these recipes; all of the nutrition calculations are figured using butter.

As with all health and nutrition advice, check with your doctor before changing your diet or adding exercise. Practice moderation in all things. If you eat a colorful diet, exercise moderately, and don't smoke, you will increase your odds of living a healthy life.

And remember that medical research is always discovering new information. Many people are tempted to throw up their hands and forget the whole thing when they hear that a food once thought good for you is not. But science doesn't proceed in a straight line. If you stick to fresh, whole foods, regular exercise, and a healthy lifestyle, you are doing all you can to promote good health. Take the latest research with a grain of salt.

# Chapter 1
## Cholesterol and You

Cholesterol is mentioned on a daily basis in the media and in ordinary conversations. But what is cholesterol? Why are high levels undesirable? What can you do to lower your cholesterol levels? Cholesterol levels are only one part of the battle against heart disease, the number-one killer of Americans. But cholesterol is a factor that you can address by changing your diet, adding healthy foods, and exercising more. Small changes will add up quickly, and your health will improve within months if you understand and follow American Heart Association and USDA guidelines.

# What Is Cholesterol?

Cholesterol is a combination of two acetate molecules that join to form a waxy substance. It is found in animals because it's produced by the liver. Plants do not have any cholesterol. It is needed by the body to produce hormones and steroids and is used in the production of cell membranes. We need cholesterol to live.

But the amount of cholesterol in our bodies, and the balance between the two main types of cholesterol and other molecules like homocysteine, triglycerides, and free radicals, can predict whether we are at risk for diseases like atherosclerosis, heart disease, or stroke. Too much of the wrong kind of cholesterol can increase the risk of disease. And the way cholesterol interacts with other substances in the body increases disease risk, too.

| Table 1-1 | | | |
|---|---|---|---|
| **Cholesterol and Fat in Foods (Before Cooking)** | | | |
| **Food** | **Total Fat** | **Saturated Fat** | **Cholesterol** |
| Chicken breast (4 ounces) | 4.05 grams | 1.15 grams | 96.39 mg |
| Flank steak (4 ounces) | 9.37 grams | 3.89 grams | 46.33 mg |
| Ground beef (4 ounces; 85 percent lean) | 16.80 grams | 6.57 grams | 76.16 mg |
| Shrimp (4 ounces) | 1.96 grams | 0.37 grams | 172.27 mg |
| Salmon (4 ounces) | 12.30 grams | 2.47 grams | 66.87 mg |
| Ground turkey (4 ounces) | 9.42 grams | 2.56 grams | 90.06 mg |
| Pork tenderloin (4 ounces) | 6.14 grams | 2.12 grams | 74.84 mg |
| Olive oil (1 tablespoon) | 13.50 grams | 1.86 grams | 0.0 mg |
| Almonds (¼ cup) | 18.42 grams | 1.42 grams | 0.0 mg |
| Egg yolk (large) | 4.51 grams | 1.62 grams | 209.78 mg |

Cholesterol must combine with a protein and a fat in order to travel through the bloodstream. These combinations of molecules are called lipoproteins. There are two main types of lipoproteins: high-density and low-density (also known as HDL and LDL).

Total cholesterol levels of up to 200 mg/dL (milligrams per decaliter) are considered normal. Depending on your health and other risk factors, your doctor may want this level to be lower. If your level falls between 200 and 239 mg/dL, you'll want to evaluate your LDL/HDL ratio. The American Heart Association has different recommendations for tests and treatment depending on the combination of these factors.

Cholesterol levels will vary depending on your genetics, age, and even gender. The levels rise as we age. Men usually have higher levels than premenopausal women, but after menopause women's cholesterol counts increase.

## HDL Cholesterol

HDL, or high density lipoprotein, is known as the "good" cholesterol because it removes LDL cholesterol from the bloodstream and takes it to the liver to be metabolized into bile salts and excreted. This type of cholesterol may actually scour your arteries, helping remove LDL cholesterol and reducing atherosclerosis and plaque formation. Here are some foods that increase HDL levels:

- Olive oil
- Nuts
- Avocados
- Peanut butter
- High-fiber foods
- Moderate alcohol consumption
- Dried beans
- Whole grains
- Citrus fruits
- Dark chocolate

For a healthy body, your HDL cholesterol levels should be above 40 mg/dL. Fortunately, your diet and lifestyle, including the right foods and exercise, can have a significant impact on HDL levels.

## LDL Cholesterol

LDL, or low density lipoprotein, is known as the "bad" cholesterol because it transports cholesterol from the liver to the bloodstream. Research indicates that plaque, which can form on arterial walls and narrow the arteries, may be filled with LDL cholesterol. Here are some foods that reduce LDL levels:

- Oatmeal and oat bran
- Orange juice
- Apples
- Walnuts and almonds
- Flaxseed
- Fatty fish
- Legumes
- Barley
- Cherries
- Vegetables

Your LDL cholesterol levels should be less than 100 mg/dL. Over 160 mg/dL is considered high. The level of this type of cholesterol responds well to changes in diet and the addition of exercise.

## The Total/HDL Cholesterol Proportion

The proportion of total cholesterol to HDL in your blood is an important risk predictor for heart disease. To calculate this, divide your total cholesterol level by your HDL level. The ratio you want to reach is below 3.5 to 1. Anything about 5 to 1 or higher indicates an increased risk of heart disease.

# Factors That Affect Cholesterol

There are other fats, hormones, and molecules in your blood that can affect your risk of heart disease. There are blood tests available for all of them. If you have more than one risk factor for heart disease, ask your doctor about tests for these factors.

## Homocysteine

Homocysteine is a protein, or amino acid, which is usually made from the meat you eat when you are deficient in B vitamins. If blood levels of this molecule are too high, the interior artery walls will be damaged, increasing the probability of blood clots. Homocysteine auto-oxides in the blood, creating free radicals.

What you eat can have a big impact on your homocysteine levels. Folate, a B vitamin present in whole grains, cereals, oranges, broccoli, beets, and nuts, can help reduce homocysteine levels in the blood. Vitamin supplements containing folic acid (a synthetic variation of folate) are beneficial as well.

If you have a personal or family history of heart disease but don't have any other major risk factors (like smoking, obesity, high blood pressure, or high cholesterol levels), your doctor should check your homocysteine levels.

## Triglycerides

Triglycerides are the fats present in your bloodstream. When you eat more calories than your body can burn, these molecules are transformed into triglycerides and stored in fat cells.

Cholesterol is present in every cell in your body. In fact 10 to 20 percent of your brain tissue is made up of cholesterol. You need cholesterol to produce bile salts, which emulsify fats in the intestines. All of your cell membranes need cholesterol for permeability and to function properly. Finally, cholesterol is used to made vitamin D.

A diet very high in carbohydrates, especially simple carbs, may cause high triglyceride levels. High triglyceride levels are usually associated with generally high cholesterol levels and an increased risk of heart disease.

Normal triglyceride levels are 150 milligrams per decaliter (mg/dL), based on a fasting blood test. If you have uncontrolled diabetes, your triglyceride level will probably be very high, over 1000 mg/dL, and must be controlled.

## Genetic Factors

There are a few compounds that may be influenced by genetic factors, which diet and exercise cannot help. If your blood cholesterol tests reveal that you have these compounds, talk to your doctor about prescription drugs that may help.

Very low density cholesterol, or VLDL, is a form of LDL cholesterol that is particularly harmful to your body. These molecules are smaller and denser than LDL cholesterol and have the highest amounts of triglycerides. Their level in the blood can't be directly measured, so is estimated as a percentage of triglyceride levels. The effects of this compound and how to control levels are being studied.

Lowering your cholesterol even by a small amount can have an impact on your health. Studies have shown that when cholesterol levels are lowered by 1 percent, there is a 2-percent decrease in the risk of heart disease. These encouraging numbers can help keep you motivated and stick to a plan.

Lp(a) cholesterol is a genetic variation of LDL cholesterol. A high level of this cholesterol is considered a significant risk factor for heart disease. Researchers are just beginning to study this molecule. It may cause fatty deposits to build up on artery walls, increasing the risk of a blood clot.

This molecule is very susceptible to oxidation, which is a process similar to rusting. Worse, the body may confuse Lp(a) cholesterol with plasminogen, a compound that helps break down blood clots, with disastrous results.

# When Cholesterol Is Too High

Cholesterol and triglyceride levels are just a part of the coronary heart disease (CHD) equation. Other important factors can be controlled with diet and exercise. The way cholesterol behaves in your body is affected by several factors.

## Inflammation

Some researchers believe that heart disease is an inflammatory disease. That means that the walls of arteries and veins are irritated, or inflamed, by free radicals and other compounds like cigarette smoke and food preservatives and additives. Your doctor can actually gauge inflammation by measuring C-reactive protein (CRP) in the blood. High CRP levels along with high cholesterol indicate a dramatically increased risk of heart disease.

When LDL cholesterol is transported to the arteries, it may be acting as a steroid, trying to help reduce the inflammation. So having a high LDL cholesterol level may indicate inflammation in your arteries. Here are some foods and spices that fight inflammation:

- Omega-3 fatty acids
- Blueberries
- Leafy greens
- Olive oil
- Fatty fish
- Curry powder
- Ginger
- Dark chocolate
- Green tea
- Nuts

Eating foods that help reduce inflammation may be one way to help prevent the risk of heart disease. Foods that contain antioxidants, phytochemicals, and that are high in fiber can all help reduce inflammation in your body.

## Plaque

Inflammation can lead to the formation of plaque in the artery walls. Plaque is a combination of fats, cholesterol, and components that clot blood. Over time, hardened (or healed) plaque can build up and restrict or even stop blood flow; this is what causes 30 percent of heart attacks.

Scientists have discovered that many heart attacks are caused by soft, or vulnerable, plaque. Other factors like high blood pressure can make the plaque covering burst or crack, causing an injury to the artery wall. The body responds by forming a blood clot, which can break free and cause a heart attack.

Soft plaque is filled with LDL cholesterol. Reducing LDL cholesterol, eating for good health, engaging in moderate exercise, and taking prescription drugs can all help slow plaque formation.

## Oxidation

Research shows that cholesterol that has oxidized becomes much more dangerous. Oxidation occurs when free radicals, which are unstable molecules missing an electron, take an electron from a cholesterol molecule, creating oxysterols. These then attack blood vessels, promoting lesions and fatty streaks. To fight this, consume foods high in antioxidants. These compounds, including beta-carotene and vitamin E, react or bind with the free radicals, stopping the oxidation reaction in its tracks. Foods high in antioxidants include:

- Berries
- Broccoli
- Tomatoes
- Garlic
- Red grapes
- Whole grains
- Cinnamon
- Carrots

Where do free radicals come from? Scientists think that pollutants like lead, pesticides, cigarette smoke, and alcohol all increase the production of free radicals. Basic chemical reactions in the body produce free radicals. Also, factors like stress, sunlight, pesticides, and food preservatives increase the production of free radicals.

Free radicals are present in every body, and they are produced in greater numbers as we age. Accumulation of free radicals is considered a major reason our bodies age and deteriorate over time.

# Risk Factors

Everyone's risk factors for heart disease are different. Some people can eat lots of saturated fats and cholesterol and still have excellent HDL/LDL ratios and blood cholesterol levels. Others react strongly to food and quickly develop problems. It's important to understand your personal risk factors in order to tackle the problem with the right combination of diet, exercise, and prescription medications.

## Family History

Family history is one of the most important indicators or predictors of who will develop heart disease. Your genes determined how much cholesterol your body produces every day. That's why a recent commercial for a cholesterol-lowering drug quips about getting cholesterol "from lemon pie and your Uncle Lem." You can't do anything about genetics, but you can optimize your health by the way you treat your body.

Every day, your liver produces between 800 to 1000 milligrams of cholesterol, far more than you could possibly eat. Because cholesterol is an essential compound for life, your body makes sure it always has enough. You don't need to eat any cholesterol at all; your body makes enough for good health.

There is a genetic mutation called familial hypercholesterolemia in which the body naturally produces much more LDL cholesterol, despite diet and exercise. People with this mutation must usually depend on prescription drugs to help control cholesterol levels.

## Smoking

Do not smoke. If you do smoke, quit as soon as possible. Smoking raises LDL cholesterol levels and reduces HDL levels. It also contributes to inflammation. Cigarette smoke contains more than 4,000 chemicals, including at least 43 class-C carcinogens. It also increases the blood's clotting system, which can lead to thrombosis and heart attack or stroke.

## Trans Fats Consumption

Trans fats are a completely artificial food made by adding hydrogen molecules to polyunsaturated fats. The resulting molecule is not recognized as a foreign object by the body and is incorporated into everything from cell membranes to hormones. This changes the function of those parts of your body, which has an effect on your health.

Trans fats raise the LDL cholesterol level and should be avoided. Eat fresh foods, including lots of fruits, lean meats and dairy products, whole grains, and vegetables. Avoid processed foods and fast foods, and learn to read labels. If the ingredient list contains the word *hydrogenated*, that food contains trans fat, even if the label states "0 grams trans fat per serving."

## Sedentary Lifestyle

Even adding mild to moderate exercise to your weekly routine will help reduce LDL cholesterol and increase HDL levels. The AHA recommends thirty minutes of moderate exercise, five times a week. You don't have to exercise for a straight thirty minutes, however. Break it up into three ten-minute sessions for the same health benefit.

Make sure that you have your doctor's approval before you begin an exercise program. Start off slow. Nothing kills your resolve more than very sore muscles after a too-strenuous workout. Your goal is to be able to exercise the next day.

## Obesity

Maintain or achieve a normal weight and BMI level. Look at charts available from insurance companies and compare your height to the weight ranges. If you are carrying more than 20 percent above the highest weight for your height, you are considered overweight. If that percentage climbs to 30, you are considered obese.

## Sodium

Americans have a love affair with salt. We eat far too much sodium. One problem is that salt is present in so many processed foods and in restaurant cooking. This "invisible" salt is usually more than enough to meet our daily requirements.

It's difficult to reduce sodium in the diet simply because it's present naturally in so many foods and is used in great quantities in processed foods. Carefully read labels, and keep a running total of the sodium you consume in one day. You'll be surprised at the total number!

If you really love the taste of salt, try sprinkling a very small amount directly on the food just before you eat. This way the salt will hit your taste buds quickly and the food will taste saltier. Herbs, spices, and acidic ingredients like lemon and vinegar are all good substitutes for salt.

Studies have shown that people on a low-salt diet have a lower risk of heart disease and a 20-percent lower chance of dying of a heart attack. Changing to a low-salt diet will take some research and effort. This may be difficult at first because our taste buds are used to salt; in fact, humans start craving salt at the age of four months. But after a while, you'll find that food tastes better with less salt, and many processed foods will taste too salty.

## Poor Diet

A diet composed largely of processed foods and minimal amounts of fruits and vegetables contributes to the development of heart disease. Most Americans do not eat the USDA recommended daily amount of produce and whole grains. With our busy lifestyles, we turn to fast foods and highly processed foods to save time. As we have turned away from whole foods, our health has deteriorated.

# The Best Dietary Habits

It's not enough to just eat low-fat foods or foods low in cholesterol. Many foods help combat the different variables that influence disease. The foods you choose to eat can reduce weight, maintain weight loss, fight inflammation and oxidation, and remove cholesterol from your bloodstream.

You will feel and look better and your health will improve, no matter how unfit you are when you start. It just takes a little knowledge, some effort, and determination to change your lifestyle and eating habits.

## The Rainbow Rule

The main rule is to make your plate as colorful as possible. If your food includes most of the colors of the rainbow, you can be confident that you are eating a well-balanced and nutritious diet. Red foods, including strawberries and red peppers; orange foods, including carrots; yellow foods, like corn and squash; green foods, such as kale and spinach; and blue foods, including blueberries and grapes, should all be eaten in good quantities every day.

The recommended daily allowance for fruits and vegetables is at least five to nine servings a day, and even more is better. A serving isn't as large as people think. It's one medium fruit or one cup of raw small fruits, half a cup of cooked vegetables, three-quarters of a cup of juice, one cup of leafy greens, or one cup of raw vegetables. It's easy to "sneak" vegetables and fruits into recipes, too. Add shredded carrots to a spaghetti sauce, make banana bread, and freeze fruit juices into popsicles for your kids.

**ALERT!**

Almost 20 percent of Americans don't eat any fruits or vegetables at all! Most of us fall short of the recommended daily allowances for fruits and vegetables, but this group is at high risk for poor health. It's not difficult to eat a serving of fruit; three-quarters of a cup of orange juice or one cup of blueberries is one serving.

## Eat More Fiber

There are two kinds of dietary fiber in the foods you eat: soluble and insoluble. Soluble fiber, which dissolves in water, is key to reducing LDL cholesterol levels. Doctors think that it works by absorbing bile salts in the intestines. The body reacts by removing cholesterol from the bloodstream to create more bile salts.

It's important to eat at least 5 to 10 grams of soluble fiber a day. You can get this amount from your diet if you eat the American Dietetic Association–recommended 25 to 30 grams of dietary fiber a day. A vegetarian diet can supply even more fiber. Dietary fiber comes from fruits, vegetables, whole grains, and legumes.

Soluble fiber is found in foods like oat bran, apples, strawberries, citrus fruit, rice bran, barley, beans, and peas. Insoluble fiber, which doesn't seem to affect cholesterol but helps you feel full and keeps you regular, is found in most whole grains as well as carrots, cauliflower, apple skin, and beets. A high-fiber food has 5 grams or more of fiber per serving. A food that has more than 2.5 grams of fiber per serving is considered a "good source" of fiber.

## Eat Healthy Fats

Doctors are realizing that the best diet isn't one that's simply low in fat but one that is rich in healthy fats. Monounsaturated fats are the best choice for your health. You should include oils like extra-virgin olive oil, unrefined safflower oil, nuts, and avocados in your diet.

Omega-3 fatty acids, found primarily in fatty fish, walnuts, soybeans, tofu, and flaxseed, are another fat you should be eating. Most Americans are deficient in omega-3 fats and eat too much omega-6, which are found in polyunsaturated oils. The balance between omega-3 and omega-6 is critical to health. Stressing monounsaturated fat consumption can help improve this balance.

**FACT**

The Mediterranean diet is considered one of the healthiest diets in the world. It is rich in fruits, vegetables, whole grains, and monounsaturated fats. It is not a low-fat diet but a healthy fat diet. There may be other factors at play in the lower heart-disease rates in the region, including more physical exercise and a more relaxed lifestyle, but eating these foods is a good place to start.

Most doctors, as well as the American Heart Association, believe that saturated fats, found in meats, butter, and tropical oils, are bad for your health and may increase LDL cholesterol levels. If your doctor tells you to avoid saturated fat, listen to her. It's important, however, to eat monounsaturated and, to a lesser extent, polyunsaturated fats for the best health. You should consume about 30 to 40 percent of your daily calories from fat. On a 2,000-calorie-per-day diet, that means about 50 to 60 grams of total fat and 20 grams of saturated fat, less for those with risk factors for heart disease.

## Include Antioxidants

Antioxidants are molecules that trap free radicals in your body so they can't cause cell damage and make cholesterol more harmful. Once again, these are found primarily in fresh fruits and vegetables. These molecules not only help reduce LDL cholesterol oxidation, but also help prevent the effects of aging.

## What to Eat

Luckily, there are many foods that are good for you, help lower cholesterol levels, and taste great too. Start thinking about using whole foods, not processed foods. Here's a good rule: If your great-grandmother wouldn't have recognized it as a food, don't eat it.

Fresh fruits and vegetables, whole grains, lean meats, good oils like olive oil and avocados, nuts, leafy greens, and low-fat dairy products are all delicious and good for you. You'll find that as you include these foods in your diet, you will lose weight, have more energy, and have smoother skin, brighter eyes, and stronger bones.

## The Best Foods

Some foods have even more effect on cholesterol levels and health than others. Honey has the same amount of antioxidants as spinach, apples, and oranges. Nuts, especially almonds, walnuts, and hazelnuts, are a powerful weapon against heart disease. A handful a day provides you with soluble fiber, antioxidants, omega-3 fatty acids, and monounsaturated fats.

Fish, especially cold-water fish like salmon, tuna, trout, mackerel, and sardines, are full of omega-3 fatty acids. But you have to be careful to limit consumption in some cases. Children and pregnant or nursing women should limit consumption of tuna, red snapper, and orange roughy, since these fish can be high in mercury contamination.

Flaxseed is rich in lignan, an antioxidant, and the omega-3 fatty acid linolenic acid, which lowers total and LDL cholesterol levels. You can add the whole seed to baked goods, and sprinkle it on yogurt or ice cream. You can also consume it in the form of flaxseed oil.

Apples contain a good amount of soluble and insoluble fiber, including pectin, which can help lower cholesterol. In fact, eating one large apple a day can lower cholesterol levels by about 10 percent. Apples also contain a flavonoid called quercetin, which reduces the risk of heart disease with antioxidant and anti-inflammatory activity.

In the 1980s, scientists thought oatmeal, especially oat bran, was the answer to fighting heart disease. Oats contain beta-glucan, a soluble fiber that is quite effective in lowering LDL cholesterol. As it turns out, oat bran is not a magic bullet, but is an important food to include in your diet. Beta-glucan is also found in barley.

## Table 1-2

## Antioxidant Capacity and Fiber in Good Foods per Serving[†]

| Food | Antioxidant Capacity* | Fiber |
|------|----------------------|-------|
| Red beans | 13,727 | 8 grams |
| Pinto beans | 11,864 | 12 grams |
| Blueberries | 9,019 | 3.5 grams |
| Artichoke heart | 7,904 | 9 grams |
| Prunes | 7,291 | 12 grams |
| Red apple | 5,900 | 5 grams |
| Russet potato | 4,649 | 6.5 grams |
| Avocado | 3,344 | 9.2 grams |
| Orange | 2,540 | 3.1 grams |
| Red grapes | 2,016 | 1.4 grams |

[†]Serving size is 1 cup cooked beans, 1 cup small or chopped fruits and vegetables, and one medium fruit or vegetable.

*Antioxidant capacity is measured in a test tube; reactions may be different in the body. However, antioxidant capacity is a good indicator of health benefits.

When you consume meat, especially red meat, think about using it as a flavoring or an addition to foods rather than the main course. A stir-fry with half the beef that the recipe normally calls for, with lots of fresh vegetables like onions, garlic, peppers, and beans, will satisfy meat cravings in a healthy way.

## What about Eggs?

Eggs are the exception to the rule. The American Heart Association's guidelines now state that people with normal cholesterol levels can eat one egg a day. Yes, an egg yolk contains 213 mg of cholesterol. But it's also rich in other nutrients and is a good source of high-quality protein.

When you do buy eggs, look for those that have been specially developed and bred to contain more omega-3 fatty acids that help reduce inflammation. Brands like Christopher's Eggs and Eggland's Best are good choices. Be sure to read labels carefully and still limit your egg yolk consumption to one per day or less.

## Plant Sterol Margarines

The saturated fat content in butter does seem to raise cholesterol levels, according to research. If you do have high cholesterol, you can substitute margarines enhanced with plant sterols for butter in cooking. Some brand names include Benecol and Take Control.

Be sure that the product says that it can be used in baking before trying it in breads, cookies, or cakes. And if you do not have high cholesterol levels, do not use these products. Plant sterols seem to work by competing with cholesterol in the intestines for inclusion in the compounds that transport cholesterol to the bloodstream.

**QUESTION?**

**Are there miracle foods?**
Every so often, research will point to a promising single food or ingredient that lowers cholesterol in controlled studies, like oatmeal or apples. And every time, the food turned out to not be the magic bullet everyone is looking for. Definitely include those foods in your diet, but don't count on a miracle food that will solve the problem.

Butter, in small amounts, does add great flavor to foods without too much saturated fat per serving. In fact, adding a bit of butter or other fats to cooked vegetables helps increase vitamin absorption. Use it as a garnish: Add a teaspoon to vegetables just before serving, brush on breads just out of the oven, and use it to finish sauces.

## Foods to Avoid

There are many foods that you should avoid if you are trying to control and improve cholesterol and triglycerides. Processed meats, fast food, and foods containing trans fat should not be part of your diet. Cut down on the number of sugar-sweetened foods you eat, and reduce the sugar in the recipes you already have. Most recipes still work well with half to two-thirds the amount of sugar called for.

Remember that unless your body increases blood cholesterol levels when you eat cholesterol in foods, it's most important to reduce saturated fat. When looking for the right foods to eat, consider saturated fat first, then the cholesterol amount.

Avoid saturated fats, especially in red meats. These meats can be inflammatory as well, so choose leaner cuts and try to find grass-fed beef. Learn the correct serving sizes as well. Three ounces of meat is a serving; that's about the size of a deck of cards. Most Americans consider a "serving" to be a quarter to half pound of meat!

Trans fats should be avoided whenever possible. The FDA's labeling plan will help you choose foods that are low in trans fats. If you eat whole foods and fresh foods, you can avoid most artificial trans fat. For more information, see *The Everything® No Trans Fat Cookbook*.

# The Plan

As with any problem, a solution is easier to reach if you have a plan of attack. Follow these steps and you will be on your way to a healthier life. Some of these steps take some time. But as you progress through your own plan, you will see and feel immediate results that should encourage you to continue.

## Schedule a Doctor's Appointment

The first step is to determine your cholesterol and triglyceride levels, as well as how your body reacts to what you eat and the fats and cholesterol in those foods.

Your doctor will take blood samples and have them evaluated for total blood cholesterol, HDL/LDL ratios and levels, and triglyceride counts. He may request a fasting blood glucose test to see if your body reacts to too many calories by producing too much insulin, which can cause inflammation in your arteries.

Your doctor may ask a nutritionist to consult with you to develop a healthy eating plan. Diet and exercise may be enough to bring your cholesterol under control. If not, there are other options.

## Lose Weight

Since your body can make cholesterol from amino acids, carbohydrates, fats, and alcohol, it's important to balance your consumption of calories and to not overindulge. It's best not to lose weight too quickly. A pound or two a week is a good goal. Adding exercise is important to tone muscles and develop strength, as well as improve your cholesterol and triglyceride levels.

Keep snacks available and ready to eat. You're more likely to choose a handful of vegetables if they are prepared and waiting for you. Baby carrots, cauliflower florets, pepper strips, and cantaloupe balls can be kept in small containers in the refrigerator so they are just as easy to eat as packaged chips or cookies.

If you are overweight, especially around the middle, and have high insulin levels along with high blood pressure, you may be suffering from metabolic syndrome, which is a group of risk factors for heart disease. It can be tricky to diagnose, but your doctor can help. This syndrome is treated by losing weight, changing your diet to include whole foods and healthy fats, and adding exercise to your daily routine.

## Stop Smoking

You've heard this time and time again, but one of the best things you can do for your health is to quit smoking. Worldwide, smoking kills 5 million people, and secondhand smoke kills 53,000 Americans each year. That's almost one in four deaths in North America and Europe. Furthermore, smoking raises LDL levels, increases free radicals, hardens the arteries, and increases blood pressure. Cigarette smoke causes disease in almost every organ in your body.

Luckily, once you quit, your body can begin to repair the damage. Starting the day you quit, you reduce your chances of developing cancer and heart disease. Within eight hours, the oxygen level in your body increases to normal. Within a year, the risk of heart attack caused by cigarette smoke drops 50 percent.

There are many programs available to help you stop smoking. Contact the American Lung Association at *www.lungusa.org*, or see the U.S. Centers for Disease Control Web site at *www.cdc.gov/tobacco/quit_smoking/index.htm*.

## Prescription Drugs

If all else fails, there are drugs, including statins, that you can take to reduce cholesterol levels, especially LDL levels. However, these drugs may have some serious side effects. Only you and your doctor can decide if a prescription drug is necessary in your fight against heart disease.

Many doctors recommend that you really try to lose weight, change your diet, and add exercise before you try statins. Don't turn to them unless you have really tried natural methods and they just didn't work for you.

## Change Your Diet

The recipes in this book will help you with a diet makeover. Start slowly, adding more healthy foods each week and each month. If you suddenly and drastically change your diet, you could have problems with digestion, so it's a good idea to make the change gradually.

The nutrition information for the recipes in this book, as well as the information in the tables in this chapter, have been calculated by NutriBase Clinical version 7.0 (*www.dietsoftware.com*). Total calories, fat, saturated fat, fiber, sodium, and cholesterol amounts are included for each recipe.

If you're used to looking for low-fat foods, study these recipes with this fact in mind. Some of the recipes that offer more than 30 percent of fat by calories per serving use olive oil or other healthy oils like grapeseed oil or avocado oil, so you don't have to be afraid to include them in your diet.

Include the foods discussed in this chapter in your everyday diet. Concentrate on adding good amounts of those listed as raising HDL cholesterol, lowering LDL cholesterol, reducing inflammation, and slowing down free radicals. Let's cook!

# Chapter 2
## Breakfast and Brunch

# Chocolate Pancakes

*Chocolate pancakes are a nice treat for breakfast or brunch.*
*Serve them with warmed maple syrup or whipped honey.*

**Serves 6–8**

**Calories:** 227.12
**Fat:** 11.05 grams
**Saturated fat:** 3.23 grams
**Dietary fiber:** 1.53 grams
**Sodium:** 177.18 mg
**Cholesterol:** 34.68 mg

*1½ cups flour*
*⅓ cup sugar*
*1 teaspoon baking powder*
*½ teaspoon baking soda*
*¼ cup cocoa powder*
*½ teaspoon salt*
*¼ cup vegetable oil*
*1 egg*
*1 egg white*
*½ cup buttermilk*
*1 teaspoon vanilla*
*2 tablespoons butter or*
  *margarine*

1. In medium bowl, combine flour, sugar, baking powder, baking soda, cocoa, and salt. In small bowl, combine oil, egg, egg white, buttermilk, and vanilla and beat until blended.

2. Add wet ingredients to dry ingredients and mix just until smooth, using an eggbeater or wire whisk. Let stand for 10 minutes.

3. Heat a large griddle or frying pan over medium heat. Grease the griddle with some of the butter. Pour batter in ¼-cup portions onto griddle. Cook until the sides look dry and bubbles begin to form and break on the surface, about 3–5 minutes. Turn and cook for 1–2 minutes on second side; serve immediately.

## Baking Powder

*Look for baking powder that uses phosphates, not aluminum, for your baking and cooking needs. This type has no harsh aftertaste. It's sold in large grocery and health-food stores. But make sure that the baking powder you buy is double-acting. This means that it reacts with liquid when first mixed with the batter to form $CO_2$ and forms more $CO_2$ when heated.*

# Vegetable Omelet

*You could use other vegetables in this colorful omelet. Chopped mushrooms, summer squash, or bell pepper would be delicious.*

1. In large nonstick skillet, heat olive oil over medium heat. Add carrot, broccoli, and onion; cook, stirring occasionally, until crisp-tender, about 4–5 minutes.

2. Meanwhile, in medium bowl, beat egg whites until a soft foam forms. In small bowl, combine egg yolk with milk and pepper and beat well. Fold egg yolk mixture into egg whites.

3. Pour the egg mixture into the pan. Cook, lifting the edges of the eggs so the uncooked mixture can flow underneath, until eggs are set but still moist. Sprinkle with cheese and cover pan; cook for 1 minute. Uncover, fold omelet, and serve immediately.

**Serves 4**

**Calories:** 156.08
**Fat:** 9.54 grams
**Saturated fat:** 3.96 grams
**Dietary fiber:** 1.11 grams
**Sodium:** 220.56 mg
**Cholesterol:** 68.04 mg

*1 tablespoon olive oil*
*½ cup grated carrot*
*½ cup chopped broccoli*
*¼ cup finely chopped red onion*
*8 egg whites*
*1 egg yolk*
*¼ cup 1% milk*
*⅛ teaspoon white pepper*
*½ cup grated extra-sharp Cheddar cheese*

# Cinnamon Granola

*Homemade granola makes not only a great breakfast but a fabulous snack, too.
And you can sprinkle it on frozen yogurt or sherbet for a super-quick dessert.*

**Serves 16; serving
size ½ cup**

**Calories:** 357.05
**Fat:** 11.14 grams
**Saturated fat:** 1.03 grams
**Dietary fiber:** 7.01 grams
**Sodium:** 78.62 mg
**Cholesterol:** 0.0 mg

*4 cups regular oats*
*¼ cup oat bran*
*¼ cup flaxseed*
*1 cup chopped walnuts*
*½ cup honey*
*¼ cup brown sugar*
*3 tablespoons orange juice*
*¼ cup canola oil*
*¼ teaspoon salt*
*1 tablespoon vanilla*
*1 tablespoon cinnamon*
*1 cup dried sweetened
    cranberries*
*1 cup raisins*

1. Preheat oven to 300°F. Spray a cookie sheet with sides with nonstick cooking spray and set aside.

2. In large bowl, combine oats, oat bran, flaxseed, and walnuts and mix well. In small saucepan, combine honey, sugar, orange juice, canola oil, and salt and heat over low heat until warm. Remove from heat and add vanilla.

3. Pour honey mixture over oat mixture and mix well until oat mixture is coated. Spoon onto prepared cookie sheet and spread into an even layer.

4. Bake granola for 45 minutes, stirring every 10 minutes. Remove from oven, sprinkle with cinnamon, and stir in cranberries and raisins. Cool completely, then store in airtight container at room temperature.

### Flaxseed

*Flaxseed can be found in health-food stores and co-ops, as well as online. You can also find flaxseed oil at these locations, which can be used in baking and cooking. Flaxseed contains lignans, a type of soluble fiber, and alpha linolenic acids, similar to omega-3 fatty acids, which can lower total LDL cholesterol and help prevent blood platelets from sticking together.*

# Curried Peach Spread

*Spread this delicious mixture on Whole-Grain Oatmeal Bread (page 63),*
*or Honey-Wheat Sesame Bread (page 66) for the perfect breakfast.*
*It's so tasty you can omit the butter!*

In blender or food processor, combine all ingredients and blend or process until smooth. Transfer to a small bowl, cover, and refrigerate up to 4 days. Let stand at room temperature for 20 minutes before using.

**Yields 1 cup; serving size 2 tablespoons**

**Calories:** 87.16
**Fat:** 1.77 grams
**Saturated fat:** 1.11 grams
**Dietary fiber:** 0.23 grams
**Sodium:** 36.12 mg
**Cholesterol:** 5.60 mg

*½ cup peach preserves*
*½ cup whipped low-fat cream cheese*
*1 teaspoon minced ginger root*
*1 teaspoon curry powder*
*1 tablespoon lemon juice*
*1 tablespoon honey*

# Spicy Raspberry Spread

*The combination of fruits and spices, especially Tabasco and*
*hot peppers, is fairly new in the food world, but it is delicious.*

In blender or food processor, combine all ingredients and blend or process until smooth. Transfer to a small bowl, cover, and refrigerate up to 4 days. Let stand at room temperature for 20 minutes before using.

**Yields 1 cup; serving size 2 tablespoons**

**Calories:** 80.09
**Fat:** 3.58 grams
**Saturated fat:** 2.22 grams
**Dietary fiber:** 0.57 grams
**Sodium:** 62.95 mg
**Cholesterol:** 11.20 mg

*⅔ cup whipped low-fat cream cheese*
*2 tablespoons minced fresh rosemary*
*2 tablespoons raspberry preserves*
*½ cup raspberries*
*½ teaspoon Tabasco sauce*
*2 tablespoons honey*

# Hot Pepper and Salsa Frittata

*If you don't want to make your own salsa, look for low-sodium salsa in the health food aisle of the supermarket. You can also find it in the organic foods aisle and at food co-ops.*

**Serves 3**

**Calories:** 201.08
**Fat:** 12.47 grams
**Saturated fat:** 2.67 grams
**Dietary fiber:** 1.47 grams
**Sodium:** 289.79 mg
**Cholesterol:** 6.33 mg

*2 tablespoons olive oil*
*½ cup finely chopped red onion*
*1 jalapeño pepper, minced*
*½ cup egg substitute*
*4 egg whites*
*¼ cup skim milk*
*3 tablespoons grated Parmesan cheese*
*½ cup Super Spicy Salsa (page 85)*
*2 tablespoons chopped cilantro*

1. In large nonstick skillet, heat olive oil over medium heat. Add onion and jalapeño pepper; cook and stir until crisp-tender, about 4 minutes.

2. Meanwhile, in medium bowl beat egg substitute, egg whites, milk, and cheese until combined. Pour into skillet. Cook, running spatula around edge of frittata as it cooks, until eggs are soft set and light brown on the bottom.

3. Preheat broiler. Place frittata 6" from heat and broil for 4–7 minutes, watching carefully, until the top is browned and set. Top with salsa and cilantro and serve immediately.

### Frittatas

*Frittatas are like omelets but more sturdy. They are usually baked in the oven or cooked on the stovetop and finished under the broiler. They can be served immediately or cooled to room temperature for about an hour, then cut and served. Garnish frittatas with chopped onion, jalapeño or green chile peppers, and Parmesan cheese.*

# Salmon Soufflé

*This dish may have more than 9 grams of fat per serving, but remember, it's the good omega-3 fats from salmon.*

1. Preheat oven to 400°F. Remove skin and bones from salmon; flake salmon and set aside.

2. In small pan, heat olive oil over medium heat. Add onion; cook and stir until tender, about 5 minutes. Remove from heat and add salmon, lemon juice, and dill weed; do not stir, but set aside.

3. In large bowl, combine egg whites with cream of tartar; beat until stiff peaks form. Add mayonnaise and pepper to salmon mixture and mix gently.

4. Fold egg whites into salmon mixture. Spray the bottom of a 2-quart casserole with nonstick cooking spray. Pour salmon mixture into dish. Bake for 20 minutes, then lower heat to 350°F and bake for 20–30 minutes longer or until soufflé is puffed and deep golden brown. Serve immediately.

**Serves 4**

**Calories:** 203.36
**Fat:** 11.28 grams
**Saturated fat:** 1.96 grams
**Dietary fiber:** 0.31 grams
**Sodium:** 255.03 mg
**Cholesterol:** 19.34 mg

1 (7-ounce) can salmon, drained
1 tablespoon olive oil
½ cup finely chopped red onion
2 tablespoons lemon juice
½ teaspoon dried dill weed
8 egg whites
¼ teaspoon cream of tartar
¼ cup low-fat mayonnaise
⅛ teaspoon cayenne pepper

# Peach and Raspberry Soufflé

*Your guests should always be waiting for the soufflé, not vice versa. This lower-fat soufflé is more delicate than the traditional version, so it may fall sooner.*

**Serves 4**

**Calories:** 282.90
**Fat:** 7.13 grams
**Saturated fat:** 4.07 grams
**Dietary fiber:** 1.95 grams
**Sodium:** 208.17 mg
**Cholesterol:** 67.70 mg

*1½ cups chopped frozen
      peaches, thawed*
*2 tablespoons butter or
      margarine*
*2 tablespoons flour*
*⅛ teaspoon salt*
*¼ cup sugar, divided*
*3 tablespoons raspberry jelly*
*1 egg yolk*
*6 egg whites*
*¼ teaspoon cream of tartar*

1. Preheat oven to 400°F. Drain peaches, reserving juice.

2. In medium pan, melt butter over medium heat. Add flour and salt; cook and stir for 3 minutes until bubbly. Add 1 tablespoon sugar, reserved peach juice, and jelly; stir until mixture bubbles and thickens. Remove from heat and whisk in egg yolk and drained peaches. Set aside.

3. In large bowl, combine salt with egg whites and cream of tartar; beat until foamy. Gradually beat in remaining 3 tablespoons sugar until stiff peaks form.

4. Stir a dollop of the egg-white mixture into peach mixture, then fold in remaining egg whites. Spray the bottom of a 2-quart casserole dish with nonstick cooking spray and pour soufflé batter into the dish. Bake for 35–45 minutes or until soufflé is puffed and deep golden brown. Serve immediately.

## Garnishing

*Soufflés and omelets can be garnished for added color and nutrition, too. Use ingredients that are in the recipe as garnishes. Whole raspberries would be a perfect garnish for the Peach and Raspberry Soufflé (above), while Salmon Soufflé (page 27) would be delicious garnished with chopped chives.*

# Dutch Apple Omelet

*Fruit, especially tart fruit like apples or peaches, can be delicious in
a fluffy omelet. Serve this excellent recipe with some apple juice.*

**Serves 4**

**Calories:** 237.84
**Fat:** 9.78 grams
**Saturated fat:** 4.14 grams
**Dietary fiber:** 3.41 grams
**Sodium:** 180.82 mg
**Cholesterol:** 15.87 mg

*2 Granny Smith apples, thinly
   sliced*
*¼ cup water*
*1 tablespoon butter or
   margarine*
*1 tablespoon brown sugar*
*½ teaspoon cinnamon*
*½ cup egg substitute*
*4 large egg whites*
*¼ cup skim milk*
*½ cup Cinnamon Granola
   (page 24)*

1. In large nonstick skillet, combine apple slices and water. Bring to a boil over high heat, reduce heat to low, and simmer for 4–5 minutes or until apples are almost tender.

2. Drain the water and add butter, brown sugar, and cinnamon to apples; cook and stir over medium heat for 1 minute. Arrange apples in even layer in skillet.

3. In large bowl, combine egg substitute, egg whites, and milk and beat with eggbeater or wire whisk. Pour into skillet and cook over medium heat, shaking pan and lifting edges of omelet occasionally, until browned on the bottom and set but still moist on top. Sprinkle with Cinnamon Granola, flip in half, slide onto serving plate, and serve immediately.

# Slow-Cooker Fruity Oatmeal

*You can warm leftover oatmeal in the microwave to serve
it again. Substitute your favorite dried fruit, like raisins
or dried cranberries, for the dried fruit bits if you'd like.*

**Serves 8**

**Calories:** 368.25
**Fat:** 5.92 grams
**Saturated fat:** 0.88 grams
**Dietary fiber:** 7.39 grams
**Sodium:** 123.11 mg
**Cholesterol:** 0.76 mg

*2 cups steel-cut oats*
*4 cups water*
*1½ cups orange juice*
*¼ teaspoon salt*
*½ teaspoon cinnamon*
*2 apples, peeled and chopped*
*1 cup dried fruit bits*
*½ cup brown sugar*
*½ cup fat-free half-and-half*
*1 cup Cinnamon Granola*
  *(page 24)*

1. The night before you want to eat, toast oats over low heat in small saucepan for 5–8 minutes, stirring frequently until light golden brown. Place in 2½-quart slow cooker.

2. Add remaining ingredients except half-and-half and Cinnamon Granola. Stir well. Cover and cook on low for 7–9 hours.

3. In the morning, stir in the half-and-half and cook for 10 minutes longer. Sprinkle with Granola and serve.

### Steel-Cut Oats

*Steel-cut oats are whole oat grains, or groats, that have been sliced into pieces. They stand up very well to the long cooking time of the slow cooker. You can also cook them on the stovetop. Use 4 cups liquid for 1 cup of oats, and simmer over medium-low heat for 40–50 minutes, stirring occasionally.*

# Apple Pie Spice Soufflé

*This soufflé smells like apple pie while it's baking! Serve with a tall glass of orange juice and some chicken or turkey sausages for the perfect breakfast.*

1. Preheat oven to 400°F. In medium bowl, combine applesauce, apple, brown sugar, lemon juice, cinnamon, nutmeg, cloves, salt, and egg yolk and mix well.

2. In large bowl, combine egg whites with cream of tartar; beat until foamy. Gradually add sugar, beating until very stiff peaks form. Fold into apple mixture.

3. Spray the bottom of a 2-quart soufflé dish with nonstick cooking spray; pour apple mixture into dish. Bake for 45–50 minutes or until soufflé is puffed and deep golden brown. Serve immediately.

**Serves 4**

**Calories:** 181.22
**Fat:** 1.29 grams
**Saturated fat:** 0.41 grams
**Dietary fiber:** 0.94 grams
**Sodium:** 260.92 mg
**Cholesterol:** 52.45 mg

*1 cup applesauce*
*½ cup finely chopped apple*
*2 tablespoons brown sugar*
*2 tablespoons lemon juice*
*½ teaspoon cinnamon*
*¼ teaspoon nutmeg*
*⅛ teaspoon cloves*
*¼ teaspoon salt*
*1 egg yolk*
*8 egg whites*
*½ teaspoon cream of tartar*
*3 tablespoons sugar*

# French Toast with Citrus Compote

*This citrus compote can be served with Buckwheat Pancakes (page 35) or Whole-Grain Waffles (page 34), or even Slow-Cooker Fruity Oatmeal (page 30).*

**Serves 4–6**

**Calories:** 262.24
**Fat:** 4.59 grams
**Saturated fat:** 2.07 grams
**Dietary fiber:** 3.96 grams
**Sodium:** 96.68 mg
**Cholesterol:** 42.49 mg

*1 orange*
*1 red grapefruit*
*½ cup sugar, divided*
*1 cup orange juice, divided*
*1 teaspoon vanilla*
*1 egg*
*6 slices Hearty-Grain French Bread (page 74)*
*2 tablespoons butter or margarine*

1. Peel and chop orange and grapefruit and place in small bowl. In small saucepan, combine ¼ cup sugar with ½ cup orange juice and bring to a simmer. Simmer for 5–6 minutes or until slightly thickened; pour over orange mixture and set aside.

2. In shallow bowl, combine remaining ¼ cup sugar with ½ cup orange juice, vanilla, and egg, and beat well. Heat a nonstick pan over medium heat and add butter.

3. Slice bread on an angle. Dip bread into egg mixture, turning to coat. Cook in hot butter over medium heat for 6–8 minutes, turning once, until bread is crisp and deep golden brown. Serve with citrus compote.

### French Toast

*When making French toast, it's important to let the bread soak up some of the liquid mixture it is dipped in before it's cooked. But if the bread is soaked too long, it will fall apart when you take it from the liquid. Place the bread into the liquid, push it down so the liquid covers the bread, and let sit for about 30 seconds. Cook immediately.*

# Fruity Stuffed French Toast

*Serve this delicious toast with warmed maple syrup or
a combination of powdered sugar and cinnamon.*

**Serves 4–6**

**Calories:** 272.41
**Fat:** 8.65 grams
**Saturated fat:** 3.94 grams
**Dietary fiber:** 2.88 grams
**Sodium:** 111.62 mg
**Cholesterol:** 60.42 mg

*4 slices Honey-Wheat Sesame
  Bread, cut 1 inch thick
  (page 66)*
*⅓ cup buttermilk*
*1 egg*
*3 tablespoons sugar, divided*
*½ cup part-skim ricotta cheese*
*¾ cup frozen blueberries, not
  thawed*
*½ teaspoon cinnamon*
*2 tablespoons butter or
  margarine*

1. Cut a pocket in the center of each piece of bread, starting from the side, making sure to not cut through to the other side. Combine buttermilk, egg, and 1 tablespoon sugar in shallow bowl and beat well.

2. In small bowl, combine remaining 2 tablespoons sugar with ricotta and cinnamon and mix well. Fold in blueberries. Gently stuff this mixture into the bread slices.

3. Place butter in nonstick pan and heat over medium heat. Dip bread into the egg mixture, turning to coat. Cook in pan until crisp and browned, turning once, about 6–9 minutes. Serve immediately.

# Whole-Grain Waffles

*Homemade waffles taste so much better than frozen.*
*You can use them for breakfast with fresh fruit, or serve*
*them for dinner with some Three-Bean Chili (page 122).*

**Serves 8**

**Calories:** 250.62
**Fat:** 4.71 grams
**Saturated fat:** 2.45 grams
**Dietary fiber:** 3.07 grams
**Sodium:** 291.70 mg
**Cholesterol:** 36.51 mg

*1 cup all-purpose flour*
*¾ cup whole-wheat flour*
*1 cup cornmeal*
*2 teaspoons baking powder*
*½ teaspoon baking soda*
*⅛ teaspoon salt*
*1 egg*
*2 tablespoons butter or*
*    margarine, melted*
*2 cups buttermilk*
*4 egg whites*
*¼ cup sugar*

1. In medium bowl, combine flour, whole-wheat flour, cornmeal, baking powder, baking soda, and salt, and mix well.

2. In small bowl, combine egg, melted butter, and buttermilk and mix well. Add to flour mixture and stir just until combined.

3. In large bowl, beat egg whites until foamy. Gradually add sugar, beating until stiff peaks form. Fold into flour mixture.

4. Spray waffle iron with nonstick cooking spray and heat according to directions. Pour about ¼ cup batter into the waffle iron, close, and cook until the steaming stops, or according to the appliance directions. Serve immediately.

### Waffles

*The first waffle you cook almost always sticks; you can consider it a test waffle. Be sure to lightly spray the waffle iron with nonstick cooking spray before you add the batter each time, and remove any bits of the previous waffle before adding batter. You might need nonstick cooking spray with flour as extra protection against sticking.*

# Buckwheat Pancakes

*Because buckwheat is a fruit, not a grain, buckwheat flour
is gluten-free. It is high in protein and fiber, making it a
good choice for people watching their cholesterol.*

1. In small bowl, combine buttermilk, butter, and egg white, and beat well. Set aside.

2. In large bowl, combine buckwheat flour, all-purpose flour, baking powder, baking soda, and sugar and mix well. Form a well in the center of the dry ingredients and add the wet ingredients. Stir just until batter is mixed; do not overmix.

3. Spray a skillet or griddle with nonstick cooking spray and heat over medium heat. Using a ¼-cup measure, pour four pancakes at once onto the griddle. Cook until bubbles form on the surface and begin to break. Flip pancakes and cook for 1–2 minutes on second side. Serve immediately.

**Serves 4**

**Calories:** 215.98
**Fat:** 6.67 grams
**Saturated fat:** 3.94 grams
**Dietary fiber:** 1.93 grams
**Sodium:** 350.46 mg
**Cholesterol:** 16.48 mg

½ cup buttermilk
2 tablespoons butter or
    margarine, melted
2 egg whites
½ cup buckwheat flour
½ cup all-purpose flour
1½ teaspoons baking powder
½ teaspoon baking soda
3 tablespoons sugar
Nonstick cooking spray

# Blueberry Corn Pancakes

*The combination of sweet roasted corn with tart blueberries is really wonderful. Serve with warmed blueberry or maple syrup.*

**Serves 6**

**Calories:** 225.39
**Fat:** 5.36 grams
**Saturated fat:** 2.83 grams
**Dietary fiber:** 1.81 grams
**Sodium:** 190.53 mg
**Cholesterol:** 45.83 mg

*1 cup frozen corn*
*1 tablespoon olive oil*
*1¼ cups all-purpose flour*
*¼ cup cornmeal*
*2 teaspoons baking powder*
*3 tablespoons sugar*
*1 egg*
*2 egg whites*
*¼ cup buttermilk*
*¼ cup orange juice*
*2 tablespoons butter or margarine, melted*
*1 teaspoon grated orange zest*
*½ cup fresh or frozen blueberries*

1. Preheat oven to 400°F. Place corn on small cookie sheet and drizzle with olive oil. Roast for 15–25 minutes or until corn begins to turn golden brown on the edges. Remove from oven and cool completely.

2. In large bowl, combine flour, cornmeal, baking powder, and sugar and mix well. In small bowl, combine egg, egg whites, buttermilk, orange juice, melted butter, and orange zest and beat until combined.

3. Stir egg mixture into flour mixture just until combined, then fold in cooled corn and blueberries.

4. Heat a large skillet or griddle. Spray with nonstick cooking spray. Pour batter by ¼-cup portions onto skillet, making four pancakes at a time. Cook until bubbles form on the surface and begin to break, about 2–4 minutes. Carefully turn pancakes and cook for 1–2 minutes on second side. Serve immediately.

## About Pancakes

*Pancakes are easy, if you follow a few rules. First of all, don't overmix the batter; there should be a few lumps. When you cook the pancakes, pour the batter onto the hot griddle, then don't touch it until the sides start to look dry and bubbles form on the surface of the pancake. Carefully flip the pancakes and cook for another couple of minutes.*

# Blueberry-Banana Smoothie

*Smoothies are a great way to eat breakfast on the run, but they can be high in calories. Use nonfat ingredients, and pile on the fruit!*

Place milk, banana, blueberries, and yogurt in blender or food processor; blend or process until smooth. Add ice cubes; blend or process until thick. Pour into glasses and serve immediately.

## Blueberries

*Blueberries, especially wild blueberries, are one of the healthiest foods on the planet. Their antioxidant count is through the roof. In fact, blueberries lower cholesterol better than statin drugs! Add a cup of blueberries a day to your diet to really improve your health. They also taste great. And try dried blueberries for a snack.*

**Serves 2**

**Calories:** 283.52
**Fat:** 4.83 grams
**Saturated fat:** 2.77 grams
**Dietary fiber:** 3.51 grams
**Sodium:** 159.60 mg
**Cholesterol:** 5.12 mg

*1½ cups skim milk*
*1 banana*
*1 cup blueberries*
*1 cup nonfat vanilla yogurt*
*4 ice cubes*

# PB&J Smoothies

*Remember, peanut butter is cholesterol-free because it is made from plant materials. You can find low-fat versions of peanut butter on the market.*

In blender or food processor, combine yogurt, milk, peanut butter, and frozen yogurt. Blend or process until smooth. By hand, stir in the jelly just until marbled. Pour into glasses and serve immediately.

**Serves 3**

**Calories:** 238.61
**Fat:** 9.89 grams
**Saturated fat:** 2.47 grams
**Dietary fiber:** 1.42 grams
**Sodium:** 92.47 mg
**Cholesterol:** 3.62 mg

*1 cup raspberry yogurt*
*1 cup skim milk*
*3 tablespoons peanut butter*
*½ cup frozen vanilla yogurt*
*2 tablespoons raspberry jelly*

# Orange-Vanilla Smoothie

*This smoothie can be varied in so many ways. Use pineapple yogurt, pineapple nectar, and crushed pineapple instead of the orange; use your imagination!*

## Serves 2

**Calories:** 346.91
**Fat:** 2.34 grams
**Saturated fat:** 1.22 grams
**Dietary fiber:** 2.33 grams
**Sodium:** 241.12 mg
**Cholesterol:** 6.81 mg

1½ cups orange yogurt
½ cup orange juice
1 orange, peeled and sliced
¼ cup vanilla-flavored whey
    protein
1 teaspoon vanilla
4 ice cubes

Place yogurt, orange juice, orange, whey protein, and vanilla in blender or food processor; blend or process until smooth. Add ice cubes; blend or process until thick. Pour into glasses and serve immediately.

### Whey Protein

*Whey protein, an isolate of this component of milk, is lactose-free, high in protein, and almost cholesterol-free. It may help reduce high blood pressure and lower cholesterol. You can stir it into smoothies, add it to hot cocoa, and add a spoonful or two to muffin batters and bread dough.*

# Apple-Cinnamon Smoothie

*Applesauce is available in several versions; you can find chunky applesauce, smooth applesauce, and organic applesauce.*

## Serves 2

**Calories:** 179.68
**Fat:** 1.08 grams
**Saturated fat:** 0.55 grams
**Dietary fiber:** 2.36 grams
**Sodium:** 44.25 mg
**Cholesterol:** 3.06 mg

1 cup applesauce
½ cup vanilla yogurt
½ teaspoon cinnamon
1 apple, peeled and chopped
4 ice cubes

Place applesauce, yogurt, cinnamon, and apple in blender or food processor; blend or process until smooth. Add ice cubes; blend or process until thick. Pour into glasses and serve immediately.

# Strawberry Granola Parfaits

*Yes, a parfait for breakfast! With fiber-rich homemade granola,*
*sweet yogurt, and fresh fruit, this recipe is a real treat.*

1.  In small bowl, combine yogurt with whipped topping; fold together until blended.

2.  In six parfait glasses, layer yogurt mixture, granola, and strawberries until glasses are full. Top with raspberries and sprinkle with coconut. Serve immediately, or cover and refrigerate for up to 2 hours before serving. (Granola will soften slightly.)

## Toasting Coconut

*Coconut toasts easily, adding a wonderful bit of crunch and sweet flavor to many dishes. To toast, spread coconut in a small pan; bake at 350°F for 4–6 minutes, stirring once during cooking time, until light golden. You can also microwave the coconut. Spread in a microwave-safe pan and microwave on high for 1 minute. Stir, then microwave again on high for 30 seconds longer, until coconut is very light brown.*

**Serves 6**

**Calories:** 342.21
**Fat:** 9.95 grams
**Saturated fat:** 2.58 grams
**Dietary fiber:** 6.24 grams
**Sodium:** 96.40 mg
**Cholesterol:** 2.45 mg

*2 (6-ounce) containers strawberry yogurt*
*¾ cup frozen nonfat whipped topping, thawed*
*1½ cups chopped strawberries*
*½ cup raspberries*
*1½ cups Cinnamon Granola (page 24)*
*2 tablespoons toasted coconut*

# Fruity Oat-Nut Trail Bars

*These hearty bars pack a lot of fiber and nutrition into one cookie.*
*Tuck them into lunchboxes or munch for breakfast on the run.*

**Yields 24 bars**

**Calories:** 124.17
**Fat:** 4.44 grams
**Saturated fat:** 0.38 grams
**Dietary fiber:** 1.18 grams
**Sodium:** 81.62 mg
**Cholesterol:** 8.81 mg

*1 cup brown sugar*
*¼ cup canola oil*
*1 egg*
*½ cup orange juice*
*¾ cup oatmeal*
*⅓ cup all-purpose flour*
*1 teaspoon baking powder*
*1 teaspoon baking soda*
*3 egg whites*
*½ cup chopped walnuts*
*½ cup dried cranberries*
*½ cup golden raisins*

1. Preheat oven to 300°F. Spray a 9" × 13" glass baking dish with nonstick cooking spray containing flour, and set aside.

2. In large bowl, combine brown sugar, canola oil, egg, and orange juice and mix well. Stir in oatmeal, flour, baking powder, and baking soda until moistened.

3. In small bowl, beat egg whites until stiff. Fold into oat mixture along with walnuts, cranberries, and raisins. Spread into prepared pan.

4. Bake for 45 to 55 minutes or until bars are set and golden brown. Let cool for 20 minutes, then cut into bars. Wrap bars individually in plastic wrap to store.

# Chapter 3
## Quick Breads and Muffins

# Navajo Chili Bread

*Serve this spicy quick bread warm with a pot of Three-Bean Chili (page 122) for a warming dinner on a cold day.*

**Yields 1 loaf; 12 servings**

**Calories:** 223.97
**Fat:** 7.59 grams
**Saturated fat:** 2.11 grams
**Dietary fiber:** 2.10 grams
**Sodium:** 232.04 mg
**Cholesterol:** 6.54 mg

*3 tablespoons olive oil*
*½ cup minced onion*
*2 cloves garlic, minced*
*2 jalapeño peppers, minced*
*½ cup finely chopped red bell pepper*
*1¼ cups all-purpose flour*
*1 cup yellow cornmeal*
*⅛ teaspoon salt*
*1 teaspoon baking powder*
*½ teaspoon baking soda*
*2 teaspoons chili powder*
*½ cup liquid egg substitute*
*¾ cup buttermilk*
*2 tablespoons molasses*
*½ cup shredded Pepper Jack cheese*

1. Preheat oven to 375°F. Spray a 9" square glass baking dish with nonstick cooking spray containing flour, and set aside.

2. In small saucepan, heat olive oil over medium heat Add onion, garlic, jalapeño, and red bell pepper; cook and stir until crisp-tender, about 4 minutes. Remove from heat.

3. In large bowl, combine flour, cornmeal, salt, baking powder, baking soda, and chili powder, and mix to combine. Add egg substitute, buttermilk, and molasses to vegetables in saucepan, and beat to combine. Stir into flour mixture until combined, then fold in cheese.

4. Pour batter into prepared pan. Bake for 30–40 minutes or until bread is light golden-brown and toothpick inserted in center comes out clean. Let cool for 15 minutes, then serve.

# Banana-Blueberry Oatmeal Bread

*Quick breads are easy to make. Their flavor and texture usually gets better if allowed to stand, covered, overnight at room temperature.*

1. Preheat oven to 350°F. Spray a 9" × 5" loaf pan with nonstick cooking spray containing flour, and set aside.

2. In large bowl, combine cream cheese with brown sugar and sugar and beat until fluffy. Beat in mashed bananas, then add egg, egg whites, and orange juice and beat until smooth.

3. Stir together flour, whole-wheat flour, baking powder, and baking soda. Add to batter and stir just until combined. Fold in blueberries and oatmeal. Pour into prepared loaf pan.

4. Bake for 50–60 minutes or until bread is deep golden-brown and toothpick inserted in center comes out clean. Remove from pan and cool on wire rack.

### Fresh or Frozen Fruit?

*When baking, you can usually use either fresh or frozen fruit. If using frozen fruit, do not thaw before adding it to the batter, or it will add too much liquid and color or stain the bread. Use frozen fruits that are dry-packed, with no added sugar or other ingredients.*

**Yields 1 loaf; 12 servings**

**Calories:** 165.78
**Fat:** 2.43 grams
**Saturated fat:** 1.05 grams
**Dietary fiber:** 2.39 grams
**Sodium:** 173.82 mg
**Cholesterol:** 21.59 mg

1 (3-ounce) package light
    cream cheese, softened
¼ cup brown sugar
¼ cup sugar
2 bananas, mashed
1 egg
2 egg whites
¼ cup orange juice
1 cup all-purpose flour
½ cup whole-wheat flour
1 teaspoon baking powder
1 teaspoon baking soda
1 cup blueberries
½ cup regular oatmeal

# Zucchini-Walnut Bread

*When your garden is overflowing with zucchini in late summer, make several batches of this bread and freeze for the long winter months.*

**Yields 1 loaf; 12 servings**

**Calories:** 217.46
**Fat:** 8.48 grams
**Saturated fat:** 0.70 grams
**Dietary fiber:** 2.13 grams
**Sodium:** 127.63 mg
**Cholesterol:** 17.63 mg

¼ cup canola oil
¼ cup sugar
½ cup brown sugar
1 egg
2 egg whites
½ cup orange juice
2 teaspoons vanilla
1 cup grated zucchini
1 teaspoon grated lemon zest
2 tablespoons wheat germ
1 cup all-purpose flour
1 cup whole-wheat flour
1 teaspoon baking powder
½ teaspoon baking soda
⅛ teaspoon salt
1 teaspoon cinnamon
¼ teaspoon cloves
½ cup chopped walnuts

1. Preheat oven to 350°F. Spray a 9" × 5" loaf pan with nonstick cooking spray containing flour, and set aside.

2. In large bowl, combine oil, sugar, brown sugar, egg, egg whites, orange juice, and vanilla and beat until smooth. Stir in zucchini, lemon zest, and wheat germ.

3. Sift together flour, whole-wheat flour, baking powder, baking soda, salt, cinnamon, and cloves, and add to oil mixture. Stir just until combined, then fold in walnuts. Pour into prepared pan.

4. Bake for 55–65 minutes or until bread is golden-brown and toothpick inserted in center comes out clean. Remove from pan and let cool on wire rack.

# Cinnamon-Hazelnut Scones

*Scones are simply sweetened biscuits. You can add
any dried fruit or nuts to this simple recipe.*

**Serves 8**

**Calories:** 286.34
**Fat:** 14.98 grams
**Saturated fat:** 3.77 grams
**Dietary fiber:** 2.95 grams
**Sodium:** 184.16 mg
**Cholesterol:** 38.49 mg

1. Preheat oven to 400°F. Line cookie sheet with parchment paper and set aside. In large bowl, combine flour, whole-wheat flour, brown sugar, cinnamon, baking powder, and baking soda and mix well. Cut in butter until particles are fine.

2. In small bowl, combine oil, egg, buttermilk, and vanilla and beat to combine. Add to dry ingredients and mix just until moistened.

3. Add cranberries and hazelnuts and mix just until blended. Turn out onto floured surface and toss several times to coat.

4. Pat dough into an 8" circle on prepared cookie sheet. Cut into 8 triangles and separate slightly. Brush with milk. Bake for 15 to 18 minutes or until scones are golden brown. Cool for 5 minutes, then serve.

*1 cup all-purpose flour*
*1 cup whole-wheat flour*
*⅓ cup brown sugar*
*1 teaspoon cinnamon*
*1 teaspoon baking powder*
*½ teaspoon baking soda*
*3 tablespoons butter or plant
    sterol margarine*
*3 tablespoons canola oil*
*1 egg*
*½ cup buttermilk*
*1 teaspoon vanilla*
*½ cup dried cranberries*
*½ cup chopped hazelnuts*
*1 tablespoon milk*

## Hazelnuts

*Hazelnuts are also known as filberts. The nuts have a dark, tough skin that should be removed before use for best results. Toast the hazelnuts in a 350°F oven for 10 minutes, then immediately wrap in a kitchen towel. Let stand for 1 minute, then, using the towel, rub off as much of the skin as possible.*

# Fruity Oatmeal Coffee Cake

*This coffee cake is full of fruit, oatmeal, and nuts.*
*It's delicious served still warm from the oven.*

**Serves 16**

**Calories:** 261.93
**Fat:** 10.24 grams
**Saturated fat:** 1.72 grams
**Dietary fiber:** 2.96 grams
**Sodium:** 161.27 mg
**Cholesterol:** 17.49 mg

½ cup brown sugar
1½ teaspoons cinnamon
1 cup oatmeal
½ cup chopped walnuts
6 tablespoons canola oil,
 divided
2 tablespoons butter or plant
 sterol margarine
1 cup blueberries
½ cup dried cranberries
1 egg
2 egg whites
¾ cup buttermilk
¼ cup orange juice
⅔ cup sugar
1 cup all-purpose flour
1 cup whole-wheat flour
2 teaspoons baking powder
1 teaspoon baking soda

1. Preheat oven to 350°F. Spray a 13" × 9" baking pan with nonstick cooking spray containing flour, and set aside.

2. In medium bowl, combine brown sugar, cinnamon, oatmeal, and walnuts and mix well. In small saucepan, melt together 2 tablespoons canola oil and the butter. Pour into oatmeal mixture and stir until crumbs form. Add blueberries and cranberries; set aside.

3. In large bowl, combine remaining 4 tablespoons oil, egg, egg whites, buttermilk, orange juice, and sugar and beat until combined. Add flour, whole-wheat flour, baking powder, and baking soda and stir just until dry ingredients are moistened.

4. Spoon and spread batter into prepared pan. Evenly sprinkle oatmeal mixture over the batter. Bake for 30–40 minutes or until coffee cake is golden-brown and toothpick inserted in center comes out clean. Serve warm.

*good & easy*

# Applesauce Cinnamon Bread

*If you don't want to use liquid egg substitute, use 1 egg and 2 egg whites.*

1. Preheat oven to 350°F. Spray a 9" × 5" loaf pan with nonstick cooking spray containing flour, and set aside.

2. In large bowl, combine applesauce, ¾ cup plus 2 tablespoons brown sugar, canola oil, milk, and egg substitute and beat well.

3. In medium bowl, combine flour, whole-wheat flour, wheat germ, 1 teaspoon cinnamon, nutmeg, baking powder, baking soda, raisins, and walnuts, and mix well. Add to applesauce mixture and stir until combined.

4. Pour batter into prepared pan. In small bowl, combine remaining 2 tablespoons brown sugar with remaining ½ teaspoon cinnamon and mix well. Sprinkle evenly over batter in pan. Bake for 55–65 minutes or until bread is golden-brown and toothpick inserted in center comes out clean. Remove from pan and let cool on wire rack.

### Wheat Germ

*Wheat germ is very high in fiber and antioxidants. It's made from the kernel of the grain. Its vitamin-E content can help reduce oxidation of cholesterol in your blood, thus reducing the risk of plaque formation. Wheat germ is also high in oil and can go rancid quite quickly. For the longest life, store it in the refrigerator.*

---

**Yields 1 loaf; 12 servings**

**Calories:** 263.33
**Fat:** 9.88 grams
**Saturated fat:** 0.75 grams
**Dietary fiber:** 2.24 grams
**Sodium:** 113.09 mg
**Cholesterol:** 0.21 mg

1¼ cups applesauce
1 cup brown sugar, divided
⅓ cup canola oil
¼ cup skim milk
½ cup liquid egg substitute
1 cup all-purpose flour
¾ cup whole-wheat flour
2 tablespoons wheat germ
1½ teaspoons cinnamon, divided
½ teaspoon nutmeg
1 teaspoon baking powder
½ teaspoon baking soda
½ cup golden raisins
½ cup chopped walnuts

# Carrot-Oatmeal Bread

*This bread is like carrot cake, but not as sweet. Try it in a chicken salad sandwich!*

**Yields 1 loaf; 12 servings**

**Calories:** 241.05
**Fat:** 8.56 grams
**Saturated fat:** 0.66 grams
**Dietary fiber:** 2.57 grams
**Sodium:** 107.36 mg
**Cholesterol:** 0.0 mg

1½ cups finely chopped
   carrots
1 cup water
1½ cups all-purpose flour
¾ cup oatmeal
2 tablespoons oat bran
½ cup brown sugar
⅓ cup sugar
½ teaspoon salt
1 teaspoon baking powder
½ teaspoon baking soda
½ teaspoon cinnamon
½ teaspoon ginger
⅔ cup applesauce
¼ cup canola oil
2 egg whites
½ cup chopped walnuts

1. Preheat oven to 350°F. Spray a 9" × 5" loaf pan with nonstick cooking spray containing flour, and set aside.

2. In small saucepan, combine carrots and water and bring to a boil. Reduce heat and simmer for 5–7 minutes or until carrots are tender. Drain carrots and mash until smooth. Set aside.

3. In large bowl, combine flour, oatmeal, oat bran, brown sugar, sugar, salt, baking powder, baking soda, cinnamon, and ginger and mix well. In medium bowl combine mashed carrots, applesauce, canola oil, and egg whites, and beat well. Stir into dry ingredients until blended. Fold in walnuts.

4. Pour batter into prepared pan. Bake for 55–65 minutes or until bread is deep golden-brown and toothpick inserted in center comes out clean. Remove from pan and let cool on wire rack.

# Mixed-Nut Spice Muffins

*Nuts are an important part of a cholesterol-reducing diet.*
*These spicy muffins are easy, perfect for breakfast on the run.*

1. Preheat oven to 400°F. Line 12 muffin cups with paper liners and set aside.

2. In large bowl, combine oil, jam, egg, egg whites, lemon juice, and orange juice and whisk to blend. Add remaining ingredients and stir until just combined.

3. Fill each prepared muffin cup ¾ full. Bake for 18–24 minutes or until muffins are set and golden brown. Remove from muffin cups immediately and cool on wire rack.

## Toasting Nuts

*Toasting nuts brings out their flavor so you use less of them. To toast nuts, spread in a single layer on a baking or cookie sheet. Bake in a preheated 350°F oven for 8–12 minutes, stirring twice during cooking time, until the nuts turn a darker color and are fragrant. You can also toast them in a dry skillet for 4–6 minutes. Let cool completely before chopping.*

---

**Yields 12 muffins**

**Calories:** 229.28
**Fat:** 11.80 grams
**Saturated fat:** 1.12 grams
**Dietary fiber:** 1.50 grams
**Sodium:** 90.32 mg
**Cholesterol:** 17.62 mg

*¼ cup canola oil*
*½ cup apricot jam*
*1 egg*
*2 egg whites*
*3 tablespoons lemon juice*
*½ cup orange juice*
*2 cups all-purpose flour*
*1½ teaspoons baking powder*
*⅛ teaspoon salt*
*1 teaspoon cinnamon*
*¼ teaspoon nutmeg*
*¼ teaspoon allspice*
*½ cup chopped hazelnuts, toasted*
*¼ cup chopped macadamia nuts, toasted*
*¼ cup chopped walnuts, toasted*

# Apple-Cranberry Nut Bread

*This fragrant bread is a wonderful use for fall apples. Serve it for a quick breakfast.*

**Yields 1 loaf; 12 servings**

**Calories:** 268.90
**Fat:** 8.39 grams
**Saturated fat:** 0.68 grams
**Dietary fiber:** 2.48 grams
**Sodium:** 93.75 mg
**Cholesterol:** 17.63 mg

*2 apples, peeled and diced*
*¼ cup sugar*
*½ cup brown sugar*
*¼ cup canola oil*
*1 egg*
*2 teaspoons vanilla*
*1 cup apple juice, divided*
*1¼ cups all-purpose flour*
*¾ cup whole-wheat flour*
*1 teaspoon baking powder*
*½ teaspoon baking soda*
*1 teaspoon cinnamon*
*½ cup dried cranberries*
*½ cup fresh chopped cranberries*
*½ cup chopped walnuts*
*1 cup powdered sugar*

1. Preheat oven to 350°F. Spray a 9" × 5" loaf pan with nonstick cooking spray containing flour, and set aside.

2. In large bowl, combine apples and ¼ cup sugar. Let stand for 15 minutes. Add brown sugar, oil, egg, vanilla, and ⅔ cup apple juice and mix well.

3. In medium bowl, combine flour, whole-wheat flour, baking powder, baking soda, cinnamon, both types of cranberries, and walnuts and stir to mix. Add to apple mixture and stir until blended.

4. Pour into prepared pan. Bake for 55–65 minutes or until bread is golden-brown and toothpick inserted in center comes out clean. Remove from pan and place on wire rack.

5. In small bowl, combine remaining ⅓ cup apple juice and powdered sugar and mix well. Drizzle over warm bread, then let stand until cool.

# Savory Herb Muffins

*These little muffins are delicious served with soup for lunch on a cold day.*

**Yields 12 muffins**

**Calories:** 161.90
**Fat:** 7.19 grams
**Saturated fat:** 1.05 grams
**Dietary fiber:** 1.39 grams
**Sodium:** 204.07 mg
**Cholesterol:** 20.27 mg

*1 cup buttermilk*
*1 egg*
*2 egg whites*
*5 tablespoons canola oil*
*2 tablespoons chopped fresh rosemary leaves*
*2 teaspoons fresh thyme leaves*
*2 tablespoons chopped flat-leaf parsley*
*¼ teaspoon dried marjoram*
*¼ cup grated Parmesan cheese*
*½ cup cornmeal*
*1¼ cups all-purpose flour*
*½ cup whole-wheat flour*
*1 teaspoon baking powder*
*1 teaspoon baking soda*

1. Preheat oven to 375°F. Place paper liners into 12 muffin cups and set aside.

2. In large bowl, combine buttermilk, egg, egg whites, canola oil, all the herbs, Parmesan, and cornmeal, and mix well until combined. Add flour, whole-wheat flour, baking powder and baking soda and stir just until dry ingredients are moistened.

3. Fill prepared muffin cups ⅔ full. Bake for 20–25 minutes or until muffins are light golden brown and set. Remove from muffin cups and serve warm.

## Rosemary

*Rosemary is one of the herbs believed to reduce arterial inflammation. Try to find fresh rosemary. Dried rosemary is so stiff and brittle it has to be chopped very fine or it can be difficult to swallow. To use fresh rosemary, pull the thin leaves backward from the stem, then pile up and chop with a chef's knife.*

## Good-Morning Muffins

*These moist muffins are packed with fiber and nutrition.
Serve them warm with some whipped honey. Yum.*

**Yields 18 muffins**

**Calories:** 210.22
**Fat:** 8.48 grams
**Saturated fat:** 0.86 grams
**Dietary fiber:** 2.78 grams
**Sodium:** 116.29 mg
**Cholesterol:** 13.06 mg

*1 cup all-purpose flour*
*1 cup whole-wheat flour*
*2 tablespoons oat bran*
*2 tablespoons ground
    flaxseed*
*½ cup brown sugar*
*½ cup sugar*
*2 teaspoons cinnamon*
*¼ teaspoon nutmeg*
*1½ teaspoons baking powder*
*1 teaspoon baking soda*
*2 apples, peeled and chopped*
*1 cup grated carrots*
*½ cup applesauce*
*1 egg*
*1 egg white*
*¼ cup low-fat sour cream*
*¼ cup canola oil*
*2 teaspoons vanilla*
*1 cup dried cranberries*
*1 cup chopped walnuts*

1. Preheat oven to 375°F. Line 18 muffin cups with paper liners and set aside. In large bowl, combine flour, whole-wheat flour, oat bran, flaxseed, sugar, brown sugar, cinnamon, nutmeg, baking powder, and baking soda and mix well.

2. In medium bowl, combine apples, carrots, applesauce, egg, egg white, sour cream, canola oil, and vanilla, and beat to combine. Add to flour mixture and stir just until dry ingredients are moistened. Fold in cranberries and walnuts.

3. Fill prepared muffin cups ¾ full. Bake for 15–25 minutes, or until muffins are golden-brown and toothpick inserted in center comes out clean. Remove from muffin cups and cool on wire rack.

# Cranberry-Orange Bread

*Cranberry and orange is an irresistible combination.*
*Serve this bread with low-fat fruit-flavored cream cheese spread.*

**Yields 1 loaf; 12 servings**

**Calories:** 232.48
**Fat:** 8.24 grams
**Saturated fat:** 0.72 grams
**Dietary fiber:** 2.69 grams
**Sodium:** 145.81 mg
**Cholesterol:** 17.63 mg

¾ cup orange juice
2 tablespoons frozen orange
   juice concentrate, thawed
½ teaspoon almond extract
¼ cup canola oil
1 egg
⅓ cup sugar
½ cup brown sugar
1 teaspoon grated orange zest
1½ cups all-purpose flour
¾ cup whole-wheat flour
1 teaspoon baking soda
1 teaspoon baking powder
2 cups chopped cranberries
½ cup chopped hazelnuts

1. Preheat oven to 350°F. Spray a 9" × 5" loaf pan with nonstick cooking spray containing flour, and set aside.

2. In medium bowl, combine orange juice, orange juice concentrate, almond extract, canola oil, egg, sugar, brown sugar, and orange zest and beat to combine.

3. In large bowl, combine flour, whole-wheat flour, baking soda, baking powder, and mix. Make a well in the center of the flour mixture and pour in the orange juice mixture. Stir just until dry ingredients are moistened.

4. Fold in cranberries and hazelnuts. Pour into prepared pan. Bake for 55–65 minutes or until bread is golden-brown and toothpick inserted in center comes out clean. Remove from pan and let cool on wire rack.

### Self-Rising Flour

*If you're watching your sodium intake, do not use self-rising flour. On average, it contains 1½ teaspoons of baking powder and ½ teaspoon of salt per cup, which together add more than 1700 mg of sodium. Just use whole-wheat or all-purpose flour, adding 1 teaspoon baking powder and a pinch of salt per cup.*

# Cheddar-Herb Biscuits

*These biscuits have to be served hot from the oven! Offer a
nonfat cream cheese spread flavored with more herbs.*

**Yields 8 biscuits**

**Calories:** 218.86
**Fat:** 9.80 grams
**Saturated fat:** 2.18 grams
**Dietary fiber:** 1.55 grams
**Sodium:** 272.53 mg
**Cholesterol:** 7.60 grams

*1½ cups all-purpose flour*
*½ cup whole wheat flour*
*1½ teaspoons baking powder*
*½ teaspoon baking soda*
*¼ teaspoon garlic salt*
*¼ cup canola oil*
*1 egg white*
*⅔ cup buttermilk*
*1 cup grated low-fat extra-*
*    sharp Cheddar cheese*
*1 tablespoon chopped fresh*
*    rosemary*
*1 tablespoons fresh thyme*
*    leaves*
*1 tablespoon butter or plant*
*    sterol margarine, melted*
*1 tablespoon chopped flat-*
*    leaf parsley*

1. Preheat oven to 400°F. Line a cookie sheet with parchment paper and set aside.

2. In large bowl, combine flour, whole-wheat flour, baking powder, baking soda, and garlic salt and mix well. In small bowl, combine oil, egg white, and buttermilk. Add all at once to dry ingredients, stirring just until moistened.

3. Fold in cheese, rosemary, and thyme leaves. Drop into eight mounds onto prepared cookie sheet. Bake for 15–20 minutes or until biscuits are light golden brown.

4. In small microwave-safe bowl, melt butter. Add parsley and stir well. Brush this mixture over the hot biscuits. Remove biscuits to wire rack to cool slightly before serving.

# Blueberry-Walnut Muffins

*Blueberry muffins for breakfast are a great treat. Serve these warm from the oven.*

**Yields 12 muffins**

**Calories:** 230.36
**Fat:** 10.80 grams
**Saturated fat:** 0.95 grams
**Dietary fiber:** 1.91 grams
**Sodium:** 197.52 mg
**Cholesterol:** 18.44 mg

*1 cup buttermilk*
*1 egg*
*2 egg whites*
*6 tablespoons canola oil*
*½ cup sugar*
*⅛ teaspoon salt*
*1¼ cups all-purpose flour*
*¾ cup whole-wheat flour*
*1 teaspoon baking powder*
*1 teaspoon baking soda*
*1 cup blueberries*
*1 tablespoon flour*
*½ cup chopped walnuts*
*2 tablespoons brown sugar*
*½ teaspoon cinnamon*

1. Preheat oven to 400°F. Line 12 muffin cups with paper liners and set aside. In large bowl, combine buttermilk, egg, egg whites, oil, sugar, and salt and mix well.

2. Stir in 1¼ cups flour, whole-wheat flour, baking powder, and baking soda just until dry ingredients are moistened. In small bowl, toss blueberries with 1 tablespoon flour. Stir into batter along with walnuts.

3. Fill prepared muffin cups ¾ full. In small bowl, combine 2 tablespoons brown sugar and cinnamon and sprinkle over muffins. Bake for 17–22 minutes or until golden-brown and set. Remove from muffin cups and cool on wire racks.

## Toss with Flour

*It's best to toss fruit or nuts with a bit of flour before stirring into any batter. The flour helps hold these ingredients suspended in the batter, so they don't sink to the bottom as the bread bakes and rises in the oven. You need to use about one tablespoon of flour per cup of fruits or nuts.*

**Serves 9**

**Calories:** 252.79
**Fat:** 7.58 grams
**Saturated fat:** 0.87 grams
**Dietary fiber:** 2.79 grams
**Sodium:** 272.96 mg
**Cholesterol:** 24.59 mg

¾ cup all-purpose flour
½ cup whole-wheat flour
¼ cup brown sugar
2 teaspoons baking powder
1 teaspoon baking soda
1 cup cornmeal
⅓ cup oat bran
1 egg
2 egg whites
¼ cup honey
1 cup buttermilk
¼ cup canola oil

**Yields 12 muffins**

**Calories:** 232.40
**Fat:** 8.66 grams
**Saturated fat:** 0.80 grams
**Dietary fiber:** 3.37 grams
**Sodium:** 159.46 mg
**Cholesterol:** 17.63 mg

1¼ cups all-purpose flour
½ cup rolled oats
¼ cup oat bran
1½ teaspoons baking powder
1 teaspoon baking soda
⅓ cup brown sugar
1 egg
¼ cup canola oil
⅓ cup applesauce
1 teaspoon grated orange zest
1 cup finely chopped dates
½ cup chopped hazelnuts

# Whole-Grain Cornbread

*Cornbread should be eaten hot from the oven. Instead of slathering it with butter, spread with whipped honey or top with Super Spicy Salsa (page 85).*

1. Preheat oven to 400°F. Spray a 9" square pan with nonstick cooking spray containing flour, and set aside. In large mixing bowl, combine flour, whole-wheat flour, brown sugar, baking powder, baking soda, cornmeal, and oat bran and mix well.

2. In small bowl, combine egg, egg whites, honey, buttermilk, and canola oil and beat to combine. Add to dry ingredients and stir just until mixed.

3. Spoon into prepared pan and smooth top. Bake for 25–35 minutes or until bread is golden brown.

# Oat-Bran Date Muffins

*Dates contain lots of soluble fiber and are naturally sweet. Keep some Medjool dates on hand for snacking.*

1. Preheat oven to 350°F. Line 12 muffin cups with paper liners and set aside. In large bowl, combine flour, oats, oat bran, baking powder, baking soda, and brown sugar, and mix well.

2. In medium bowl, combine egg, canola oil, applesauce, and orange zest and beat to combine. Add to dry ingredients and stir just until moistened. Fold in dates and hazelnuts.

3. Fill prepared muffin cups ⅔ full. Bake for 25–35 minutes or until muffins are set and toothpick inserted in center comes out clean. Remove from muffin cups to wire racks to cool.

# Cranberry-Cornmeal Muffins

*Masa harina is corn flour; it's not the same as cornmeal.*
*You can find it in the international foods aisle of the supermarket.*

1. Preheat oven to 400°F. Line 12 muffin cups with paper liners and set aside. In large bowl, combine cornmeal, masa harina, flour, flaxseed, brown sugar, baking powder, and baking soda and mix well.

2. In small bowl, combine egg, oil, buttermilk, orange zest, honey, and vanilla, and beat to combine. Add to dry ingredients and stir just until moistened. Add chopped and dried cranberries.

3. Fill muffin cups ⅔ full. Bake for 15–22 minutes or until toothpick inserted in center comes out clean. Let cool on wire racks for 10 minutes before serving.

**Yields 12 muffins**

**Calories:** 181.75
**Fat:** 6.06 grams
**Saturated fat:** 0.66 grams
**Dietary fiber:** 2.05 grams
**Sodium:** 165.51 mg
**Cholesterol:** 18.44 mg

½ cup cornmeal
½ cup masa harina
1 cup all-purpose flour
2 tablespoons crushed flaxseed
¼ cup brown sugar
1 teaspoon baking powder
1 teaspoon baking soda
1 egg
¼ cup canola oil
1 cup buttermilk
1 teaspoon grated orange zest
2 tablespoons honey
1 teaspoon vanilla
⅓ cup chopped cranberries
⅓ cup dried cranberries

# Dark-Chocolate Orange Scones

*Sanding sugar is a large-grain sugar used for decoration.*
*If you can't find it, use 1 tablespoon regular sugar.*

**Yields 10 scones**

**Calories:** 271.10
**Fat:** 11.59 grams
**Saturated fat:** 6.93 grams
**Dietary fiber:** 3.60 grams
**Sodium:** 193.64 mg
**Cholesterol:** 15.74 mg

*1¼ cups all-purpose flour*
*1 cup whole-wheat flour*
*⅓ cup brown sugar*
*¼ cup cocoa powder*
*⅛ teaspoon salt*
*1 teaspoon baking powder*
*½ teaspoon baking soda*
*5 tablespoons butter or plant*
*    sterol margarine*
*1 egg white*
*¼ cup orange juice*
*½ cup buttermilk*
*1 teaspoon vanilla*
*1 teaspoon grated orange zest*
*1 cup dark chocolate chips*
*2 tablespoons sanding sugar*

1. Preheat oven to 375°F. Line a cookie sheet with parchment paper and set aside.

2. In large bowl, combine flour, whole-wheat flour, brown sugar, cocoa, salt, baking powder, and baking soda and mix well. Cut in the butter until particles are fine.

3. In small bowl, combine egg white, orange juice, buttermilk, vanilla, and orange zest and mix well. Pour over dry ingredients and stir until moistened. Fold in chocolate chips.

4. Gather dough into a ball and pat into a 9" circle on the prepared cookie sheet. Cut into 10 wedges and separate slightly. Sprinkle with sanding sugar. Bake for 20–25 minutes or until scones are set.

## Dark Chocolate

*You can now find dark chocolate chips, which contain at least 60 percent cocoa, in the baking aisle of your supermarket. The more cocoa the better, since that means the chocolate has more flavonoids and antioxidant vitamins. In fact, the cacao bean has the same antioxidants found in apples and red wine!*

# Pumpkin Bread

*This spicy and velvety bread has the best aroma
while it's baking, and it tastes even better.*

1. Preheat oven to 350°F. Spray a 9" × 5" loaf pan with nonstick cooking spray containing flour, and set aside.

2. In large bowl, combine brown sugar, ¼ cup sugar, canola oil, egg, egg whites, and vanilla and beat until combined. Add pumpkin and beat until smooth.

3. Sift together flour, whole-wheat flour, baking powder, baking soda, ½ teaspoon cinnamon, nutmeg, and cardamom. Add to pumpkin mixture and beat until smooth.

4. Spoon batter into prepared pan. In small bowl combine 2 tablespoons sugar and ½ teaspoon cinnamon and mix well. Sprinkle over batter. Bake for 60–70 minutes or until bread is set and toothpick inserted in center comes out clean. Remove from pan and let cool on wire rack.

**Yields 1 loaf; 12 servings**

**Calories:** 178.02
**Fat:** 5.63 grams
**Saturated fat:** 0.64 grams
**Dietary fiber:** 1.48 grams
**Sodium:** 108.61 mg
**Cholesterol:** 35.25 mg

*½ cup brown sugar*
*¼ cup sugar*
*¼ cup canola oil*
*1 egg*
*2 egg whites*
*2 teaspoons vanilla*
*1 cup canned solid-pack
    no-salt pumpkin*
*1¼ cups all-purpose flour*
*½ cup whole-wheat flour*
*1 teaspoon baking powder*
*½ teaspoon baking soda*
*1 teaspoon cinnamon,
    divided*
*¼ teaspoon nutmeg*
*¼ teaspoon cardamom*
*2 tablespoons sugar*

# Savory Zucchini Muffins

*Serve these flavorful muffins with grilled fish or chicken along with a spinach salad for a nice dinner.*

**Yields 12 muffins**

**Calories:** 153.97
**Fat:** 7.08 grams
**Saturated fat:** 1.07 grams
**Dietary fiber:** 1.46 grams
**Sodium:** 156.44 mg
**Cholesterol:** 2.75 mg

1 tablespoon olive oil
⅓ cup finely chopped onion
4 cloves garlic, minced
¼ cup canola oil
1 cup buttermilk
½ cup egg substitute
1 cup grated zucchini, drained
1¼ cups all-purpose flour
1 cup whole-wheat flour
1 teaspoon baking powder
½ teaspoon baking soda
1 tablespoon fresh chopped rosemary
¼ cup minced flat-leaf parsley
¼ cup grated Parmesan cheese
¼ teaspoon pepper

1. Preheat oven to 375°F. Line 12 muffin cups with paper liners and set aside. In small saucepan, combine olive oil, onion, and garlic; cook and stir until tender, about 6 minutes. Remove from heat and place in large mixing bowl. Let cool for 30 minutes.

2. Stir in canola oil, buttermilk, egg substitute, and zucchini and mix well. Then add flour, whole-wheat flour, baking powder, baking soda, rosemary, and parsley and mix until dry ingredients are moistened. Stir in cheese and pepper.

3. Fill prepared muffin cups ¾ full. Bake for 20–25 minutes or until muffins are golden brown and set. Remove from cups and serve immediately.

### Vegetables in Breads

*When using vegetables in breads, especially grated vegetables, be sure to drain them well before adding them to the batter. Some vegetables, especially zucchini and tomatoes, can add significant amounts of water to the batter and may throw off the proportion of flour to liquid. Follow the recipe carefully.*

# Chapter 4
## Yeast Breads

# Whole-Wheat Cinnamon Platters

*These crisp and flat rolls are a perfect treat for a special occasion, like Christmas morning or Mother's Day.*

**Yields 18 platters**

**Calories:** 189.56
**Fat:** 5.30 grams
**Saturated fat:** 0.77 grams
**Dietary fiber:** 2.41 grams
**Sodium:** 42.47 mg
**Cholesterol:** 13.44 mg

*1 cup whole-wheat flour*
*1 (¼-ounce) package instant-blend dry yeast*
*1¼ to 1¾ cups all-purpose flour, divided*
*¼ teaspoon salt*
*1 teaspoon cinnamon*
*⅛ teaspoon cardamom*
*2 tablespoons honey*
*¼ cup orange juice*
*1 tablespoon butter*
*½ cup water*
*1 egg*
*1 cup dried currants*
*1 cup sugar*
*1 cup finely chopped walnuts*
*2 teaspoons cinnamon*

1. In large bowl, combine whole-wheat flour, yeast, ½ cup all-purpose flour, salt, 1 teaspoon cinnamon, and cardamom and mix well. In small saucepan, combine honey, orange juice, butter, and water; heat until very warm. Add to flour mixture and beat for 2 minutes.

2. Add egg and beat for 1 minute. Stir in enough remaining all-purpose flour to form a stiff batter. Stir in currants. Cover and let rise for 1 hour.

3. Stir down dough. Line cookie sheets with parchment paper or Silpat liners. On plate, combine sugar, walnuts, and 2 teaspoons cinnamon and mix well. Drop dough by spoonfuls into the sugar mixture and toss to coat. Place on prepared cookie sheets and flatten to ⅛" thick circles.

4. Preheat oven to 400°F. Bake pastries for 13–16 minutes or until light golden-brown and caramelized. Let cool on cookie sheets for 3 minutes, then remove to wire rack to cool.

# Whole-Grain Oatmeal Bread

*This hearty bread is delicious toasted and spread with whipped honey or jam.*

**Yields 2 loaves; 32 servings**

**Calories:** 136.74
**Fat:** 3.46 grams
**Saturated fat:** 0.77 grams
**Dietary fiber:** 2.25 grams
**Sodium:** 85.39 mg
**Cholesterol:** 8.67 mg

*1 cup warm water*
*2 (¼-ounce) packages active
    dry yeast*
*¼ cup honey*
*1 cup skim milk*
*1 cup oatmeal*
*1 teaspoon salt*
*3 tablespoons canola oil*
*1 egg*
*1½ cups whole-wheat flour*
*½ cup medium rye flour*
*¼ cup ground flaxseed*
*3 to 4 cups bread flour*
*2 tablespoons butter*

1. In small bowl, combine water and yeast; let stand until bubbly, about 5 minutes. Meanwhile, in medium saucepan combine honey, milk, oatmeal, salt, and canola oil. Heat just until very warm (about 120°F). Remove from heat and beat in egg. Combine in large bowl with whole-wheat flour, rye flour, flaxseed, and 1 cup bread flour. Add yeast mixture and beat for 1 minute. Cover and let rise for 30 minutes.

2. Gradually stir in enough remaining bread flour to make a firm dough. Turn onto floured surface and knead until dough is elastic, about 10 minutes. Place in greased bowl, turning to grease top. Cover and let rise for 1 hour. Punch down dough, divide in half, and form into loaves. Place in greased 9" × 5" loaf pans, cover, and let rise for 30 minutes.

3. Bake in preheated 350°F oven for 25–30 minutes or until golden brown. Brush with butter, then remove to wire racks to cool.

### Rolls or Bread?

*Any yeast bread mixture can be made into rolls. Just divide the dough into 2" balls and roll between your hands to smooth. Place on greased cookie sheets about 4" apart. Cover and let rise for 30–40 minutes. Then bake at 375°F for 15–25 minutes until deep golden brown. Let cool on wire racks. Freeze if not using within 1 day.*

# Oat-Bran Dinner Rolls

*These excellent rolls are light yet hearty,*
*with a wonderful flavor and a bit of crunch.*

**Yields 30 rolls**

**Calories:** 100.84
**Fat:** 1.48 grams
**Saturated fat:** 0.64 grams
**Dietary fiber:** 1.83 grams
**Sodium:** 54.45 mg
**Cholesterol:** 2.36 mg

1½ cups water
¾ cup quick-cooking oats
½ cup oat bran
¼ cup brown sugar
2 tablespoons butter or plant
    sterol margarine
1 cup buttermilk
2 (¼-ounce) packages active
    dry yeast
2 to 3 cups all-purpose flour,
    divided
1½ cups whole-wheat flour
½ teaspoon salt
2 tablespoons honey
1 egg white, beaten
2 tablespoons oat bran

1. In medium saucepan, bring water to a boil over high heat. Add oats, oat bran, brown sugar, and butter and stir until butter melts. Remove from heat and let cool to lukewarm.

2. Meanwhile, in microwave-safe glass cup, place buttermilk. Microwave on medium for 1 minute or until lukewarm (about 110°F). Sprinkle yeast over milk; stir and let stand for 10 minutes.

3. In large mixing bowl, combine 1 cup all-purpose flour, whole-wheat flour, and salt. Add honey, cooled oatmeal mixture, and softened yeast mixture and beat until smooth. Gradually add enough remaining all-purpose flour to form a soft dough.

4. Turn onto lightly floured board and knead until smooth and elastic, about 5–7 minutes. Place in greased bowl, turning to grease top. Cover and let rise for 1 hour or until dough doubles.

5. Punch down dough and divide into thirds. Divide each third into 10 pieces. Roll balls between your hands to smooth. Place balls into two 9-inch round cake pans. Brush with egg white and sprinkle with 2 table-spoons oat bran. Cover and let rise until doubled, about 45 minutes.

6. Preheat oven to 375°F. Bake rolls for 15–25 minutes or until firm to the touch and golden brown. Remove from pans and cool on wire racks.

# Cornmeal-Cranberry Rolls

*This is a yeast batter bread, which doesn't require kneading. These little rolls are delicious warm from the oven, spread with whipped honey.*

1. In medium saucepan, combine buttermilk, water, cornmeal, and oil over medium heat. Cook, stirring, until very warm. Remove from heat.

2. In large bowl, combine 2 cups flour, yeast, and salt and mix well. Add the buttermilk mixture along with egg, egg whites, and honey. Beat for 2 minutes. Then gradually add enough remaining flour until a stiff batter forms. Stir in cranberries.

3. Cover and let rise until doubled, about 1 hour. Grease 18 muffin cups with nonstick cooking spray. Spoon batter into the prepared cups, filling each ⅔ full. Cover and let rise for 30 minutes.

4. Preheat oven to 350°F. Bake rolls for 20–30 minutes or until golden brown and set. Immediately brush with butter. Remove from pans and let cool on wire racks.

## Instant-Blend Yeast

*When a recipe calls for mixing dry yeast with flour and then adding a warm liquid, you should use instant-blend yeast instead of active dry yeast. It performs exactly the same as active dry yeast, but it hydrates much more quickly, so it will come back to life even when surrounded by other ingredients.*

**Yields 18 rolls**

**Calories:** 194.31
**Fat:** 6.20 grams
**Saturated fat:** 1.37 grams
**Dietary fiber:** 1.49 grams
**Sodium:** 113.41 mg
**Cholesterol:** 16.23 mg

½ cup buttermilk
½ cup water
½ cup yellow cornmeal
⅓ cup canola oil
2½ to 3½ cups all-purpose flour
1 (¼-ounce) package instant-blend dried yeast
½ teaspoon salt
1 egg
2 egg whites
⅓ cup honey
⅔ cup chopped dried cranberries
2 tablespoons butter, melted

# Honey-Wheat Sesame Bread

*Sesame seeds add not only flavor and crunch to these delicious loaves but fiber and healthy monounsaturated fat as well.*

**Yields 2 loaves; 32 servings**

**Calories:** 131.38
**Fat:** 3.02 grams
**Saturated fat:** 1.03 grams
**Dietary fiber:** 1.77 grams
**Sodium:** 34.51 mg
**Cholesterol:** 9.85 mg

*1 cup milk*
*1 cup water*
*½ cup honey*
*3 tablespoons butter*
*¼ teaspoon salt*
*1 egg*
*2 cups whole-wheat flour*
*2 (¼-ounce) packages*
  *instant-blend dry yeast*
*½ cup sesame seeds*
*3 to 4 cups all-purpose flour*
*1 egg white*
*2 tablespoons sesame seeds*

1. In medium saucepan, combine milk, water, honey, butter, and salt. Heat over medium heat until butter melts. Remove from heat and let stand for 30 minutes or until just lukewarm. Beat in egg.

2. Meanwhile, in large bowl combine whole-wheat flour, instant-blend yeast, and ½ cup sesame seeds. Add milk mixture and beat for 1 minute. Then gradually stir in enough all-purpose flour to make a firm dough.

3. Turn out onto floured surface and knead, adding additional flour if necessary, until dough is elastic. Place in greased bowl, turning to grease top; cover and let rise until double, about 1 hour.

4. Grease two 9" × 5" loaf pans with unsalted butter and set aside. Punch down dough and divide into two parts. On floured surface, roll or pat to 7" × 12" rectangle. Roll up tightly, starting with 7" side. Place in prepared pans. Brush with egg white and sprinkle each with 1 tablespoon sesame seeds.

5. Cover with towel, and let rise until double, about 30 minutes. Preheat oven to 350°F. Bake loaves for 35–45 minutes or until golden brown. Turn onto wire rack to cool completely.

# Raisin-Cinnamon Oatmeal Bread

*Batter breads are really simple to make because they require less of your time.*

**Yields 2 loaves; 32 servings**

**Calories:** 138.98
**Fat:** 1.60 grams
**Saturated fat:** 0.63 grams
**Dietary fiber:** 1.65 grams
**Sodium:** 54.50 mg
**Cholesterol:** 8.71 grams

2 (¼-ounce) packages active
   dry yeast
½ cup warm water
1¼ cups skim milk
¼ cup brown sugar
¼ cup honey
1 egg
2 egg whites
⅓ cup oat bran
1¼ cups oatmeal
3½ to 4½ cups all-purpose
   flour
½ teaspoon salt
2 teaspoons cinnamon
2 cups raisins
2 tablespoons butter, melted

1. In large bowl, combine yeast and warm water; let stand for 10 minutes. In small saucepan, combine milk, brown sugar, and honey; heat over low heat until warm. Add to yeast along with egg and egg whites; beat until combined.

2. Add oat bran, oatmeal, and 1 cup all-purpose flour and beat for 1 minute. Let stand, covered, for 30 minutes. Then stir in salt, cinnamon, raisins, and enough all-purpose flour to form a stiff batter; beat for 2 minutes.

3. Spray two 9" × 5" loaf pans with nonstick cooking spray. Divide batter among the pans, smoothing the top. Cover and let rise for 45 minutes until batter is doubled.

4. Preheat oven to 375°F. Bake bread for 30–40 minutes or until bread is firm and golden brown. Remove from pans, brush tops with melted butter, and let cool on wire racks.

### Batter Breads

*Batter breads are just breads with less flour, so instead of forming a dough they make a stiff batter that becomes difficult to stir. Because the bread isn't kneaded and there is more liquid, the texture of the bread will be coarser. These breads are quicker to make and are less intimidating to beginning cooks.*

# Sunflower Rye Bread

**Yields 1 loaf; 16 servings**

**Calories:** 199.73
**Fat:** 6.57 grams
**Saturated fat:** 0.73 grams
**Dietary fiber:** 2.89 grams
**Sodium:** 83.83 mg
**Cholesterol:** 13.42 mg

½ cup lukewarm water
1 (¼-ounce) package active
    dry yeast
⅔ cup skim milk
¼ cup honey
½ teaspoon salt
2 tablespoons canola oil
1 egg, beaten, divided
1 cup medium rye flour
½ cup whole-wheat flour
2 to 3 cups bread flour
1 cup hulled unsalted
    sunflower seeds

*Forming the dough into a round and baking it on a cookie sheet
makes a 'rustic' loaf that is crustier than bread baked in a loaf pan.*

1. In small bowl combine water and yeast and let stand until bubbly, about 5 minutes. In microwave-safe glass bowl, combine milk, honey, salt, and canola oil and heat on 30 percent power until warm, about 30–40 seconds. Pour milk mixture into large bowl.

2. Remove 1 tablespoon egg and refrigerate for glaze. Add remaining egg to milk mixture along with yeast mixture and rye flour; beat for 1 minute. Add whole-wheat flour and 1 cup bread flour; beat for 1 minute.

3. Gradually stir in enough remaining bread flour to form a firm dough. On lightly floured surface, knead in sunflower seeds. Knead bread until smooth and elastic, about 10 minutes. Place in greased bowl, turning to grease top. Cover and let rise for 1 hour.

4. Punch down dough and let rest for 10 minutes. Spray a cookie sheet with nonstick cooking spray. On floured surface, shape dough into an 8" round. Place on prepared cookie sheet. Brush with reserved egg, cover, and let rise for 30 minutes. Bake for 35–45 minutes or until dark golden brown. Let cool on wire rack.

# Whole-Grain Pizza Crust

*Make a couple of batches of this crust, prebake, and store in
the freezer to make your own homemade pizzas in a flash.*

1. In large bowl, combine water and yeast; let stand for 10 minutes until bubbly. Add milk, honey, olive oil, and salt and mix well. Stir in whole-wheat flour, cornmeal, and ½ cup bread flour; beat for 1 minute.

2. Stir in enough bread flour to make a firm dough. Turn onto floured surface and knead for 10 minutes. Place dough in greased bowl, turning to grease top. Cover and let rise for 1 hour.

3. Turn dough onto floured work surface and let rest for 10 minutes. Spray two 12" round pizza pans with nonstick cooking spray and sprinkle with some cornmeal. Divide dough in half and roll to 12" circles; place on pizza pans; press to edges if necessary. Let stand for 10 minutes.

4. Preheat oven to 400°F. Bake crusts for 10 minutes or until set. Remove from oven, add toppings, return to oven, and bake as the pizza recipe directs.

### Freezing Pizza Dough

*To freeze pizza dough, bake it for 10 minutes until the crust is set but not browned. Let cool completely, then place in heavy-duty food storage freezer bags, seal, label, and freeze for up to 3 months. To use, you can top the crust right from the freezer and bake as recipe directs, adding 5–10 minutes to the baking time.*

**Yields 2 crusts; 12 servings**

**Calories:** 213.01
**Fat:** 3.17 grams
**Saturated fat:** 0.46 grams
**Dietary fiber:** 3.48 grams
**Sodium:** 104.52 mg
**Cholesterol:** 0.20 mg

*1 cup warm water*
*2 (¼-ounce) packages active
    dry yeast*
*½ cup skim milk*
*2 tablespoons honey*
*2 tablespoons olive oil*
*½ teaspoon salt*
*1½ cups whole-wheat flour*
*1 cup cornmeal*
*1½ to 2½ cups bread flour*

# Light Whole-Grain Bread

**Yields 2 loaves; 32 servings**

**Calories:** 137.87
**Fat:** 2.75 grams
**Saturated fat:** 0.74 grams
**Dietary fiber:** 2.16 grams
**Sodium:** 76.58 mg
**Cholesterol:** 8.98 mg

*1 cup lukewarm water*
*2 (¼-ounce) packages active dry yeast*
*1½ cups buttermilk*
*½ cup orange juice*
*½ teaspoon salt*
*⅓ cup honey*
*3 tablespoons canola oil*
*1 egg*
*2 cups whole-wheat flour*
*½ cup oat bran*
*½ cup cracked wheat*
*3½ to 4½ cups bread flour*
*½ teaspoon baking soda*
*2 tablespoons butter*

*This hearty, crunchy loaf is packed full of flavor, nutrition, and fiber.*

1. In large bowl, combine water and yeast; mix well and let stand for 10 minutes. Add buttermilk, orange juice, salt, honey, oil, and egg and beat well. Add 1 cup whole-wheat flour, oat bran, cracked wheat, 1 cup bread flour, and baking soda; beat for 1 minute. Let bread stand for 30 minutes.

2. Gradually add enough remaining whole-wheat flour and bread flour to form a firm dough. Turn onto floured surface and knead for 10 minutes. Place dough in greased bowl, turning to grease top. Cover and let rise for 1 hour.

3. Turn dough onto floured work surface and let rest for 10 minutes. Grease two 9" × 5" loaf pans with unsalted butter and set aside. Punch down dough and divide into two parts. On floured surface, roll or pat to 7" × 12" rectangle. Roll up tightly, starting with 7" side. Place in prepared pans.

4. Cover with towel, and let rise until double, about 30 minutes. Preheat oven to 350°F. Bake loaves for 35–45 minutes or until golden brown. Brush each loaf with butter, then turn onto wire rack to cool completely.

# Whole-Grain Ciabatta

*Ciabatta means "slipper" in Italian. The loaves are fairly
flat and oblong, with large air holes and a nice crust.*

1. In large bowl, combine water and yeast; stir and let stand for 10 minutes. When yeast is bubbly, add milk, olive oil, whole-wheat flour, oat bran, ½ cup bread flour, and salt and beat for 2 minutes. Cover and let stand at room temperature for 1 hour.

2. Add enough remaining bread flour to make a soft dough; beat for 1 minute. Cover bowl and let rise for 1 hour.

3. Remove dough to lightly floured surface (dough will be soft and sticky). Grease two 4" × 10" shapes on a large cookie sheet and sprinkle with cornmeal. Divide dough in half and shape into two 3" × 9" rectangles on the greased areas of the cookie sheet. Let rise for 30 minutes.

4. Preheat oven to 400°F. Place a 9" pan filled with ½" of water on bottom rack. Bake bread on middle rack for 20–30 minutes or until loaves are light golden brown and sound hollow when tapped with fingers. Cool on wire rack.

## Creating Steam When Baking Bread

*Adding steam to the oven when baking bread makes a crisper, thicker crust. There are several ways to do this. You can place a pan with some water in it on the rack below the bread. You can also spritz the loaves with water a few times while the bread is baking. The steam helps keep the bread softer longer, so the crust develops more slowly.*

**Yields 2 loaves; 8 servings**

**Calories:** 212.26
**Fat:** 4.62 grams
**Saturated fat:** 0.68 grams
**Dietary fiber:** 3.28 grams
**Sodium:** 152.68 mg
**Cholesterol:** 0.20 mg

*1 cup lukewarm water*
*1 (¼-ounce) package active
   dry yeast*
*⅓ cup milk*
*2 tablespoons olive oil*
*¾ cup whole-wheat flour*
*½ cup oat bran*
*2 to 2½ cups bread flour*
*½ teaspoon salt*
*2 tablespoons cornmeal*

# Cornmeal Focaccia

*Focaccia dough is not kneaded; this makes the air holes large and the texture of the finished bread coarse.*

**Yields 2 loaves; 12 servings**

**Calories:** 182.86
**Fat:** 6.29 grams
**Saturated fat:** 1.50 grams
**Dietary fiber:** 1.55 grams
**Sodium:** 154.62 mg
**Cholesterol:** 4.91 mg

1½ to 2½ cups all-purpose
     flour
1 (¼-ounce) package instant-
     blend dry yeast
1 cup water
1 tablespoon honey
4 tablespoons olive oil,
     divided
½ teaspoon salt
1 tablespoon chopped fresh
     rosemary
2 teaspoons chopped fresh
     oregano leaves
½ cup cornmeal
½ cup masa harina (corn
     flour)
2 tablespoons cornmeal
¼ cup grated Romano or
     Cotija cheese

1. In large bowl, combine 1 cup flour and yeast and mix well. In microwave-safe glass measuring cup, combine water, honey, 2 tablespoons olive oil, and salt. Microwave on 50-percent power for 1 minute or until mixture is very warm.

2. Add to flour mixture; beat for 2 minutes. Stir in rosemary, oregano, ½ cup cornmeal, and masa harina and beat for 1 minute.

3. Add enough remaining all-purpose flour to make a soft dough. Cover and let rise for 30 minutes.

4. Divide dough in half. Grease two 12" round pizza pans with unsalted butter and sprinkle with 2 tablespoons cornmeal. Divide dough into two parts and press each part into prepared pans. Push your fingertips into the dough to make dimples. Drizzle remaining olive oil over the dough; sprinkle with cheese. Let stand for 20 minutes.

5. Preheat oven to 425°F. Bake bread for 13–18 minutes or until deep golden brown. Cool on wire racks.

# Three-Grain French Bread

*Yogurt and orange juice add a bit of sourdough
texture and flavor to this easy and delicious loaf.*

1. In large bowl, combine water, yeast, and sugar; stir and let stand for 10 minutes. Add orange juice, yogurt, lemon juice, and egg and beat for 1 minute. Add oat bran, salt, whole-wheat flour, and 1 cup bread flour and beat. Cover for 1 hour.

2. Gradually add enough remaining bread flour to form a firm dough. Turn onto floured surface and knead for 10 minutes until smooth and elastic. Place in greased bowl, turning to grease top. Cover and let rise for 1 hour.

3. Punch down dough and let rest for 10 minutes. With nonstick cooking spray, spray two 14" × 4" rectangles on a cookie sheet and sprinkle with cornmeal. Divide dough in half and roll each half to a 14" × 6" rectangle. Roll up tightly, starting at longer side. Pinch edges and ends to seal and place, seam side-down, onto prepared cookie sheet.

4. Cover and let rise for 30 minutes, or until doubled. Preheat oven to 375°F. Slash bread in shallow cuts several times, cutting across the loaves, using a sharp knife. Bake for 30–40 minutes or until loaves are golden brown and sound hollow when tapped with fingers. Let cool on wire rack.

### Storing French Bread

*Homemade French bread will not last very long after it's baked. Within two days of baking the bread, slice into 1" slices and flash freeze on a cookie sheet. When bread is frozen, pack into hard-sided containers, label, seal, and freeze up to 3 months. To use, spread with olive oil and toast right out of the freezer.*

**Yields 2 loaves; 16 servings**

**Calories:** 158.22
**Fat:** 1.61 grams
**Saturated fat:** 0.53 grams
**Dietary fiber:** 2.52 grams
**Sodium:** 85.22 mg
**Cholesterol:** 15.06 mg

¾ cup warm water
2 (¼-ounce) packages active
   dry yeast
1 tablespoon sugar
¼ cup orange juice
1 cup plain yogurt
2 tablespoons lemon juice
1 egg
⅓ cup oat bran
½ teaspoon salt
1½ cups whole-wheat flour
3 to 3½ cups bread flour
1 tablespoon cornmeal

# Hearty-Grain French Bread

*Cottage cheese, sour cream, and orange juice*
*add a nice tang to this hearty French bread.*

**Yields 2 loaves; 32 servings**

**Calories:** 94.80
**Fat:** 1.23 grams
**Saturated fat:** 0.43 grams
**Dietary fiber:** 2.11 grams
**Sodium:** 53.23 mg
**Cholesterol:** 1.62 mg

*1 cup quick-cooking oats*
*1 cup water*
*½ cup cottage cheese*
*½ cup low-fat sour cream*
*2 tablespoons orange juice*
*½ teaspoon salt*
*2 cups bread flour*
*2 (¼-ounce) packages*
*    instant-blend dry yeast*
*¼ cup oat bran*
*2 to 3 cups whole wheat flour*
*2 tablespoons cornmeal*

1. In small microwave-safe bowl, combine oats and 1 cup water; microwave on high for 3–4 minutes until creamy. Let cool for 10 minutes. Then combine oatmeal mixture and cottage cheese in a blender or food processor; blend or process until creamy.

2. Place oatmeal mixture in large bowl and stir in sour cream, orange juice, and salt; mix well. Add bread flour, yeast, and oat bran and beat for one minute. Then stir in enough whole wheat flour to form a firm dough.

3. Knead dough on lightly floured surface until smooth and elastic, about 8 minutes. Place dough in greased bowl, turning to grease top. Cover and let rise until doubled, about 1 hour.

4. Punch down dough and place on counter. Cover with bowl and let stand for 10 minutes. Grease two 12" long rectangles on a cookie sheet and sprinkle with cornmeal. Divide dough into two balls. Roll each ball into a 12" cylinder and place on prepared cookie sheet. Cover and let rise until doubled, about 30 minutes.

5. Preheat oven to 375°F. Spray loaves with some cold water and bake for 30–40 minutes or until loaves are deep golden brown and sound hollow when tapped with fingers. Cool on wire rack.

# Dark Dinner Rolls

*Before serving, place these rolls in a 350°F oven
for 5–6 minutes to warm and refresh.*

1. In large saucepan, place milk and heat over medium heat until warm. Pour out ½ cup of the warm milk into a large mixer bowl and combine with yeast; let stand for 10 minutes.

2. Add remaining milk, honey, salt, canola oil, egg, and egg whites and beat well. Add whole-wheat flour and rye flour and beat well. Gradually add enough all-purpose flour to form a soft dough.

3. Turn dough onto floured surface and knead until smooth, about 5–7 minutes. Place dough in greased bowl, turning to grease top. Cover and let rise for 1 hour or until doubled.

4. Turn dough out onto lightly floured surface. Divide dough into fourths, then divide each fourth into six pieces. Roll pieces between your hands to form a smooth ball. Place on cookie sheets about 3" apart. Let rise for 30–40 minutes or until doubled.

5. Preheat oven to 400°F. Bake rolls for 15–25 minutes or until golden brown and set. Remove to wire racks and brush with melted butter. Let cool.

## Flour Substitutions

*You can usually substitute most flours for others, measure for measure. Rye flour, corn flour (masa harina), whole-wheat flour, and buckwheat flour can be used instead of all-purpose flour and bread flour. If you are substituting a lot of whole-grain flours for regular flour, consider using bread flour to help add enough gluten.*

**Yields 24 rolls**

**Calories:** 165.50
**Fat:** 4.05 grams
**Saturated fat:** 1.30 grams
**Dietary fiber:** 2.94 grams
**Sodium:** 76.60 mg
**Cholesterol:** 13.64 mg

*2 cups milk*
*2 (¼-ounce) packages active dry yeast*
*¼ cup honey*
*½ teaspoon salt*
*3 tablespoons canola oil*
*1 egg*
*2 egg whites*
*2½ cups whole-wheat flour*
*1½ cups medium rye flour*
*2½ to 3 cups all-purpose flour*
*3 tablespoons butter, melted*

**Yields 2 loaves; 32 servings**

**Calories:** 156.26
**Fat:** 4.05 grams
**Saturated fat:** 1.28 grams
**Dietary fiber:** 2.26 grams
**Sodium:** 92.19 mg
**Cholesterol:** 10.88 mg

*1 recipe Light Whole-Grain
   Bread (page 70)*
*2 recipes Roasted Garlic
   (page 89)*
*2 tablespoons butter*

# Roasted Garlic Bread

*Whole roasted garlic cloves add incredible flavor and texture to this bread.
Toast it, drizzle with olive oil, and serve with a spaghetti dinner.*

1. Prepare bread dough and let rise once. Punch down dough and let rest for 10 minutes. Remove cloves of garlic from papery skins, keeping cloves whole. Knead cloves into bread.

2. Divide dough in half and shape into two ovals. Grease two oval shapes on a cookie sheet and place dough on the greased spots. Cover and let rise for 1 hour, until doubled in size.

3. Preheat oven to 350°F. Bake loaves for 35–45 minutes or until golden brown. Brush each loaf with butter, then place on wire rack to cool completely.

**Yields 18 rolls**

**Calories:** 267.32
**Fat:** 6.83 grams
**Saturated fat:** 2.53 grams
**Dietary fiber:** 3.94 grams
**Sodium:** 149.80 mg
**Cholesterol:** 21.04 mg

*1 recipe Light Whole-Grain
   Bread (page 70)*
*3 tablespoons cornmeal*
*3 tablespoons butter, melted*

# Whole-Grain Hoagie Buns

*These delicious sandwich buns freeze beautifully. Cut them in half lengthwise,
then freeze until firm. To thaw, let stand at room temperature for 1–2 hours.*

1. Prepare dough for Light Whole-Grain Bread, knead, and let rise once.

2. Punch down dough and let stand for 10 minutes. Divide in thirds, then in half again. Divide each portion into three pieces, to make 18 pieces in all. Roll pieces on floured surface to 5"-long ropes.

3. Dip the bottom of each rope in cornmeal and place on cookie sheets. With a rolling pin, gently flatten the dough to form rectangles. Cover and let rise for 30–40 minutes until light and doubled.

4. Preheat oven to 375°F. Bake rolls for 20–30 minutes or until golden brown and set. Immediately brush with melted butter, then remove to wire racks to cool.

# Seeded Breadsticks

*These breadsticks freeze very well. To thaw, let stand at room temperature for 1 hour, then heat in the toaster oven for 2–3 minutes until hot.*

**Yields 18 breadsticks**

**Calories:** 166.16
**Fat:** 4.15 grams
**Saturated fat:** 0.57 grams
**Dietary fiber:** 2.86 grams
**Sodium:** 138.76 mg
**Cholesterol:** 0.14 mg

*1 recipe Whole-Grain Pizza
   Crust dough (page 69)*
*1 egg white*
*1 tablespoon water*
*¼ cup sesame seeds*
*3 tablespoons poppy seeds*
*2 tablespoons dill seed*
*½ teaspoon salt*

1. Prepare Whole-Grain Pizza Crust dough (page 69) and let rise once. Punch down dough and let stand for 10 minutes.

2. On shallow plate, combine egg white and water and beat until foamy. On another shallow plate, combine sesame seeds, poppy seeds, dill seed, and salt and mix well.

3. Divide dough in half, then divide those halves into thirds, then into thirds again to make 18 pieces. Roll each piece into a 1" wide rope. Dip in egg-white mixture, then in seed mixture to coat. Place on cookie sheet.

4. Let breadsticks rise for 30 minutes. Preheat oven to 375°F. Bake breadsticks for 12–17 minutes or until deep golden brown and crisp. Let cool on wire racks.

## Healthy Seeds

*Seeds, along with nuts, are good for your heart. These tiny powerhouses are rich in fiber and antioxidants and have lots of heart-healthy monounsaturated fats. They do, however, go rancid fairly easily, so buy them in small quantities and store in a cool, dark place. The refrigerator or freezer is ideal.*

**Calories:** 215.29
**Fat:** 6.06 grams
**Saturated fat:** 1.72 grams
**Dietary fiber:** 2.64 grams
**Sodium:** 81.90 mg
**Cholesterol:** 12.37 mg

1 recipe Honey-Wheat
   Sesame Bread (page 66)
1 (8-ounce) package nonfat
   cream cheese, softened,
   divided
2 tablespoons butter or
   plant sterol margarine,
   softened
¾ cup brown sugar
1 cup dried blueberries
1 cup chopped hazelnuts
1 cup powdered sugar
2 tablespoons milk
1 teaspoon vanilla

# Cream-Cheese Cinnamon Rolls

*Cinnamon rolls made with whole-wheat dough and dried blueberries
are absolutely delicious, and even fairly good for you!*

1.  Prepare the bread dough, omitting sesame seeds. Let rise once, then punch down and let rest for 10 minutes.

2.  In small bowl, combine 6 ounces cream cheese with butter and beat until combined. Spray a large cookie sheet with nonstick cooking spray and set aside.

3.  Divide dough in half and roll out dough on lightly floured surface to two 16" × 7" rectangles. Spread with cream cheese mixture. Sprinkle with brown sugar, blueberries, and hazelnuts. Roll up tightly, starting with long side.

4.  Cut each roll into 16" pieces. Place, cut side up, on prepared cookie sheet. Let rise for 30 minutes.

5.  Preheat oven to 350°F. Bake rolls for 15–20 minutes or until golden brown. Remove to wire rack to cool.

6.  While rolls are still warm, combine remaining 2 ounces cream cheese, powdered sugar, vanilla, and 1 tablespoon milk in small bowl and beat well. Add more milk if necessary to make frosting consistency. Frost warm rolls, then cool completely.

### Dried Blueberries

*Dried blueberries are usually made from wild blueberries, which have a higher antioxidant count than cultivated blueberries. They are sweet, chewy, and delicious, and they make for an unusual touch in cinnamon rolls. Serve them as snacks to eat out of hand, use them in snack mixes, and stir into cereal, cookie dough, and muffin batter.*

# Ciabatta Rolls

*Ciabatta is a chewy bread with a nice crust and big air
holes that is perfect shaped into rolls for sandwiches.*

1. Prepare Ciabatta through the first rising. Punch down dough and turn onto lightly floured surface.

2. Divide dough into 6 portions. Using floured fingers, shape each portion into a 3" × 3" rectangle. Grease six 4" × 4" squares on a cookie sheet with olive oil and sprinkle with cornmeal. Place dough onto each cornmeal coated square. Drizzle with remaining olive oil.

3. Let rise in warm place until doubled in size, about 45 minutes. Preheat oven to 425°F. Bake rolls for 10–15 minutes or until very light brown. Turn off oven and prop open oven door. Let rolls stand in oven for another 5 minutes. Then remove from oven and let cool on wire racks.

### Freezing Ciabatta

*To freeze ciabatta rolls, let them cool completely, then slice in half horizontally. Freeze individually on a cookie sheet, then package into hard-sided freezer containers, label, seal, and freeze for up to 3 months. To thaw, remove from package and place on wire racks. Let thaw at room temperature for about 1 hour.*

**Yields 6 rolls**

**Calories:** 283.00
**Fat:** 6.17 grams
**Saturated fat:** 0.91 grams
**Dietary fiber:** 4.38 grams
**Sodium:** 203.58 mg
**Cholesterol:** 0.27 mg

*1 recipe Whole-Grain
    Ciabatta (page 71)*
*2 tablespoons olive oil*
*3 tablespoons cornmeal*

# Light Yeast Rolls

*These rolls are perfect for entertaining. Serve them warm from the oven with some softened butter for a real treat.*

### Yields 24 rolls

**Calories:** 110.92
**Fat:** 2.42 grams
**Saturated fat:** 1.31 grams
**Dietary fiber:** 1.63 grams
**Sodium:** 111.38 mg
**Cholesterol:** 14.26 mg

*1 cup low-fat cottage cheese*
*¼ cup low-fat sour cream*
*3 tablespoons butter*
*⅔ cup buttermilk*
*3 tablespoons honey*
*1 teaspoon fennel seeds, crushed*
*2 cups whole-wheat flour*
*2 to 2½ cups all-purpose flour*
*2 (¼-ounce) packages instant-blend dry yeast*
*½ teaspoon salt*
*1 egg*
*1 egg white*

1. In medium saucepan, combine cottage cheese, sour cream, butter, buttermilk, honey, and fennel seeds over medium heat. Cook, stirring, until very warm. Remove from heat and let cool for 20 minutes.

2. In large bowl, combine whole-wheat flour, ½ cup all-purpose flour, yeast, and salt and mix well. Add the buttermilk mixture along with egg and egg whites. Beat for 2 minutes. Then gradually add enough remaining flour until a stiff batter forms.

3. Cover and let rise until doubled, about 1 hour. Grease 24 muffin cups with nonstick cooking spray. Spoon batter into the prepared cups, filling each two-thirds full. Cover and let rise for 30 minutes.

4. Preheat oven to 350°F. Bake rolls for 20–30 minutes or until golden brown and set. Remove from pans and let cool on wire racks.

# Chapter 5
# Appetizers and Canapés

# Lemon Bruschetta with Chopped Olives

**Serves 12**

**Calories:** 200.09
**Fat:** 11.94 grams
**Saturated fat:** 1.65 grams
**Dietary fiber:** 2.88 grams
**Sodium:** 152.59 mg
**Cholesterol:** 1.62 mg

*12 slices Hearty-Grain French
    Bread (page 74)*
*6 tablespoons olive oil,
    divided*
*3 tablespoons lemon juice,
    divided*
*1 pasteurized egg white*
*2 tablespoons Dijon mustard*
*10 large black olives, chopped*
*10 large cracked green olives,
    chopped*
*½ cup chopped flat-leaf
    parsley*
*1 tablespoon fresh oregano
    leaves*
*¼ teaspoon crushed red
    pepper flakes*
*½ cup chopped toasted
    walnuts*

*Olives are high in sodium, but they contain a lot of heart-healthy oil.
This elegant appetizer is quick and easy to make.*

1. Preheat oven to 375°F. In small bowl, combine 2 tablespoons of the olive oil and 1 tablespoon lemon juice, and brush this mixture on both sides of the bread. Place on cookie sheet and bake for 10 minutes, then turn and bake for another 10–15 minutes or until bread is toasted. Remove from oven and cool on wire rack.

2. Meanwhile, in blender or food processor, combine remaining 4 tablespoons olive oil, remaining 2 tablespoons lemon juice, the egg white, and mustard, and blend or process until blended and thick.

3. Stir in the remaining ingredients, cover, and refrigerate for 1 hour. Serve the olive spread with the toasted bread.

# Smoked Salmon and Turkey Wasabi Wraps

*Wasabi is a super-hot root vegetable that tastes like a very pungent horseradish. It's used sparingly to add a lot of flavor with very few calories and no fat.*

**Serves 12**

**Calories:** 75.82
**Fat:** 3.97 grams
**Saturated fat:** 0.65 grams
**Dietary fiber:** 0.46 grams
**Sodium:** 385.38 mg
**Cholesterol:** 6.24 mg

*1 medium cantaloupe*
*1 tablespoon lime juice*
*4 ounces thinly sliced cold-smoked salmon*
*4 ounces thinly sliced smoked turkey*
*½ cup light mayonnaise*
*1 teaspoon wasabi paste*

1. Peel cantaloupe and remove seeds. Cut cantaloupe in half, then cut each half crosswise into 12 pieces. Sprinkle with lime juice.

2. Arrange salmon slices on work surface. In small bowl, combine mayonnaise with wasabi paste and mix very well with wire whisk. Be sure the wasabi is evenly distributed. Spread over salmon and turkey slices.

3. Wrap one coated salmon slice or turkey slice around a slice of cantaloupe, mayonnaise side in. Serve immediately or cover and refrigerate for 2 hours before serving.

### Cold-Smoked Salmon

*Cold-smoked salmon is also known as lox. It is dark pink and very soft. The fish has been cured before being cold-smoked. It's easiest to let the deli person slice it because it should be sliced very thin. Look for Nova lox, which is usually cured in a milder brine and may have a lower sodium content.*

# Salmon Pâté

*Sockeye salmon is the most expensive type, but it has the most flavor.
It's perfect in this simple recipe; serve with crackers and toasted French bread.*

**Serves 8**

**Calories:** 167.26
**Fat:** 9.07 grams
**Saturated fat:** 1.83 grams
**Dietary fiber:** 0.16 grams
**Sodium:** 301.51 mg
**Cholesterol:** 24.08 mg

*1 (14-ounce) can no-salt-*
*added red sockeye salmon*
*1 (8-ounce) package nonfat*
*cream cheese, softened*
*½ cup finely minced red onion*
*½ cup low-fat mayonnaise*
*1 tablespoon fresh dill weed,*
*minced*
*2 tablespoons lime juice*
*½ teaspoon Tabasco sauce*
*⅛ teaspoon white pepper*

1. Drain salmon well; remove skin and bones, if desired. Combine all ingredients in blender or food processor. Blend or process until mixture is smooth.

2. Spoon into serving bowl, cover, and chill for 2–3 hours before serving.

# Fig Crostini with Prosciutto

*This classic Italian recipe has the most wonderful sweet and
salty flavor. You can find prosciutto at most supermarket delis.*

**Serves 12**

**Calories:** 133.75
**Fat:** 4.22 grams
**Saturated fat:** 0.97 grams
**Dietary fiber:** 1.44 grams
**Sodium:** 227.80 mg
**Cholesterol:** 8.65 mg

*12 ½-inch slices Hearty-Grain*
*French Bread (page 74)*
*2 tablespoons olive oil*
*½ cup fig jam*
*2 fresh or dried figs, thinly*
*sliced*
*6 thin slices prosciutto, cut*
*in half*
*1 tablespoon aged balsamic*
*vinegar*

1. Brush both sides of bread slices with olive oil. Place on cookie sheet and broil 6" from heat until toasted, about 2–4 minutes; turn and broil second side until toasted. Remove to serving plate.

2. Spread each piece of bread with the fig jam and top with fig slices and prosciutto. Sprinkle each piece with a bit of balsamic vinegar and serve immediately.

# Super Spicy Salsa

*Salsa can be used in so many ways. It's fabulous in Hot Pepper and Salsa Frittata (page 26) and delicious as a garnish for chili or grilled chicken.*

**Yields 3 cups; serving size ¼ cup**

**Calories:** 25.23
**Fat:** 0.21 grams
**Saturated fat:** 0.05 grams
**Dietary fiber:** 1.44 grams
**Sodium:** 53.25 mg
**Cholesterol:** 0.0 mg

*2 jalapeño peppers, minced*
*1 habanero pepper, minced*
*1 green bell pepper, minced*
*4 cloves garlic, minced*
*1 red onion, chopped*
*5 ripe tomatoes, chopped*
*3 tablespoons lemon juice*
*¼ teaspoon salt*
*⅛ teaspoon white pepper*
*¼ cup chopped fresh cilantro*

1. In large bowl, combine jalapeños, habanero pepper, bell pepper, garlic, red onion, and tomatoes. In small bowl, combine lemon juice, salt, and pepper; stir to dissolve salt. Add to tomato mixture along with cilantro.

2. Cover and refrigerate for 3–4 hours before serving.

### Pepper Heat

*The heat in a pepper is concentrated in its seeds and inner membranes. If you prefer a milder taste, just remove and discard the seeds and membranes before mincing. Remember, the smaller the pepper, the hotter. Habaneros and Scotch bonnet peppers are the hottest, while pepperoncini and Poblano peppers are milder.*

# Marinated Baby Artichokes

*Artichokes are a member of the thistle family. They have no fat or cholesterol and lots of fiber. They are nutrient-dense and contain an ingredient that may protect your liver.*

**Serves 4**

**Calories:** 129.79
**Fat:** 10.39 grams
**Saturated fat:** 1.43 grams
**Dietary fiber:** 3.77 grams
**Sodium:** 100.09 mg
**Cholesterol:** 0.0 mg

*1 lemon, cut in half*
*6 baby artichokes*
*8 cups water*
*1 teaspoon ground coriander*
*3 tablespoons extra-virgin olive oil*
*1 tablespoon Dijon mustard*
*1 shallot, peeled and minced*
*⅛ teaspoon pepper*

1. Cut the lemon in half and squeeze the juice. Place half of juice in large bowl filled with cold water. Prepare artichokes by pulling off outer leaves until you reach yellow leaves. Cut off stem. Cut off top one-third of artichoke and discard. As you work, drop trimmed artichokes into bowl of lemon water.

2. In large pot, combine cold water, ground coriander, and squeezed lemon halves. Bring to a boil. Add the artichokes and bring back to a boil. Cover, reduce heat, and simmer for 10–15 minutes or until artichokes are tender.

3. Meanwhile, in small bowl, combine remaining half of lemon juice, olive oil, mustard, shallot, and pepper, and whisk to blend.

4. When artichokes are tender, drain and rinse with cold water. Cut artichokes in quarters lengthwise. If necessary, with a spoon, carefully remove the prickly choke from the center. Arrange artichokes on serving plate and drizzle with olive oil mixture.

### Baby Artichokes

*Baby artichokes are not young artichokes, but small buds that grow on the sides of the plant's main stem. They are more tender and mild than regular artichokes. They usually don't have a choke, or collection of prickly leaves, in the center. When you cut the cooked baby artichokes, check if there is a choke; if there is, remove carefully with a spoon.*

# Cucumber Dill Canapés

*This cool, crisp, and creamy appetizer is very simple to make. If you pipe the cream cheese mixture on the cucumbers, it's suitable for a fancy party.*

**Serves 6**

**Calories:** 80.23
**Fat:** 5.94 grams
**Saturated fat:** 2.09 grams
**Dietary fiber:** 0.34 grams
**Sodium:** 114.68 mg
**Cholesterol:** 7.94 mg

1. Wash cucumber and slice into ¼" slices. Arrange on serving platter. In small bowl, combine cream cheese with lemon juice and beat well. Add salad dressing, dill, and pepper and beat until smooth.

2. Spoon or pipe cream cheese mixture on cucumber slices. Serve immediately or cover and chill up to 4 hours before serving.

*1 English cucumber*
*1 (3-ounce) package low-fat cream cheese, softened*
*1 tablespoon lemon juice*
*¼ cup nonfat whipped salad dressing*
*1 tablespoon minced fresh dill weed*
*Pinch white pepper*

## English Cucumbers

*Cucumbers are very high in water content and vitamin C. The skins of regular cucumbers are usually waxed, so they must be peeled before serving. English cucumbers are not waxed, so you can serve them with the peel, which increases the fiber content. A component of cucumbers may help lower blood pressure.*

# Stuffed Jalapeño Peppers

*These little peppers are super spicy.*
*Serve them at the beginning of a Mexican meal.*

**Serves 6**

**Calories:** 45.98
**Fat:** 2.70 grams
**Saturated fat:** 1.60 grams
**Dietary fiber:** 1.03 grams
**Sodium:** 51.15 mg
**Cholesterol:** 7.94 mg

*12 small jalapeños*
*1 (3-ounce) package low-fat*
  *cream cheese, softened*
*1 tablespoon lemon juice*
*¼ cup Super Spicy Salsa*
  *(page 85)*
*1 teaspoon chopped fresh*
  *oregano*

1. Cut jalapeños in half lengthwise. For a milder taste, remove membranes and seeds. Set aside.

2. In small bowl, combine cream cheese with lemon juice; beat until fluffy. Add salsa and oregano and mix well.

3. Using a small spoon, fill each jalapeño half with the cream cheese mixture. Serve immediately or cover and chill for up to 8 hours before serving.

### Working with Hot Peppers

*You must be very careful when working with hot peppers like jalapeños, Scotch bonnet, and habaneros. Capsaicin is the ingredient that gives peppers their heat; it's also an ingredient in pepper spray! Use gloves when working with peppers and never, ever touch your face, especially your eyes, until you have removed the gloves and thoroughly washed your hands.*

# Roasted Garlic

*Believe it or not, roasted garlic is a fabulous treat eaten all by itself.
You can also spread it on bread, mash it into some low-fat
cream cheese for a sandwich spread, or add to sauces.*

**Serves 6**

**Calories:** 32.10
**Fat:** 1.56 grams
**Saturated fat:** 0.22 grams
**Dietary fiber:** 0.27 grams
**Sodium:** 28.00 mg
**Cholesterol:** 0.0 mg

*1 head garlic*
*2 teaspoons olive oil*
*Pinch salt*
*1 teaspoon lemon juice*

1. Preheat oven to 400°F. Peel off some of the outer skins from the garlic head, leaving the head whole. Cut off the top ½" of the garlic head; discard top.

2. Place on a square of heavy-duty aluminum foil, cut side up. Drizzle with the olive oil, making sure the oil runs into the cloves. Sprinkle with salt and lemon juice.

3. Wrap garlic in the foil, covering completely. Place on a baking sheet and roast for 40–50 minutes or until garlic is very soft and golden brown. Let cool for 15 minutes, then serve or use in recipes.

## Freezing Roasted Garlic

*Make a lot of Roasted Garlic. When the garlic is cool, squeeze the cloves out of the papery covering; discard the covering. Place the garlic in a small bowl and work into a paste. Freeze in ice cube trays until solid, then place in heavy-duty freezer bags, label, and freeze up to 3 months. To use, just cut off the amount you want and thaw in the fridge.*

# Roasted Garlic Spread

*Combine nutty and sweet roasted garlic with some creamy
cheese and you have a fabulous appetizer spread.*

**Serves 6**

**Calories:** 73.35
**Fat:** 3.82 grams
**Saturated fat:** 1.60 grams
**Dietary fiber:** 0.52 grams
**Sodium:** 92.01 mg
**Cholesterol:** 8.24 mg

*1 recipe Roasted Garlic (page
   89)*
*½ cup part-skim ricotta
   cheese*
*½ cup shredded carrots*
*2 tablespoons grated
   Parmesan cheese*
*1 tablespoon fresh chopped
   chives*

1. Remove garlic cloves from the skins; discard skins. In blender or food processor, combine garlic and ricotta cheese. Blend or process until smooth.

2. Scrape into bowl and stir in carrots and Parmesan cheese. Top with chives and serve immediately, or cover and refrigerate 2–4 hours before serving.

# Sugared Pork and Apple Skewers

*Pork tenderloin is very lean yet quite tender. It's delicious paired
with tart and sweet apples in this simple appetizer recipe.*

**Serves 6**

**Calories:** 172.66
**Fat:** 3.92 grams
**Saturated fat:** 1.34 grams
**Dietary fiber:** 1.14 grams
**Sodium:** 140.43 mg
**Cholesterol:** 46.78 mg

*⅓ cup brown sugar*
*3 tablespoons apple cider*
*2 tablespoons apple cider
   vinegar*
*1 tablespoon low-sodium soy
   sauce*
*1 pound pork tenderloin*
*2 Granny Smith apples*

1. For marinade, in medium bowl, combine sugar, cider, vinegar, and soy sauce and mix well. Cut pork into 1" cubes and add to sugar mixture. Stir well, then cover and refrigerate for at least 4 hours.

2. When ready to eat, prepare and preheat grill. Core apple and cut into ½" slices. Using small metal skewers, alternately thread pork and apples. Brush with all remaining marinade.

3. Place skewers on grill 6" from medium coals. Grill for 6–10 minutes, turning once, until pork registers 155°F on meat thermometer or is just slightly pink inside. Serve immediately.

# Grilled Cherry Tomatoes with Parmesan Cheese

*When cherry tomatoes are grilled, their flavor is intensified.*
*Each little tomato will burst with flavor in your mouth.*

1. Tear off an 18" × 12" sheet of heavy-duty aluminum foil. Poke cherry tomatoes with the tip of a knife (to prevent splitting) and arrange on foil. In small bowl, combine oil, vinegar, salt, and pepper and mix well. Spoon over tomatoes.

2. Bring together foil edges and fold over several times, sealing the package. Leave some room for expansion during cooking.

3. Prepare and preheat grill. Grill the foil packet over medium coals for 4–6 minutes or until tomatoes are hot. Remove from grill, open package, and sprinkle with mint and shaved Parmesan. Serve immediately.

**Serves 6**

**Calories:** 43.92
**Fat:** 3.78 grams
**Saturated fat:** 0.69 grams
**Dietary fiber:** 0.82 grams
**Sodium:** 107.03 mg
**Cholesterol:** 1.33 mg

*24 cherry tomatoes*
*1 tablespoon extra-virgin olive oil*
*1 tablespoon red-wine vinegar*
*⅛ teaspoon salt*
*Pinch white pepper*
*1 tablespoon chopped fresh mint*
*2 tablespoons shaved Parmesan cheese*

# Hawaiian Chicken Skewers

*Serve these little skewers before a cookout featuring grilled hamburgers or turkey burgers and New-Potato Salad (page 229).*

**Serves 8**

**Calories:** 119.37
**Fat:** 3.54 grams
**Saturated fat:** 1.33 grams
**Dietary fiber:** 0.44 grams
**Sodium:** 40.24 mg
**Cholesterol:** 45.18 mg

*¼ cup coconut milk*
*1 tablespoon toasted sesame oil*
*½ teaspoon Tabasco sauce*
*¼ cup pineapple juice*
*1 pound chicken tenders*
*½ fresh pineapple, cut into chunks*
*2 tablespoons lime juice*

1. In medium bowl, combine coconut milk, sesame oil, Tabasco sauce, and pineapple juice. Cut chicken tenders crosswise and add to coconut milk mixture. Cover and refrigerate for 8 hours.

2. Alternate chicken pieces and pineapple chunks on metal skewers, using 2 chicken pieces and 1 pineapple chunk per skewer.

3. Prepare and preheat grill. Grill skewers 6" from medium coals for 8–12 minutes, turning frequently, until chicken is thoroughly cooked. Sprinkle with lime juice and serve immediately.

## Skewers

*Creating skewers with meats and fruits or vegetables is a great way to reduce your total meat intake. To make skewers, you can use wooden picks or metal skewers. If you choose wooden picks, soak them in cold water for at least 30 minutes before using. They will soak up some of the water and won't burn on the high heat of the grill.*

# Stuffed Eggs with Salmon Mousse

*Put the salmon mixture into a cake-decorating bag and
pipe it into the egg whites for a beautiful presentation.*

**Serves 12**

**Calories:** 59.79
**Fat:** 3.37 grams
**Saturated fat:** 1.12 grams
**Dietary fiber:** 0.0 grams
**Sodium:** 286.50 mg
**Cholesterol:** 6.14 mg

*4 ounces cold-smoked
   salmon*
*1 (3-ounce) package light
   cream cheese, softened*
*¼ cup low-fat mayonnaise*
*¼ teaspoon pepper*
*2 tablespoons chopped
   chives*
*9 hard-cooked eggs, halved,
   yolks removed*
*2 cups curly parsley*

1. In blender or food processor, combine salmon, cream cheese, mayonnaise, and pepper. Blend or process until smooth. Stir in chives.

2. Fill egg white halves with the salmon mixture. Arrange on parsley on a serving plate; cover with plastic wrap, and chill for 2 hours before serving.

### Hard-Cooked Eggs

*To hard-cook eggs, place large eggs in a saucepan and cover with cold water. Bring to a boil over high heat. When water is boiling furiously, cover pan, remove from heat, and let stand for 15 minutes. Then place the saucepan in the sink and run cold water into it until the eggs feel cold. Crack shells under water, then peel the eggs.*

# Baby Artichokes Stuffed with Tuna

Serves 12

Calories: 90.34
Fat: 4.60 grams
Saturated fat: 1.08 grams
Dietary fiber: 2.34 grams
Sodium: 90.88 mg
Cholesterol: 7.52 mg

1 lemon
9 baby artichokes
8 cups water
1 (6-ounce) can white
    albacore tuna, drained
1 slice Honey-Wheat
    Sesame Bread (page 66),
    crumbled
2 shallots, minced
1 teaspoon fresh oregano
⅓ cup grated Parmesan
    cheese
3 tablespoons olive oil,
    divided

*You can make this appetizer ahead of time and broil just before serving.*

1. Cut the lemon in half and squeeze the juice. Place half of the juice in a large bowl filled with cold water. Prepare artichokes by pulling off the outer leaves until you reach yellow leaves. Cut off the stem. Cut off the top one-third of the artichoke and discard. As you work, drop the trimmed artichokes into the bowl of lemon water.

2. In large pot, combine cold water and the squeezed lemon halves. Bring to a boil. Add the artichokes and bring back to a boil. Cover, reduce heat, and simmer for 10–15 minutes or until artichokes are tender.

3. Meanwhile, in small bowl combine drained tuna, breadcrumbs, shallots, oregano, Parmesan cheese, and 2 tablespoons olive oil and mix well.

4. When artichokes are tender, drain well. Cut artichokes in half and remove the choke, if necessary. Fill each artichoke half with some of the tuna mixture.

5. Preheat broiler. Place filled artichokes, stuffed side up, on a broiler pan. Drizzle with more olive oil. Broil 6" from heat for 4–7 minutes or until filling starts to sizzle. Serve immediately.

# High-Fiber Guacamole

*Lima beans and peas add fiber to this delicious low-fat guacamole. Remember that avocados have lots of heart-healthy monounsaturated fat and are low in saturated fat.*

**Yields 3 cups; serving size ¼ cup**

**Calories:** 129.39
**Fat:** 7.59 grams
**Saturated fat:** 1.94 grams
**Dietary fiber:** 4.88 grams
**Sodium:** 79.72 mg
**Cholesterol:** 3.93 mg

*1 tablespoon olive oil*
*1 onion, finely chopped*
*3 cloves garlic, minced*
*1 (10-ounce) package frozen baby lima beans*
*1 cup frozen peas*
*2 avocados*
*2 tablespoons lemon juice*
*¼ teaspoon salt*
*½ cup low-fat sour cream*
*½ teaspoon crushed red pepper flakes*

1. In medium saucepan, heat olive oil over medium heat. Add onion and garlic; cook and stir until crisp-tender, about 4 minutes. Add lima beans; cook and stir for 3 minutes, then add peas; cook and stir for 2–4 minutes longer until peas and lima beans are hot and tender. Remove from heat and let cool for 20 minutes.

2. Peel avocado, cut in half, remove pit, and place in medium bowl and top with lemon juice and salt. Add lima-bean mixture, and mash with a potato masher or fork. Blend in sour cream and red pepper flakes. Serve immediately, or cover and refrigerate up to 4 hours before serving.

### Keeping Guacamole Green

*Guacamole turns brown because compounds in its cells oxidize when exposed to air. This is called enzymatic browning. To prevent this, you can either add an acidic ingredient like lemon juice to slow down the enzymes, or limit air exposure. When covering guacamole, press plastic wrap directly on its surface to limit exposure to air.*

# Yogurt Cheese Balls

*Make sure that the yogurt you use to make yogurt cheese is free of fillers and thickening agents; find the purest yogurt possible.*

**Serves 8**

**Calories:** 84.35
**Fat:** 6.03 grams
**Saturated fat:** 1.31 grams
**Dietary fiber:** 0.06 grams
**Sodium:** 44.06 mg
**Cholesterol:** 3.67 mg

*2 cups plain low-fat yogurt*
*¼ cup minced flat-leaf parsley*
*¼ cup minced chives*
*3 tablespoons extra-virgin olive oil*
*1 tablespoon aged balsamic vinegar*

1. To make the yogurt cheese, the day before, line a strainer with cheese-cloth or a coffee filter. Place the strainer in a large bowl and add the yogurt. Cover and refrigerate overnight. The next day, place the thickened yogurt in a medium bowl. Discard the liquid, or whey, or reserve for use in soups and gravies.

2. Roll the yogurt cheese into 1" balls. On shallow plate, combine parsley and chives. Roll yogurt balls in herbs to coat. Place on serving plate and drizzle with olive oil and vinegar. Serve immediately.

### Yogurt Cheese

*Yogurt cheese is thick and rich-tasting, even though it's low in fat and cholesterol. It can be used in so many ways. Use it as a substitute for sour cream in most recipes. Mix it with some herbs and spices and use it to top a baked potato. And it's a perfect appetizer dip combined with everything from salsa to pesto.*

# Fresh Creamy Fruit Dip

*Serve this creamy dip with fresh fruit like apple and pear slices, honeydew melon wedges, and whole strawberries.*

In medium bowl, beat cream cheese until light and fluffy. Gradually add yogurt, beating until smooth. Add honey, orange juice, and brown sugar and beat well. Cover and chill for at least 4 hours before serving.

**Serves 6**

**Calories:** 99.31
**Fat:** 3.14 grams
**Saturated fat:** 1.98 grams
**Dietary fiber:** 0.02 grams
**Sodium:** 72.66 mg
**Cholesterol:** 10.39 mg

*1 (3-ounce) package light cream cheese, softened*
*1 cup vanilla yogurt*
*2 tablespoons honey*
*2 tablespoons orange juice*
*2 tablespoons brown sugar*

# Spicy Salsa Bruschetta

*Ricotta cheese adds a nice creamy and mild contrast to the crisp toasted bread and spicy, crunchy salsa in this super-easy appetizer recipe.*

1. Preheat broiler. Brush bread slices on both sides with olive oil and place on broiler pan. Broil 6" from heat until golden brown, about 3–5 minutes, then turn and broil the second side until golden brown, about 3–5 minutes.

2. Spread each toasted bread slice with 2 teaspoons ricotta cheese, then top with a spoonful of salsa. Serve immediately.

**Serves 12**

**Calories:** 99.90
**Fat:** 4.86 grams
**Saturated fat:** 1.21 grams
**Dietary fiber:** 1.54 grams
**Sodium:** 57.35 mg
**Cholesterol:** 4.01 mg

*12 (½-inch thick) slices Hearty-Grain French Bread (page 74)*
*3 tablespoons olive oil*
*½ cup part-skim ricotta cheese*
*1 cup Super Spicy Salsa (page 85)*

# Greek Quesadillas

*Quesadillas can be made with any ethnic ingredients. Try sun-dried tomatoes, basil, and Parmesan cheese for Italian quesadillas.*

**Calories:** 181.26
**Fat:** 6.34 grams
**Saturated fat:** 3.62 grams
**Dietary fiber:** 2.75 grams
**Sodium:** 208.14 mg
**Cholesterol:** 17.67 mg

1 cucumber
1 cup plain yogurt
½ teaspoon dried oregano
    leaves
1 tablespoon lemon juice
½ cup crumbled feta cheese
4 green onions, chopped
3 plum tomatoes, chopped
1 cup fresh baby spinach
    leaves
1 cup shredded part-skim
    mozzarella cheese
12 (6-inch) no-salt corn
    tortillas

1. Peel cucumber, remove seeds, and chop. In small bowl, combine cucumber with yogurt, oregano, and lemon juice and set aside.

2. In medium bowl, combine feta cheese, green onions, tomatoes, baby spinach, and mozzarella cheese and mix well.

3. Preheat griddle or skillet. Place six tortillas on work surface. Divide tomato mixture among them. Top with remaining tortillas and press down gently.

4. Cook quesadillas, pressing down occasionally with spatula, until tortillas are lightly browned. Flip quesadillas and cook on second side until tortillas are crisp and cheese is melted. Cut quesadillas in quarters and serve with yogurt mixture.

### Tortillas

*Tortillas are made with flour or with corn. They may be fat-free, but the typical 10" flour tortilla made with salt has about 400 mg of sodium! Read labels carefully to find no-salt tortillas. Flour tortillas can be flavored with everything from spinach to red peppers to tomatoes. The corn tortillas have more nutrition and more fiber.*

## Fried Tomatoes with Goat Cheese

*Make sure the tomatoes are really green, with no touch of red,
for best results. Serve these hot with a knife and fork.*

**Serves 8**

**Calories:** 127.27
**Fat:** 6.58 grams
**Saturated fat:** 2.29 grams
**Dietary fiber:** 1.25 grams
**Sodium:** 107.70 mg
**Cholesterol:** 31.63 mg

*3 green tomatoes
1 egg
¼ cup buttermilk
½ cup cornmeal
¼ cup all-purpose flour
1 teaspoon baking powder
⅛ teaspoon cayenne pepper
½ cup olive oil
⅓ cup goat cheese*

1. Cut tomatoes into ⅓" slices; discard ends. In shallow bowl, combine egg and buttermilk and whisk to combine. On plate, combine cornmeal, flour, baking powder, and pepper and mix well.

2. Place olive oil in large saucepan over medium heat. When hot, dip tomato slices into egg mixture, then into cornmeal mixture to coat. Place carefully in oil and fry, turning once, until golden brown, about 3–5 minutes per side.

3. Drain fried tomatoes on paper towels and top each with a bit of goat cheese. Serve immediately.

## Creamy Garlic Hummus

*Hummus, made from garbanzo beans, is an excellent
source of folate and soluble fiber. Plus it tastes great!*

**Serves 6–8**

**Calories:** 231.54
**Fat:** 11.71 grams
**Saturated fat:** 1.57 grams
**Dietary fiber:** 5.41 grams
**Sodium:** 26.76 mg
**Cholesterol:** 16.78 mg

*1 head Roasted Garlic
    (page 89)
1 (15-ounce) can no-salt
    garbanzo beans
½ cup Yogurt Cheese (as
    described in recipe for
    Yogurt Cheese Balls, page
    96)
2 tablespoons lemon juice
¼ cup tahini
2 tablespoons olive oil
3 tablespoons toasted
    sesame seeds*

1. Remove garlic from the papery skins and place in blender or food processor. Rinse and drain garbanzo beans and add to blender along with Yogurt Cheese, lemon juice, and tahini.

2. Blend or process until smooth. Place in serving bowl and drizzle with olive oil. Sprinkle with sesame seeds and serve with Seeded Breadsticks (page 77), pita chips, and crackers.

# Chinese Skewered Chicken

*Intensely flavored chicken is paired with sweet bell peppers in this simple skewer.*

**Serves 6–8**

**Calories:** 122.72
**Fat:** 4.20 grams
**Saturated fat:** 0.87 grams
**Dietary fiber:** 0.53 grams
**Sodium:** 115.36 mg
**Cholesterol:** 45.18 mg

*2 tablespoons olive oil*
*2 tablespoons dry sherry or apple juice*
*1 tablespoon low-sodium soy sauce*
*1 teaspoon sesame oil*
*1 teaspoon five-spice powder*
*1 tablespoon honey*
*1 tablespoon minced ginger root*
*2 cloves garlic, minced*
*½ teaspoon cayenne pepper*
*1 pound chicken tenders*
*2 green bell peppers, sliced*

1. In medium bowl, combine olive oil, sherry, soy sauce, sesame oil, five-spice powder, honey, ginger root, garlic, and cayenne pepper and mix well.

2. Cut tenders crosswise into 3 pieces each. Add to olive oil mixture, stir well, cover, and refrigerate for at least 4 hours.

3. When ready to serve, prepare and preheat grill. Thread chicken pieces and bell pepper strips on metal skewers. Grill 6" from medium coals, turning once, until chicken is thoroughly cooked. Brush food once with marinade during cooking time, then discard marinade. Serve immediately.

### Asian Spices

*Five-spice powder is a blend of Szechuan peppercorns, star anise, cloves, cinnamon, and fennel. It's used in stir-fries and marinades. Szechuan peppercorn is actually the dried berry of a prickly ash tree; it's not as sharp as black pepper. Star anise is the fruit of an evergreen, and it is literally star-shaped. You can find it whole or ground.*

# Chapter 6
# Soup

# Artichoke-Lentil Soup

*There is enough sodium in the canned artichoke hearts to flavor
the entire soup. Drain and rinse them well before using.*

**Serves 6**

**Calories:** 292.83
**Fat:** 9.65 grams
**Saturated fat:** 2.16 grams
**Dietary fiber:** 13.34 grams
**Sodium:** 180.02 mg
**Cholesterol:** 4.77 mg

*3 tablespoons olive oil*
*2 onions, chopped*
*4 cloves garlic, minced*
*1 cup green lentils, rinsed*
*3 cups Low-Sodium Chicken
    Broth (page 120)*
*3 cups water*
*2 tablespoons lemon juice*
*2 tablespoons cornstarch*
*1 cup fat-free half-and-half*
*1 (14-ounce) can artichoke
    hearts, drained*
*⅛ teaspoon white pepper*
*½ cup chopped flat-leaf
    parsley*
*3 tablespoons grated
    Parmesan cheese*
*1 teaspoon grated lemon zest*

1. In large stockpot, heat olive oil over medium heat. Add onions and garlic; cook and stir until crisp-tender, about 4 minutes. Add lentils Chicken Broth, and water and bring to a simmer. Cover and simmer for 1 hour.

2. In small bowl, combine lemon juice with cornstarch and half-and-half. Stir into soup with wire whisk. Finely chop artichoke hearts and add to soup along with pepper. Heat until soup steams.

3. In small bowl, combine parsley and cheese with lemon zest and mix well. Ladle the soup into heated bowls, sprinkle with parsley mixture and serve.

### Lentils

*Green lentils, also known as French green lentils or Puy lentils, are considered the most delicate and flavorful of the lentil family. They remain firm after cooking, holding their shape better than brown lentils. Pick over them carefully and rinse thoroughly before using. Most lentils cook in just about an hour; taste to make sure they're tender.*

# Spring Asparagus Soup

*In February, the first asparagus comes in with a taste of spring. This pureed soup can also be made with other vegetables, like sugar-snap peas or baby peas.*

1. In large soup pot, heat olive oil over medium heat. Add scallions, sweet onion, and garlic; cook and stir for 3 minutes. Then add potatoes; cook and stir for 5 minutes longer.

2. Snap the asparagus spears and discard ends. Chop asparagus into 1" pieces and add to pot along with broth. Bring to a boil, reduce heat, cover, and simmer for 10 minutes.

3. Using an immersion blender, puree the soup until smooth. Add lemon juice, lemon zest, thyme, pepper, and half-and-half, heat until steaming, and serve. You can also serve this soup chilled. (Without an immersion blender, puree the soup in four batches in a blender or food processor, then return to the pot and continue with the recipe.)

**Serves 4**

**Calories:** 201.50
**Fat:** 6.04 grams
**Saturated fat:** 1.52 grams
**Dietary fiber:** 4.90 grams
**Sodium:** 182.69 mg
**Cholesterol:** 3.03 mg

*1 tablespoon olive oil*
*3 scallions, chopped*
*½ cup finely chopped sweet onion*
*1 clove garlic, minced*
*2 new potatoes, peeled and chopped*
*1 pound asparagus*
*4 cups Low-Sodium Chicken Broth (page 120)*
*1 tablespoon lemon juice*
*1 teaspoon lemon zest*
*1 tablespoon fresh thyme leaves*
*⅛ teaspoon white pepper*
*1 cup fat-free half-and-half*

# Chicken Curry Apple Soup

*This soup is delicately flavored, perfect for lunch on the porch.*
*If you can't find fresh herbs, use dried; reduce the amount by ⅔.*

**Serves 6**

**Calories:** 262.31
**Fat:** 3.95 grams
**Saturated fat:** 1.09 grams
**Dietary fiber:** 2.95 grams
**Sodium:** 114.86 mg
**Cholesterol:** 59.50 mg

*2 cups chopped cooked
    chicken breast*
*3 cups Low-Sodium Chicken
    Broth (page 120)*
*2 cups unsweetened apple
    juice*
*2 tablespoons lemon juice*
*1 tablespoon curry powder*
*2 Granny Smith apples,
    chopped*
*1 tablespoon fresh thyme
    leaves*
*1 teaspoon finely chopped
    rosemary leaves*
*⅛ teaspoon pepper*
*½ cup chopped celery leaves*

In large pot, combine all ingredients except for celery leaves. Bring to a boil, then reduce heat, cover, and simmer for 10–14 minutes or until apple is tender and chicken is hot. Garnish each serving with celery leaves.

### Curry Powder

*Curry powder is actually a mixture of spices that varies according to regional preferences or traditions. Most producers of curry powder usually include coriander, turmeric, cumin, and fenugreek in their blends. Other spices such as garlic, fennel, ginger, cinnamon, glove, cardamom, mustard, or varieties of peppers can also be added. You'll also notice a difference in taste between "raw" curry powder and that which has been toasted or sautéed. Sauteing curry powder boosts the flavors, releasing the natural aromatic oils in the spices.*

# Cantaloupe-Melon Soup

*This soup is light, cool, and refreshing. You can substitute other melons like Casaba, orange honeydew, or Santa Claus if you'd like.*

1. In blender or food processor, combine ice, cantaloupe, melon, mint, and pineapple-orange juice; cover and blend or process until smooth.

2. Place in serving bowl and add Tabasco sauce, lime juice, and salt. Cover and chill for 2–3 hours before serving.

### Ripening Melons

*When you buy melons, be sure to choose those that are heavy, with a sweet smell and evenly webbed skin. The stem end should be smooth, not torn or rough. Let melons stand at room temperature for a day or two to ripen a bit more so they are super-sweet. You can place them together in a paper bag and add an apple for faster ripening.*

**Serves 4**

**Calories:** 109.47
**Fat:** 0.43 grams
**Saturated fat:** 0.11 grams
**Dietary fiber:** 2.19 grams
**Sodium:** 187.74 mg
**Cholesterol:** 0.0 mg

1 cup cracked ice
4 cups chopped ripe
   cantaloupe
2 cups chopped honeydew
   melon
4 fresh mint leaves
1 (6-ounce) can pineapple-
   orange juice
⅛ teaspoon Tabasco sauce
1 tablespoon lime juice
¼ teaspoon salt

# Cabbage-Tomato-Bean Chowder

*Cabbage becomes sweet when cooked, and is a great complement to tender beans and tangy tomatoes. A tiny bit of sugar helps counteract the acid in the tomatoes.*

**Serves 4**

**Calories:** 272.75
**Fat:** 4.96 grams
**Saturated fat:** 0.95 grams
**Dietary fiber:** 13.58 grams
**Sodium:** 148.66 mg
**Cholesterol:** 1.01 mg

*1 tablespoon olive oil*
*1 onion, chopped*
*4 cloves garlic, minced*
*3 cups shredded green cabbage*
*1 (14-ounce) can no-salt diced tomatoes, undrained*
*1 (6-ounce) can no-salt tomato paste*
*2 cups Low-Sodium Chicken Broth (page 120)*
*1 teaspoon sugar*
*⅛ teaspoon white pepper*
*2 cups Beans for Soup (page 111)*
*⅓ cup fat-free half-and-half*

1. In large saucepan, heat olive oil over medium heat. Add onion and garlic; cook and stir until crisp-tender, about 4 minutes. Add cabbage; cook and stir for 3 minutes longer.

2. Add tomatoes, tomato paste, chicken broth, sugar, and pepper. Cook and stir until tomato paste dissolves in soup. Then stir in beans and bring to a simmer. Simmer for 10 minutes, then add half-and-half. Heat until the soup steams, and serve.

### Low-Sodium Tomato Products

*Most supermarkets now carry many low-sodium or no-salt products; they're on the shelves right next to the regular products. You just need to be on the alert when purchasing these products and be sure to read labels. You can also find some of these products, especially organic foods, on the Internet and at co-ops and health-food stores.*

# Corn Polenta Chowder

*Turkey bacon helps reduce the fat in this excellent thick chowder,
but it is high in salt, so no additional salt is needed.*

**Serves 6**

**Calories:** 276.10
**Fat:** 6.03 grams
**Saturated fat:** 1.42 grams
**Dietary fiber:** 5.22 grams
**Sodium:** 184.32 mg
**Cholesterol:** 6.22 mg

*2 strips turkey bacon*
*1 tablespoon olive oil*
*1 red onion, chopped*
*3 cloves garlic, minced*
*1 red bell pepper, chopped*
*2 jalapeño peppers, minced*
*2 Yukon Gold potatoes,*
*    chopped*
*5 cups Low-Sodium Chicken*
*    Broth (page 120), divided*
*⅓ cup cornmeal*
*2 tablespoons adobo sauce*
*2 (10-ounce) packages frozen*
*    corn, thawed*
*1 cup fat-free half-and-half*
*¼ cup chopped cilantro*
*⅛ teaspoon cayenne pepper*

1. In large soup pot, cook bacon until crisp. Remove from heat, crumble, and set aside. To drippings remaining in pot, add olive oil, then onion and garlic; cook and stir until tender, about 5 minutes.

2. Stir in bell peppers, jalapeños, potatoes, and 3 cups of the broth. Bring to a boil, then reduce heat, cover, and simmer for 20 minutes until potatoes are tender.

3. Meanwhile, in small microwave-safe bowl, combine cornmeal and 1 cup chicken broth. Microwave on high for 2 minutes, remove and stir, then microwave for 2–4 minutes longer or until mixture thickens; stir in adobo sauce and remaining 1 cup chicken broth. Add to soup along with corn. Simmer for another 10 minutes.

4. Add the half-and-half, cilantro, and pepper and stir well. Heat until steam rises, then sprinkle with reserved bacon and serve immediately.

# Roasted Cauliflower Soup

*Roasting vegetables gives them a whole new flavor by bringing out the natural sugars as they caramelize.*

**Serves 4**

**Calories:** 223.27
**Fat:** 12.12 grams
**Saturated fat:** 2.19 grams
**Dietary fiber:** 5.73 grams
**Sodium:** 163.14 mg
**Cholesterol:** 3.05 mg

*1 head cauliflower*
*3 large carrots*
*1 chopped onion*
*4 cloves garlic, minced*
*3 tablespoons olive oil*
*½ teaspoon salt*
*3 cups Low-Sodium Chicken Broth (page 120)*
*1 tablespoon fresh thyme leaves*
*1 cup 1% milk*
*⅛ teaspoon white pepper*

1. Preheat oven to 400°F. Remove leaves from cauliflower, wash, trim, and cut into florets. Peel carrots and cut into 2" pieces. Toss cauliflower, onion, carrots, and garlic with olive oil in large roasting pan. Sprinkle with salt.

2. Roast for 45–55 minutes, until cauliflower is lightly golden, stirring twice during roasting time. Scrape all of the vegetables into large soup pot. Rinse roasting pan with ½ cup chicken broth, scraping to remove browned bits. Add to soup pot along with remaining chicken broth and thyme.

3. Bring to a simmer over medium heat; simmer for 10 minutes. Remove from heat and, using an immersion blender, puree the soup. Add milk and pepper and stir well with wire whisk. Heat until soup steams, and serve.

## Cauliflower

*Cauliflower is a member of the broccoli family and is full of antioxidants and fiber that help contribute to heart health. Purchase cauliflower florets at your supermarket, wash them, and keep in small plastic containers in the refrigerator for instant snacking. This vegetable is fresh, delicious, crunchy, and so good for you.*

# Red Lentil Soup

*This is a great, hearty soup that freezes really well. Make an extra batch and freeze it for those days when you just don't feel like cooking.*

**Serves 4**

**Calories:** 271.98
**Fat:** 8.05 grams
**Saturated fat:** 1.24 grams
**Dietary fiber:** 15.32 grams
**Sodium:** 41.12 mg
**Cholesterol:** 0.0 mg

2 tablespoons olive oil
4 cloves garlic, minced
1 cup chopped onion
2 tablespoons minced ginger
    root
2 parsnips, peeled and
    chopped
3 carrots, peeled and chopped
2 cups vegetable broth
2 cups water
2 sprigs fresh thyme
1 cup red lentils

1. In large soup pot, heat olive oil over medium heat. Add garlic and onion; cook and stir until crisp-tender, about 4 minutes. Add ginger root, parsnips, and carrots and cook for 2 minutes. Then stir in vegetable broth, water, and thyme sprigs and bring to a boil. Reduce heat, cover, and simmer for 10 minutes.

2. Meanwhile, pick over lentils and wash thoroughly. Add lentils to pot and bring back to a simmer. Simmer for 15–25 minutes or until lentils and vegetables are tender. Remove the thyme stems and discard. You can puree this soup if you'd like, but you can also serve just as it is.

# Creamy Chilled Avocado Soup

*This is as good as it gets for a summer starter or a light lunch with a nice pink shrimp or chunk of crabmeat floated on top.*

**Serves 4**

**Calories:** 257.10
**Fat:** 14.68 grams
**Saturated fat:** 2.55 grams
**Dietary fiber:** 8.72 grams
**Sodium:** 156.00 mg
**Cholesterol:** 3.92 mg

2 ripe avocados
2 tablespoons lime juice
1 cup frozen lima beans,
    thawed
½ cup chopped sweet onion
1 clove garlic, minced
¼ teaspoon Tabasco sauce
⅛ teaspoon white pepper
2½ cups low-sodium
    vegetable broth
1 cup plain low-fat yogurt

Peel avocados and chop coarsely; place in blender or food processor. Sprinkle with lime juice. Add all remaining ingredients, cover, and blend or process until soup is smooth. Place in medium bowl and place plastic wrap directly on the surface of the soup. Cover and chill for 2 hours before serving.

# White Bean, Sausage, and Escarole Soup

*This is filling and tasty, a good home-style country soup. Serve it with a whole-grain bread toasted and drizzled with olive oil and a crisp salad on the side.*

1. Place sausage in soup pot over medium heat. Add ¼ cup water and bring to a simmer. Simmer sausage, turning occasionally, until water evaporates. Then cook sausage, turning frequently, until browned. Remove sausage from pot and discard drippings; do not wash pot. Cut sausage into ½" slices.

2. Add olive oil to pot and add garlic and onion. Cook and stir until tender, about 5 minutes. Add tomatoes and stir. Add beans to pot along with broth, water, escarole, and oregano. Simmer for 15–25 minutes until escarole is tender.

3. Add sausage and parsley to soup and simmer for 5 minutes. Serve each soup bowl with a sprinkling of Parmesan cheese.

### Dark Leafy Greens

*Dark leafy greens are so good for you. They are very high in essential vitamins and minerals like vitamin C, calcium, and lutein, and have lots of fiber, which can help lower cholesterol levels. The best greens include kale, Swiss chard, chicory, turnip greens, mustard greens, and romaine lettuce.*

# Beans for Soup

*Since beans and legumes are so full of fiber and a great way to reduce cholesterol, you should eat lots of them. Unfortunately, canned beans are very high in sodium. Make up a batch of these beans and freeze them, then use instead of canned beans.*

**Yields 10 cups; serving size 1 cup**

**Calories:** 219.48
**Fat:** 0.16 grams
**Saturated fat:** 0.03 grams
**Dietary fiber:** 16.46 grams
**Sodium:** 7.08 mg
**Cholesterol:** 0.0 mg

*1 pound dried beans*
*Water*

1. Sort beans, then rinse well and drain. Combine in a large pot with water to cover by 1". Bring to a boil over high heat, then cover pan, remove from heat, and let stand for 2 hours.

2. Place pot in refrigerator and let beans soak overnight. In the morning, drain beans and rinse; drain again. Place in 5- to 6-quart slow cooker with water to just cover. Cover and cook on low for 8–10 hours until beans are tender. Do not add salt or any other ingredient.

3. Package beans in 1-cup portions into freezer bags, including a bit of the cooking liquid in each bag. Seal, label, and freeze for up to 3 months. To use, defrost in refrigerator overnight, or open bag and microwave on defrost until beans begin thawing, then stir into soup to heat.

## Sodium in Canned Beans

*A cup of canned beans, even after they have been rinsed and drained, contain about 300 to 500 mg of sodium. A cup of dried beans, cooked until tender, has about 7 mg of sodium. Let your slow cooker do the cooking, and dramatically reduce your sodium intake. Cooking a large batch of beans all at once makes them almost as convenient as canned.*

# Mediterranean Fish-and-Bean Stew

*This rich recipe is packed full of flavor, fiber, and nutrition.
Serve it with a nice green salad and Oat-Bran Dinner Rolls
(page 64) for a complete and hearty meal.*

**Serves 8**

**Calories:** 330.85
**Fat:** 6.92 grams
**Saturated fat:** 1.09 grams
**Dietary fiber:** 11.68 grams
**Sodium:** 192.53 mg
**Cholesterol:** 45.50 mg

*2 tablespoons olive oil
1 onion, chopped
1 fennel bulb, chopped,
    fronds reserved
4 cloves garlic, minced
¼ teaspoon salt
¼ teaspoon white pepper
1 teaspoon dried thyme
    leaves
4 cups Beans for Soup
    (page 111)
1 (14-ounce) can diced
    tomatoes, undrained
1 (6-ounce) can no-salt
    tomato paste
4 cups Low-Sodium Chicken
    Broth (page 120)
1 cup dry white wine
3 cups water
1½ pounds cod or haddock
    fillets
¼ cup chopped flat-leaf
    parsley
2 tablespoons chopped
    fennel fronds*

1. In large soup pot, heat olive oil over medium heat. Add onion, fennel, and garlic; cook and stir until crisp-tender, about 5 minutes. Sprinkle with salt, pepper, and thyme leaves.

2. Add remaining ingredients except for fish fillets, parsley, and fennel fronds. Bring to a boil, reduce heat, and simmer for 20 minutes.

3. Add fish fillets; simmer for 8–10 minutes or until fish flakes and is opaque. Stir gently to break up fish. Sprinkle with parsley and fennel fronds and serve.

### About Fennel

*Fennel is a root vegetable with a spicy licorice taste. Both the bulb and the fronds are edible. To prepare, cut off the root end and the fronds. Remove the outer layer of the bulb and discard; slice the flesh. Submerge in water to remove the sand and grit between the layers. Drain and slice or coarsely chop. The fronds are excellent as a garnish; rinse and chop.*

# Spanish Garlic-Lentil Soup

*This simple soup is a Spanish classic and very delicious. You can also garnish it with fresh green grapes. In Spain, the recipe changes slightly from cook to cook, village to village.*

1. Pick over lentils and rinse; drain thoroughly. Place in large pot with the beef broth and water and bring to a simmer. Cover and simmer for 20–25 minutes or until lentils are tender.

2. Meanwhile, rub bread slices between your hands to make breadcrumbs. In another large saucepan, place the olive oil over medium heat. Add garlic, breadcrumbs, and sausage and cook, stirring frequently, until garlic is soft and breadcrumbs are toasted.

3. When lentils are tender, stir garlic mixture into broth along with cayenne pepper. Simmer for 5 minutes, then garnish with almonds and serve.

**Serves 6**

**Calories:** 338.34
**Fat:** 12.91 grams
**Saturated fat:** 3.02 grams
**Dietary fiber:** 11.69 grams
**Sodium:** 151.54 mg
**Cholesterol:** 19.31 mg

*1 cup lentils*
*3 cups Low-Sodium Beef Broth (page 119)*
*3 cup water*
*4 slices Honey-Wheat Sesame Bread (page 66)*
*2 tablespoons olive oil*
*1 head garlic, peeled and sliced*
*2 ounces chorizo sausage, thinly sliced*
*⅛ teaspoon cayenne pepper*
*¼ cup sliced almonds, toasted*

# Scandinavian Summer Fruit Soup

**Serves 6**

**Calories:** 241.46
**Fat:** 2.49 grams
**Saturated fat:** 1.19 grams
**Dietary fiber:** 4.13 grams
**Sodium:** 111.65 mg
**Cholesterol:** 5.85 mg

*4 cups apple cider*
*1 cup cranberry juice*
*½ cup orange juice*
*¼ cup lemon juice*
*¼ cup sugar*
*¼ teaspoon salt*
*4 peaches, peeled and*
*    chopped*
*1 pint strawberries, chopped*
*2 pears, peeled and chopped*
*2 cinnamon sticks*
*½ teaspoon ground*
*    cardamom*
*1 bunch fresh mint*
*6 tablespoons low-fat sour*
*    cream*

*This is wonderful for a summer brunch. To make this a winter soup, use dried fruits like raisins and apricots. Each serving of soup gives you more than 100 percent of your daily requirement of vitamin C.*

1. Make the soup the day before. In a large bowl, combine apple cider, cranberry juice, orange juice, lemon juice, sugar, and salt.

2. Place half of the peaches, strawberries, and pears in a food processor or blender. Add 1 cup of the apple cider mixture and blend or process until smooth. Add to apple cider mixture along with remaining ingredients except mint and sour cream. Cover and chill for at least 8 hours.

3. Remove cinnamon sticks and stir soup. Then spoon soup into chilled bowls and garnish with mint and sour cream.

# Chunky Irish Potato-Leek Soup

*Versions of this soup have nourished generations. The onion and leek become sweet through long cooking, and the potatoes add a rich heartiness.*

**Serves 6**

**Calories:** 367.19
**Fat:** 10.70 grams
**Saturated fat:** 3.10 grams
**Dietary fiber:** 4.81 grams
**Sodium:** 316.15 mg
**Cholesterol:** 14.22 mg

*3 tablespoons olive oil*
*2 leeks, sliced*
*2 onions, chopped*
*2 tablespoons flour*
*3 cups Low-Sodium Chicken Broth (page 120)*
*1 cup water*
*6 Yukon Gold potatoes, chopped*
*⅛ teaspoon cayenne pepper*
*1 cup 1% milk*
*1 cup fat-free half-and-half*
*¼ teaspoon nutmeg*
*1 bunch chives, minced*
*¼ cup chopped parsley*

1. In a large soup pot, heat olive oil over medium heat and add sliced leeks and onion. Cook and stir for 5 minutes.

2. Blend in flour; cook and stir for 3 minutes until bubbly. Add broth, water, and potatoes. Bring to a simmer, then reduce heat to low, cover, and simmer for 15–20 minutes or until potatoes are tender. Mash some of the potatoes with a potato masher, leaving some whole.

3. Stir in cayenne pepper, milk, half-and-half, and nutmeg and heat until soup steams. Add chives and parsley and serve immediately.

### Preparing Leeks

*Leeks are a large mild member of the onion family. They can be difficult to prepare because they are grown in sandy soil. Sand gets in between all the layers of the leek. To prepare, slice leeks in half lengthwise, then cut into ¼" slices. Place in a large bowl of cold water and swish with your hands so the sand falls to the bottom of the bowl.*

# Pumpkin-Ginger-Bean Soup

*Pumpkin is delicious in soup; it adds a rich flavor and creamy texture. One serving of this soup gives you 300 percent of your daily requirement for vitamin A.*

**Serves 4–6**

**Calories:** 254.04
**Fat:** 7.97 grams
**Saturated fat:** 1.29 grams
**Dietary fiber:** 8.43 grams
**Sodium:** 63.52 mg
**Cholesterol:** 0.0 mg

*2 tablespoons olive oil*
*3 tablespoons minced fresh ginger root*
*4 shallots, minced*
*1 pear, chopped*
*3 cups Low-Sodium Chicken Broth (page 120)*
*1 tablespoon brown sugar*
*¼ cup dry sherry or apple juice*
*1 (15-ounce) can solid-pack pumpkin*
*2 cups Beans for Soup (page 111)*
*¼ teaspoon ground nutmeg*
*⅛ teaspoon ground cloves*

1. In a large soup pot, heat olive oil over medium heat. Add ginger and shallots; cook and stir for 2 minutes. Then stir in pear; cook and stir for 3 minutes. Add the chicken broth, sugar, and sherry and simmer for 3 minutes.

2. Add the pumpkin and, using a potato masher, mash thoroughly until pumpkin is combined and mixture is smooth. Stir in beans, nutmeg, and cloves and bring to a simmer.

3. Cover, reduce heat to very low, and simmer for 20–25 minutes until soup is slightly thickened, stirring occasionally. Serve immediately.

# Five-Onion Soup   OK

*This is a classic, especially good when made with homemade Low-Sodium Beef Broth. It's filling enough for an entrée; don't serve it as an appetizer!*

1. In large soup pot, heat olive oil over medium heat. Add red onion, Vidalia onion, shallots, scallions, and garlic; cook and stir for 15–20 minutes or until onions are very soft. Sprinkle with sugar and continue cooking for 5–10 minutes longer until the onions start to caramelize and turn brown at the edges.

2. Add beef broth, bay leaves, Worcestershire sauce, wine, and pepper and bring to a simmer. Reduce heat to low, cover, and simmer for one hour.

3. When ready to serve, toast the French bread slices in a toaster oven or under the broiler. Divide cheese among bread slices and toast again just until the cheese melts. Pour soup into bowls and top with bread; serve immediately.

### Bay Leaves

*Since herbs and spices are flavor replacers, adding them to your food is a great way to reduce sodium and fat. But some herbs, like bay leaves, shouldn't be eaten. The spine in the leaves doesn't soften with cooking and can be dangerous if ingested. So be careful to remove the bay leaf before serving, whether you're making soup or a casserole.*

**Serves 4**

**Calories:** 357.41
**Fat:** 15.34 grams
**Saturated fat:** 5.72 grams
**Dietary fiber:** 3.74 grams
**Sodium:** 254.39 mg
**Cholesterol:** 30.80 mg

*2 tablespoons olive oil*
*1 red onion, chopped*
*1 Vidalia or Walla Walla onion, chopped*
*2 shallots, chopped*
*4 scallions, chopped*
*4 cloves garlic, chopped*
*1 teaspoon sugar*
*4 cups Low-Sodium Beef Broth (page 119)*
*2 bay leaves*
*1 tablespoon Worcestershire sauce*
*1 cup dry red wine*
*¼ teaspoon pepper*
*4 slices Hearty-Grain French Bread (page 74)*
*½ cup shredded Muenster cheese*

# Fresh Yellow-Tomato Soup

*This light soup is a fine starter for a formal dinner party or for a late-summer lunch when tomatoes, basil, and peppers are at their peak.*

**Serves 6**

**Calories:** 197.11
**Fat:** 11.57 grams
**Saturated fat:** 3.08 grams
**Dietary fiber:** 3.99 grams
**Sodium:** 158.84 mg
**Cholesterol:** 7.63 mg

*8 yellow tomatoes*
*1 tablespoon olive oil*
*1 tablespoon butter*
*4 cloves garlic, peeled and minced*
*1 yellow bell pepper, chopped*
*1 red bell pepper, chopped*
*4 cups Low-Sodium Chicken Broth (page 120)*
*1 tablespoon lemon juice*
*⅛ teaspoon white pepper*
*1 large bunch basil, torn*
*¼ cup toasted sliced almonds*

1. Prepare large bowl of ice water. Bring large pot of water to a boil. Cut X into bottom of each tomato and drop tomatoes into boiling water. Bring water back to a boil and simmer for 1 minute, then remove each tomato and drop into ice water. Let cool for 5 minutes, then peel tomatoes; discard skin.

2. Heat large soup pot over medium heat and add olive oil and butter and let melt. Add garlic; cook and stir for 3 minutes. Cut tomatoes into quarters and add to pot along with peppers. Cook and stir for 4 minutes.

3. Add the broth, lemon juice, and pepper. Bring to a boil and cook for 10 minutes, then add half of the basil.

4. Using an immersion blender, puree soup. Or puree soup in batches in a blender or food processor. Garnish with remaining basil and toasted almonds and serve.

# Low-Sodium Beef Broth

*Even low-sodium varieties of canned beef broth have large amounts of sodium, about 400 mg per cup. This rich broth has hardly any sodium, but it does have lots of flavor.*

1. Preheat oven to 400°F. In large roasting pan, place soup bones, beef shank, carrots, and onions. Drizzle with olive oil and toss to coat. Roast for 2 hours or until bones and vegetables are brown.

2. Place roasted bones and vegetables along with bay leaves, garlic, and peppercorns in a 5- to 6-quart slow cooker. Pour 1 cup water into roasting pan and scrape up brown bits; add to slow cooker. Then pour remaining water into slow cooker. Cover and cook on low for 8–9 hours.

3. Strain broth into large bowl; discard solids. Cover broth and refrigerate overnight. In the morning, remove fat solidified on surface and discard. Pour broth into freezer containers, seal, label, and freeze up to 3 months. To use, defrost in refrigerator overnight.

## Making Broth

*The secrets to making a rich broth include thoroughly browning the bones and vegetables and also letting the broth simmer a long time. You can also clarify the broth; when the fat has been removed, bring the broth to a boil with the shell of an egg. Simmer for 5 minutes, then strain the broth through several layers of cheesecloth or a coffee strainer.*

---

**Yields 10 cups**

**Calories:** 31.45
**Fat:** 0.88 grams
**Saturated fat:** 0.29 grams
**Dietary fiber:** 0.11 grams
**Sodium:** 15.65 mg
**Cholesterol:** 8.85 mg

*3 pounds soup bones*
*1 pound beef shank*
*4 carrots, cut into 1" chunks*
*2 onions, chopped*
*2 tablespoons olive oil*
*2 bay leaves*
*5 cloves garlic, crushed*
*5 peppercorns*
*8 cups water*

# Low-Sodium Chicken Broth

*Browning the chicken before making stock adds rich flavor and deepens the color.*

**Yields 8 cups; serving size 1 cup**

**Calories:** 82.89
**Fat:** 5.22 grams
**Saturated fat:** 0.92 mg
**Dietary fiber:** 0.66 grams
**Sodium:** 39.09 mg
**Cholesterol:** 17.86 mg

*2 tablespoons olive oil*
*3 pounds cut-up chicken*
*2 onions, chopped*
*5 cloves garlic, minced*
*4 carrots, sliced*
*4 stalks celery, sliced*
*1 tablespoon peppercorns*
*1 bay leaf*
*6 cups water*
*2 tablespoons lemon juice*

1. In large skillet, heat olive oil over medium heat. Add chicken, skin-side down, and cook until browned, about 8–10 minutes. Place chicken in 5- to 6-quart slow cooker.

2. Add onions and garlic to drippings in skillet; cook and stir for 2–3 minutes, scraping bottom of skillet. Add to slow cooker along with remaining ingredients except lemon juice. Cover and cook on low for 8–9 hours.

3. Strain broth into large bowl. Remove meat from chicken; refrigerate or freeze for another use. Cover broth and refrigerate overnight. In the morning, remove fat solidified on surface and discard. Stir in lemon juice. Pour broth into freezer containers, seal, label, and freeze up to 3 months. To use, defrost in refrigerator overnight.

# Vegetable-Barley Stew

*This amount of meat adds rich flavor without increasing the cholesterol or saturated-fat content of the stew.*

1. Trim beef and cut into 1" pieces. Sprinkle with flour and paprika and toss to coat. In large skillet, heat olive oil over medium heat. Add beef; brown beef, stirring occasionally, for about 5–6 minutes. Remove to 4- to 5-quart slow cooker.

2. Add onions to skillet along with ½ cup beef broth. Bring to a boil, then simmer, scraping the bottom of the skillet, for 3–4 minutes. Add to slow cooker along with all remaining ingredients.

3. Cover and cook on low for 8–9 hours, or until barley and vegetables are tender. Stir, remove bay leaf, and serve immediately.

### Barley

*Barley contains a substance called beta-glucan that has been shown to be effective in reducing cholesterol levels in clinical studies. You can buy barley in several forms. Hulled barley is the most nutritious, while pearl barley is more polished and cooks more quickly. Barley flakes and grits are also available for quick-cooking recipes.*

---

**Serves 8**

---

**Calories:** 295.45
**Fat:** 9.45 grams
**Saturated fat:** 2.59 grams
**Dietary fiber:** 6.02 grams
**Sodium:** 250.21 mg
**Cholesterol:** 42.67 mg

¾ pound beef round steak
2 tablespoons flour
1 teaspoon paprika
2 tablespoons olive oil
2 onions, chopped
4 cups Low-Sodium Beef
    Broth (page 119), divided
4 carrots, thickly sliced
3 potatoes, cubed
1 (8-ounce) package sliced
    mushrooms
3 cups water
1 teaspoon dried marjoram
    leaves
1 bay leaf
¼ teaspoon salt
¼ teaspoon pepper
¾ cup hulled barley

# Three-Bean Chili

*Chili without meat but with beans is rich and satisfying. If you love hot food, use habanero peppers instead of the jalapeños.*

**Serves 6**

**Calories:** 326.20
**Fat:** 1.50 grams
**Saturated fat:** 0.36 grams
**Dietary fiber:** 16.52 grams
**Sodium:** 64.96 mg
**Cholesterol:** 4.42 mg

*1 cup dried black beans*
*1 cup dried kidney beans*
*1 cup dried pinto beans*
*2 jalapeño peppers, minced*
*2 onions, chopped*
*4 cloves garlic, minced*
*4 cups water*
*4 cups Low-Sodium Beef Broth (page 119), divided*
*2 (14-ounce) cans low-sodium diced tomatoes, undrained*
*1 (6-ounce) can low-sodium tomato paste*
*⅛ teaspoon pepper*

1. Pick over beans and rinse well; drain and place in large bowl. Cover with water and let stand overnight. In the morning, drain and rinse the beans and place them into a 4- to 5-quart slow cooker.

2. Add peppers, onions, and garlic to slow cooker. Add water and 3 cups broth to the slow cooker. Stir well. Cover and cook on low for 8 hours, or until beans are tender.

3. Add canned tomatoes to slow cooker. In small bowl, combine remaining 1 cup broth with the tomato paste; stir with whisk to dissolve the tomato paste. Add to slow cooker along with pepper. Cover and cook on low for 1–2 hours longer or until chili is thick.

# Chapter 7
# **Fish**

# Seafood Risotto

*Risotto is an elegant dish, perfect for entertaining. Do all your prep work ahead of time and store ingredients in the fridge, and the dish will only take about 30 minutes of cooking time.*

**Serves 6**

**Calories:** 397.22
**Fat:** 11.11 grams
**Saturated fat:** 3.20 grams
**Fiber:** 2.41 grams
**Sodium:** 354.58 mg
**Cholesterol:** 94.39 mg

*2 cups water*
*2½ cups Low-Sodium Chicken Broth (page 120)*
*2 tablespoons olive oil*
*1 onion, minced*
*3 cloves garlic, minced*
*1½ cups Arborio rice*
*1 cup chopped celery*
*1 tablespoon fresh dill weed*
*¼ cup dry white wine*
*½ pound sole fillets*
*¼ pound small raw shrimp*
*½ pound bay scallops*
*¼ cup grated Parmesan cheese*
*1 tablespoon butter*

1. In medium saucepan, combine water and broth and heat over low heat. Keep mixture on heat.

2. In large saucepan, heat olive oil over medium heat. Add onion and garlic; cook and stir until crisp-tender, about 3 minutes. Add rice; cook and stir for 3 minutes.

3. Start adding broth mixture, a cup at a time, stirring frequently, adding liquid when previous addition is absorbed. When only 1 cup of broth remains to be added, stir in celery, dill, wine, fish fillets, shrimp, and scallops to rice mixture. Add last cup of broth.

4. Cook, stirring constantly, for 5–7 minutes or until fish is cooked and rice is tender and creamy. Stir in Parmesan and butter, stir, and serve.

# Citrus-Blueberry Fish en Papillote

*This gorgeous presentation of a healthy dish is worthy of company!*
*Serve it with brown-rice pilaf and a baby-spinach salad.*

1. Preheat oven to 400°F. Cut parchment paper into four large heart shapes measuring about 12" × 18". Fold hearts in half, open up, then set aside.

2. In small saucepan, heat olive oil over medium heat. Add onion and garlic; cook and stir for 4 minutes until crisp-tender. Remove from heat and stir in lemon and orange juice along with orange zest.

3. Place one fillet at the center of each parchment heart, next to the fold. Divide onion mixture among fillets. In small bowl, combine blueberries and blueberry jam and mix gently. Divide on top of onion mixture.

4. Fold one half of the parchment heart over the other. Crimp and fold the edges to seal. Place on cookie sheets. Bake for 18–23 minutes or until the bundles are puffed and the paper is browned.

5. Serve immediately, warning diners to be careful of the steam that will billow out when the packages are opened.

### En Papillote

*This French term means "in parchment," and as a cooking term it means food cooked while completely sealed in parchment paper. This method keeps the food moist and prevents overcooking, while sealing in the flavors. You can also use heavy-duty aluminum foil instead of parchment paper.*

**Serves 4**

**Calories:** 220.81
**Fat:** 5.18 grams
**Saturated fat:** 0.87 grams
**Dietary fiber:** 1.37 grams
**Sodium:** 116.46 mg
**Cholesterol:** 72.25 mg

*1 tablespoon olive oil*
*1 onion, finely chopped*
*4 cloves garlic, minced*
*2 tablespoons lemon juice*
*2 tablespoons orange juice*
*1 teaspoon orange zest*
*4 (4-ounce) sole or mahi mahi fillets*
*1 cup blueberries*
*2 tablespoons blueberry jam*

# Broiled Swordfish

*This flavorful sauce and cooking method can be used with any fish.*

**Serves 4**

**Calories:** 210.97
**Fat:** 9.10 grams
**Saturated fat:** 2.03 grams
**Dietary fiber:** 0.24 grams
**Sodium:** 273.91 mg
**Cholesterol:** 55.25 mg

*1 tablespoon olive oil*
*2 tablespoons dry white wine*
*1 teaspoon lemon zest*
*¼ teaspoon salt*
*⅛ teaspoon white pepper*
*1 teaspoon dried dill weed*
*1¼ pounds swordfish steaks*
*4 ½-inch-thick tomato slices*

1. Preheat broiler. In small bowl, combine oil, wine, zest, salt, pepper, and dill weed and whisk to blend.

2. Place steaks on broiler pan. Brush steaks with oil mixture. Broil 6" from heat for 4 minutes. Turn fish and brush with remaining oil mixture. Top with tomatoes. Return to broiler and broil for 4–6 minutes or until fish flakes when tested with fork.

### Cooking Fish

*The general rule for broiling, grilling, or sautéing fish is to cook it for 10 minutes per inch of thickness. Fish should be cooked until it is opaque and a fork inserted into the flesh and twisted flakes the fish easily. In other words, the fish should break apart into thin layers, or flakes.*

# Cajun-Rubbed Fish

*Fish should never be marinated longer than one hour; otherwise, the flesh
may become mushy. This is a perfect last-minute dish for entertaining.*

1. Prepare and preheat grill. In small bowl, combine pepper, cayenne
   pepper, lemon zest, dill weed, salt, and brown sugar and mix well.
   Sprinkle onto both sides of the swordfish steaks and rub in. Set aside
   for 30 minutes.

2. Brush grill with oil. Add swordfish; cook without moving for 4 minutes.
   Then carefully turn steaks and cook for 2–4 minutes on second side
   until fish just flakes when tested with fork. Serve immediately.

**Serves 4**

**Calories:** 233.57
**Fat:** 7.31 grams
**Saturated fat:** 2.00 grams
**Dietary fiber:** 0.10 grams
**Sodium:** 237.08 mg
**Cholesterol:** 70.83 mg

*½ teaspoon black pepper*
*¼ teaspoon cayenne pepper*
*½ teaspoon lemon zest*
*½ teaspoon dried dill weed*
*⅛ teaspoon salt*
*1 tablespoon brown sugar*
*4 (5-ounce) swordfish steaks*

# Baked Halibut in Mustard Sauce

*Combining breadcrumbs with milk to form a
sauce is a trick from Scandinavian cooks.*

1. Preheat oven to 400°F. Spray a 1-quart baking dish with nonstick cooking spray. Cut fish into serving-size pieces and sprinkle with salt, pepper, and lemon juice.

2. In small bowl, combine melted butter, milk, and mustard, and whisk
   until blended. Stir in the breadcrumbs. Pour this sauce over the fish.

3. Bake for 20–25 minutes, or until fish flakes when tested with fork and
   sauce is bubbling. Serve immediately.

**Serves 4**

**Calories:** 219.84
**Fat:** 9.38 grams
**Saturated fat:** 4.30 grams
**Dietary fiber:** 0.71 grams
**Sodium:** 244.95 mg
**Cholesterol:** 54.29 mg

*1 pound halibut fillet*
*Pinch of salt*
*⅛ teaspoon white pepper*
*1 tablespoon lemon juice*
*1 teaspoon orange zest*
*2 tablespoons butter or
    margarine, melted*
*¼ cup skim milk*
*2 tablespoons Dijon mustard*
*1 slice Honey-Wheat
    Sesame Bread (page 66),
    crumbled*

# Bluefish with Asian Seasonings

*Bluefish has a light and delicate texture and flavor. Serve this easy dish with Baby Peas with Water Chestnuts (page 253) and Citrus Shimmer (page 239).*

**Serves 4**

**Calories:** 193.98
**Fat:** 7.17 grams
**Saturated fat:** 1.46 grams
**Dietary fiber:** 0.12 grams
**Sodium:** 181.39 mg
**Cholesterol:** 83.58 mg

*1¼ pounds bluefish fillets*
*1 tablespoon lime juice*
*2 teaspoons low-sodium soy sauce*
*2 teaspoons grated ginger root*
*3 cloves garlic, minced*
*1 teaspoon sesame oil*
*1 teaspoon Thai chile paste*
*1 tablespoon orange juice*
*⅛ teaspoon white pepper*

1. Preheat broiler. Place bluefish fillets on a broiler pan. In small bowl, combine all remaining ingredients, being very careful to make sure that the chile paste is evenly distributed in the sauce.

2. Pour sauce over the fillets. Broil 6" from heat for 6–9 minutes or until fish is opaque and flakes when tested with fork. Serve immediately.

## Sesame Oil

*Sesame oil is made from sesame seeds. It has a very strong taste, so a small amount will easily flavor a sauce. Because it can go rancid very easily, it's best to buy it in small quantities and store it in the refrigerator. Be sure to smell the oil before you use it. If it smells off, discard it and buy another bottle.*

# Cod and Potatoes

*Thinly sliced potatoes are layered with olive oil and herbs and baked until crisp, then topped with cod and lemon juice. Yum!*

**Serves 4**

**Calories:** 362.62
**Fat:** 17.28 grams
**Saturated fat:** 3.88 grams
**Dietary fiber:** 3.55 grams
**Sodium:** 91.56 mg
**Cholesterol:** 56.36 mg

*3 Yukon Gold potatoes*
*¼ cup olive oil*
*⅛ teaspoon white pepper*
*1½ teaspoons dried herbs de Provence, divided*
*4 (4-ounce) cod steaks*
*1 tablespoon butter or margarine*
*2 tablespoons lemon juice*

1. Preheat oven to 350°F. Spray a 9" glass baking dish with nonstick cooking spray. Thinly slice the potatoes. Layer in the baking dish, drizzling each layer with a tablespoon of olive oil, a sprinkle of pepper, and some of the herbs de Provence.

2. Bake for 35–45 minutes or until potatoes are browned on top and tender when pierced with a fork. Arrange cod steaks on top of potatoes. Dot with butter and sprinkle with lemon juice and remaining herbs de Provence.

3. Bake for 15–25 minutes longer or until fish flakes when tested with fork.

### Yukon Gold Potatoes

*This variety of potato is literally gold-colored. The potato tastes buttery and rich even when cooked without fat. You can find it in specialty stores and in the produce aisle of many supermarkets. It was introduced into American grocery stores in 1980 after a Canadian researcher bred a wild South American potato with a North American variety.*

# Poached Fish with Tomatoes and Capers

*White fish fillets include cod, haddock, and pollock.*
*This mild and sweet fish cooks quickly.*

**Serves 4**

**Calories:** 191.05
**Fat:** 7.70 grams
**Saturated fat:** 1.13 grams
**Dietary fiber:** 1.35 grams
**Sodium:** 199.73 mg
**Cholesterol:** 48.73 mg

*2 tablespoons olive oil*
*½ cup chopped red onion*
*2 cloves garlic, minced*
*1 cup chopped fresh tomatoes*
*2 tablespoons no-salt tomato paste*
*¼ cup dry white wine*
*2 tablespoons capers, rinsed*
*4 (4-ounce) white fish fillets*
*¼ cup chopped parsley*

1. In large skillet, heat olive oil over medium heat. Add onion and garlic; cook and stir until tender, about 5 minutes. Add tomatoes, tomato paste, and wine and bring to a simmer; simmer for 5 minutes, stirring frequently.

2. Add capers to sauce and stir, then arrange fillets on top of sauce. Spoon sauce over fish. Reduce heat to low, cover, and poach for 7–10 minutes, or until fish flakes when tested with fork. Sprinkle with parsley and serve immediately.

# Northwest Salmon

*Juniper berries add a nice bittersweet flavor to the sweet*
*onions and blueberries in this gourmet sauce.*

**Serves 4**

**Calories:** 362.66
**Fat:** 22.63 grams
**Saturated fat:** 3.27 grams
**Dietary fiber:** 1.19 grams
**Sodium:** 105.81
**Cholesterol:** 77.92 mg

*4 tablespoons olive oil, divided*
*5 juniper berries, crushed*
*½ cup chopped red onion*
*1 cup blueberries*
*½ cup chopped hazelnuts*
*¼ cup dry white wine*
*4 (5-ounce) salmon fillets*
*Pinch salt*
*⅛ teaspoon white pepper*
*2 cups watercress*

1. Preheat grill or broiler. In small saucepan, heat 3 tablespoons of the olive oil. Add juniper berries and red onion; cook and stir for 3 minutes. Add blueberries, hazelnuts, and wine and bring to a simmer.

2. Meanwhile, sprinkle salmon with salt and pepper and brush with olive oil. Broil or grill 6" from heat until salmon flakes when tested with a fork. Place salmon on watercress and pour blueberry sauce over all; serve immediately.

# Salmon Vegetable Stir-Fry

*Sturdy vegetables are used in this stir-fry because they
can continue cooking while the salmon steams.*

1. In small bowl, combine rice vinegar, sugar, ginger root, cornstarch, hoisin sauce, and pepper. Mix well and set aside.

2. In large skillet or wok, heat peanut oil over high heat. Add onion, peas, and carrots. Stir-fry for 3–4 minutes or until vegetables begin to soften. Add red bell pepper.

3. Immediately place salmon fillet on top of vegetables. Reduce heat to medium, cover skillet or wok and cook for 4–5 minutes or until salmon flakes when tested with fork.

4. Stir the vinegar mixture and add to skillet or wok. Turn heat to medium-high and stir-fry to break up the salmon for 2–3 minutes until the sauce bubbles and thickens. Serve immediately over hot cooked rice.

## Hoisin Sauce

*Hoisin sauce is used in Asian cooking. It's a rich, thick, dark and sweet sauce that stands up to the rich flavors of salmon. It is used sparingly, usually mixed into a stir-fry sauce or marinade. Hoisin sauce is made from fermented soybeans, vinegar, sugar, garlic, and chile peppers.*

**Serves 4**

**Calories:** 371.71
**Fat:** 11.73 grams
**Saturated fat:** 3.24 grams
**Dietary fiber:** 4.51 grams
**Sodium:** 237.60 mg
**Cholesterol:** 67.11 mg

*2 tablespoons rice vinegar*
*1 tablespoon sugar*
*1 tablespoon grated ginger
    root*
*1 tablespoon cornstarch*
*2 tablespoons hoisin sauce*
*⅛ teaspoon white pepper*
*2 tablespoons peanut oil*
*1 onion, sliced*
*½ pound sugar-snap peas*
*3 carrots, sliced*
*1 red bell pepper, sliced*
*¾ pound salmon fillet*

# Sole Medallions Poached in Wine

*You can add other ingredients to the sauce served with this fish.*
*Sun-dried tomatoes, chopped cherry tomatoes,*
*or jalapeño peppers make great additions.*

**Serves 3**

**Calories:** 240.38
**Fat:** 8.93 grams
**Saturated fat:** 1.64 grams
**Dietary fiber:** 0.62 grams
**Sodium:** 207.97 mg
**Cholesterol:** 76.96 mg

*1 pound sole fillet*
*Pinch salt*
*⅛ teaspoon white pepper*
*½ cup Low-Sodium Chicken Broth (page 120)*
*½ cup dry white wine*
*2 shallots, minced*
*½ cup low-fat, low-sodium mayonnaise*
*½ teaspoon dried thyme leaves*
*2 tablespoons lemon juice*
*½ cup blueberries*

1. Cut sole fillet into 1" wide strips. Roll up strips; secure with toothpicks. Sprinkle fish with salt and pepper.

2. In saucepan just large enough to hold the fish, combine chicken broth, wine, and shallots. Bring to a simmer, then lower heat to low. Add fish, cover, and poach for 10–15 minutes or until fish is just opaque. Remove from poaching liquid and remove toothpicks.

3. In small bowl, combine mayonnaise, thyme, lemon juice, and blueberries, and stir to blend. Serve with fish.

## Poaching

*Poaching is an excellent way to cook fragile, low-fat foods without drying them out. The liquid used should be just below a simmer. The French say that it is "shivering," which is a good description of what the liquid should look like. If the liquid doesn't cover the food, spoon some liquid over as it cooks.*

## Baked Lemon Sole with Herbed Crumbs

*Adding herbs to breadcrumbs is a wonderful way to make a flavorful crust on fish without adding calories, fat, or sodium.*

1. Preheat oven to 350°F. In small bowl, combine breadcrumbs, parsley, garlic, and dill weed, and mix well. Drizzle with olive oil and toss to coat.

2. Spray a 9" baking dish with nonstick cooking spray and arrange fillets in dish. Sprinkle with lemon juice, salt, and pepper. Divide crumb mixture on top of fillets.

3. Bake for 12–17 minutes or until fish flakes when tested with a fork and crumb topping is browned. Serve immediately.

**Serves 4**

**Calories:** 294.58
**Fat:** 9.86 grams
**Saturated fat:** 1.65 grams
**Dietary fiber:** 1.09 grams
**Sodium:** 288.21 mg
**Cholesterol:** 110.78 mg

*2 slices Light Whole-Grain*
*   Bread (page 70), crumbled*
*2 tablespoons minced parsley*
*2 cloves garlic, minced*
*1 teaspoon dried dill weed*
*2 tablespoons olive oil*
*4 (6-ounce) sole fillets*
*2 tablespoons lemon juice*
*Pinch salt*
*⅛ teaspoon white pepper*

## Salmon with Mustard and Orange

*Mustard adds great flavor and helps cut the rich texture of salmon, and orange adds a nice touch of sweetness.*

1. Preheat broiler. Place fillets on a broiler pan. In small bowl, combine remaining ingredients and mix well. Spread over salmon.

2. Broil fish 6" from heat for 7–10 minutes or until fish flakes when tested with fork and topping bubbles and begins to brown. Serve immediately.

**Serves 4**

**Calories:** 277.64
**Fat:** 14.02 grams
**Saturated fat:** 2.09 grams
**Dietary fiber:** 0.32 grams
**Sodium:** 197.84 mg
**Cholesterol:** 90.53 mg

*4 (5-ounce) salmon fillets*
*1 tablespoon olive oil*
*2 tablespoons Dijon mustard*
*1 tablespoon flour*
*1 teaspoon orange zest*
*2 tablespoons orange juice*
*Pinch salt*
*⅛ teaspoon white pepper*

# Red Snapper with Fruit Salsa

*This colorful and healthy salsa is sweet and spicy, perfect with the roasted fish.*

**Serves 4**

**Calories:** 254.40
**Fat:** 12.01 grams
**Saturated fat:** 1.82 grams
**Dietary fiber:** 1.41 grams
**Sodium:** 186.42 mg
**Cholesterol:** 72.25 mg

*1 cup blueberries*
*1 cup chopped watermelon*
*1 jalapeño pepper, minced*
*½ cup chopped tomatoes*
*3 tablespoons olive oil, divided*
*2 tablespoons orange juice*
*⅛ teaspoon salt, divided*
*⅛ teaspoon white pepper*
*4 (4-ounce) red snapper fillets*
*1 lemon, thinly sliced*

1. Preheat oven to 400°F. Spray a 9" glass baking pan with nonstick cooking spray and set aside. In medium bowl, combine blueberries, watermelon, jalapeño pepper, tomatoes, 1 tablespoon olive oil, orange juice, and half of the salt. Mix well and set aside.

2. Arrange fillets in prepared pan. Sprinkle with remaining salt and the white pepper and drizzle with 2 tablespoons olive oil. Top with lemon slices.

3. Bake for 15 to 20 minutes, or until fish is opaque and flesh flakes when tested with fork. Place on serving plate and top with blueberry mixture; serve immediately.

## Salsa

*Salsas are delicious for appetizers and can be used as a topping on any grilled or roasted meat. Use your imagination and remember to create a rainbow plate when making your salsas. The mixture should be as colorful as possible to give you the most antioxidants and polyphenols in each spoonful.*

# Seared Scallops with Fruit

*Serve this super-quick and colorful dish with brown-rice pilaf and a green salad.*

1. Rinse scallops and pat dry. Sprinkle with salt and pepper and set aside.

2. In large skillet, heat olive oil and butter over medium-high heat. Add the scallops and don't move them for 3 minutes. Carefully check to see if the scallops are deep golden brown. If they are, turn and cook for 1–2 minutes on the second side.

3. Remove scallops to serving plate. Add peaches to skillet and brown quickly on one side, about 2 minutes. Turn peaches and add wine to skillet; bring to a boil. Remove from heat and add blueberries. Pour over scallops, sprinkle with lime juice, and serve immediately.

## Scallops

*Scallops are shellfish that are very low in fat. Sea scallops are the largest, followed by bay scallops and calico scallops. They should smell very fresh and slightly briny, like the sea. If they smell fishy, do not buy them. There may be a small muscle attached to the side of each scallop; pull that off and discard it because it can be tough.*

**Serves 3–4**

**Calories:** 207.89
**Fat:** 7.36 grams
**Saturated fat:** 2.40 grams
**Dietary fiber:** 1.62 grams
**Sodium:** 242.16 mg
**Cholesterol:** 45.03 mg

*1 pound sea scallops*
*Pinch salt*
*⅛ teaspoon white pepper*
*1 tablespoon olive oil*
*1 tablespoon butter or margarine*
*¼ cup dry white wine*
*2 peaches, sliced*
*1 cup blueberries*
*1 tablespoon lime juice*

# Fennel-Grilled Haddock

*Fennel is sweet and tastes like licorice, especially when grilled. It imparts its distinctive flavor to the mild fish using this grilling method.*

**Serves 4**

**Calories:** 246.68
**Fat:** 11.35 grams
**Saturated fat:** 1.58 grams
**Dietary fiber:** 3.66 grams
**Sodium:** 192.31 mg
**Cholesterol:** 78.63 mg

*2 bulbs fennel*
*4 (5-ounce) haddock or*
 *halibut steaks*
*3 tablespoons olive oil*
*Pinch salt*
*⅛ teaspoon cayenne pepper*
*1 teaspoon paprika*
*2 tablespoons lemon juice*

1. Prepare and preheat grill. Slice fennel bulbs lengthwise into ½" slices, leaving the stalks and fronds attached.

2. Brush fennel and haddock with olive oil on all sides to coat. Sprinkle fish with salt, pepper, and paprika. Place fennel on grill 6" above medium coals, cut side down. Arrange fish on top of fennel and close the grill.

3. Grill for 5–7 minutes or until fennel is deep golden brown and fish flakes when tested with fork. Remove fish to serving platter, sprinkle with lemon juice, and cover.

4. Cut the root end and stems from the fennel and discard. Slice fennel and place on top of fish; serve immediately.

### Purchasing Haddock

*Haddock has a fine white flesh. Fresh haddock will hold together well and will be firm. Fillets should be translucent; if you notice the fillet has a chalky hue to it, it is old. Refrigerate your haddock as soon as possible after purchase, either in the original wrapping from the fishmonger or in an airtight container, and use it within 24 hours. If you freeze the fish it should last 3 months.*

# Pistachio-Crusted Red Snapper

*This could also be made with other heart-healthy nuts,
including hazelnuts, walnuts, or pecans.*

1. Preheat oven to 375°F. In small bowl, combine lemon juice, orange zest, lemon zest, and olive oil. In another small bowl, combine chopped pistachios and crumbled bread. Drizzle lemon mixture over bread mixture and toss to coat.

2. Spray a 9"-square glass baking dish with nonstick cooking spray. Arrange fish in dish and sprinkle with salt and pepper. Top evenly with the crumb mixture, patting into place.

3. Bake for 15–25 minutes, or until fish is opaque and flakes when tested with fork and crumb mixture is browned. Serve immediately.

**Serves 4**

**Calories:** 283.52
**Fat:** 15.79 grams
**Saturated fat:** 2.20 grams
**Dietary fiber:** 2.29 grams
**Sodium:** 172.06 mg
**Cholesterol:** 54.40 mg

1 tablespoon lemon juice
1 teaspoon grated orange zest
1 teaspoon grated lemon zest
2 tablespoons olive oil
⅓ cup chopped pistachios
1 slice Light Whole-Grain Bread
    (page 70), crumbled
1 pound red snapper fillets
Pinch salt
⅛ teaspoon pepper

# Sesame-Crusted Mahi Mahi

*The sesame seeds toast while the fish cooks, and the mustard
mixture seals in the moisture in this fabulously easy recipe.*

1. Rinse fillets and pat dry. In small bowl, combine mustard and sour cream and mix well. Spread this mixture on all sides of fish. Roll in sesame seeds to coat.

2. Heat olive oil in large skillet over medium heat. Pan-fry fish, turning once, for 5–8 minutes or until fish flakes when tested with fork and sesame seeds are toasted. Serve immediately with lemon wedges.

**Serves 4**

**Calories:** 282.75
**Fat:** 17.17 grams
**Saturated fat:** 2.84 grams
**Dietary fiber:** 2.42 grams
**Sodium:** 209.54 mg
**Cholesterol:** 73.75 mg

4 (4-ounce) mahi mahi or sole
    fillets
2 tablespoons Dijon mustard
1 tablespoon low-fat sour
    cream
½ cup sesame seeds
2 tablespoons olive oil
1 lemon, cut into wedges

# Poached Chilean Sea Bass with Pears

*Leave the skin on the pears for a pretty presentation
and to keep the fruit from falling apart.*

**Serves 4**

**Calories:** 235.38
**Fat:** 5.81 grams
**Saturated fat:** 2.55 grams
**Dietary fiber:** 2.58 grams
**Sodium:** 194.06 mg
**Cholesterol:** 65.71 mg

½ cup dry white wine
¼ cup water
2 bay leaves
⅛ teaspoon salt
½ teaspoon Tabasco sauce
1 lemon, thinly sliced
4 (4–5) ounce sea bass steaks
    or fillets
2 firm pears, cored and cut
    in half
1 tablespoon butter

1. In large skillet, combine wine, water, bay leaves, salt, Tabasco, and lemon slices. Bring to a simmer over medium heat.

2. Add fish and pears. Reduce heat to low and poach for 9–12 minutes or until fish flakes when tested with a fork.

3. Remove fish and pears to serving platter. Remove bay leaves from poaching liquid and increase heat to high. Boil for 3–5 minutes or until liquid is reduced and syrupy. Swirl in butter and pour over fish and pears; serve immediately.

### Fish and Cholesterol

*You may notice that the cholesterol counts on many of these recipes are relatively high. That is because fish is low in fat; by contrast, the cholesterol ratio is higher. Remember, the number to pay attention to is the grams of saturated fat. Your total intake of saturated fat per day should be less than 15 percent of calories.*

# Sesame-Pepper Salmon Kabobs

*Serve these skewers on brown-rice pilaf with a wedge of lemon on the side. A fruit salad will round out the meal.*

**Serves 4**

**Calories:** 319.33
**Fat:** 20.26 grams
**Saturated fat:** 3.67 grams
**Dietary fiber:** 2.39 grams
**Sodium:** 141.88 mg
**Cholesterol:** 66.94 mg

*1 pound salmon steak*
*2 tablespoons olive oil, divided*
*¼ cup sesame seeds*
*1 teaspoon pepper*
*1 red bell pepper*
*1 yellow bell pepper*
*1 red onion*
*8 cremini mushrooms*
*⅛ teaspoon salt*

1. Prepare and preheat grill. Cut salmon steak into 1" pieces, discarding skin and bones. Brush salmon with half of the olive oil.

2. In small bowl, combine sesame seeds and pepper and mix. Press all sides of salmon cubes into the sesame seed mixture.

3. Slice bell peppers into 1" slices and cut red onion into 8 wedges; trim mushroom stems and leave caps whole. Skewer coated salmon pieces, peppers, onion, and mushrooms on metal skewers. Brush vegetables with remaining olive oil and sprinkle with salt.

4. Grill 6" from medium coals, turning once during cooking time, until the sesame seeds are very brown and toasted and fish is just done, about 6–8 minutes. Serve immediately.

# Scallops on Skewers with Tomatoes

*This sauce is a variation on Chimichurri Sauce (page 179), originally from Argentina. It's fragrant and delicious.*

**Serves 4**

**Calories:** 202.03
**Fat:** 11.11 grams
**Saturated fat:** 1.52 grams
**Dietary fiber:** 1.34 grams
**Sodium:** 251.50 mg
**Cholesterol:** 35.06 mg

*1 pound sea scallops*
*12 cherry tomatoes*
*4 green onions, cut in half crosswise*
*½ cup chopped parsley*
*1 tablespoon fresh oregano leaves*
*3 tablespoons olive oil*
*2 tablespoons lemon juice*
*2 cloves garlic*
*⅛ teaspoon salt*
*⅛ teaspoon pepper*

1. Prepare and preheat broiler. Rinse scallops and pat dry. Thread on skewers along with cherry tomatoes and green onions.

2. In blender or food processor, combine remaining ingredients. Blend or process until smooth. Reserve ¼ cup of this sauce.

3. Brush remaining sauce onto the food on the skewers. Place on broiler pan. Broil 6" from heat for 3–4 minutes per side, turning once during cooking time. Serve with remaining sauce.

## Uncooked Sauces

*Uncooked sauces like Chimichurri Sauce (page 179) and pesto can be stored in the refrigerator up to 3 days. For longer storage, freeze them. Pour about 2 tablespoons into ice cube trays and freeze until solid. Pop the frozen cubes into a heavy-duty freezer bag, label, and freeze up to 6 months. To defrost, let stand in refrigerator overnight.*

# Almond Snapper with Shrimp Sauce

*You could use any mild white fish in this delicious recipe.*

1. Place egg white in shallow bowl; beat until foamy. On shallow plate, combine breadcrumbs, almonds, salt, and pepper and mix well. Dip fish into egg white, then into crumb mixture, pressing to coat. Let stand on wire rack for 10 minutes.

2. In small saucepan, heat 1 tablespoon olive oil over medium heat. Add onion, garlic, and bell pepper; cook and stir until tender, about 5 minutes. Add shrimp; cook and stir just until shrimp curl and turn pink, about 1–2 minutes. Remove from heat and add lemon juice; set aside.

3. In large saucepan, heat remaining 2 tablespoons olive oil over medium heat. Add coated fish fillets. Cook for 4 minutes on one side, then carefully turn and cook for 2–5 minutes on second side until coating is browned and fish flakes when tested with a fork.

4. While fish is cooking, return saucepan with shrimp to medium heat. Add sour cream and dill weed. Heat, stirring, until mixture is hot.

5. Remove fish from skillet and place on serving plate. Top each with a spoonful of shrimp sauce and serve immediately.

**Serves 6**

**Calories:** 272.57
**Fat:** 13.80 grams
**Saturated fat:** 3.09 grams
**Dietary fiber:** 1.56 grams
**Sodium:** 216.17 mg
**Cholesterol:** 88.71 mg

*1 egg white*
*¼ cup dry breadcrumbs*
*⅓ cup ground almonds*
*⅛ teaspoon salt*
*⅛ teaspoon white pepper*
*6 (4-ounce) red snapper fillets*
*3 tablespoons olive oil, divided*
*1 onion, chopped*
*4 cloves garlic, minced*
*1 red bell pepper, chopped*
*¼ pound small raw shrimp*
*1 tablespoon lemon juice*
*½ cup low-fat sour cream*
*½ teaspoon dried dill weed*

# Scallops on Skewers with Lemon

*Because scallops are so low in fat, sodium, and cholesterol, you can add a bit of low-sodium bacon to this dish for a flavor treat.*

**Serves 4**

**Calories:** 173.65
**Fat:** 6.48 grams
**Saturated fat:** 1.51 grams
**Dietary fiber:** 0.07 grams
**Sodium:** 266.64 mg
**Cholesterol:** 46.20 mg

*2 tablespoons lemon juice*
*1 teaspoon grated lemon zest*
*2 teaspoons sesame oil*
*2 tablespoons chili sauce*
*⅛ teaspoon cayenne pepper*
*1 pound sea scallops*
*4 strips low-sodium bacon*

1. Prepare and preheat grill or broiler. In medium bowl, combine lemon juice, zest, sesame oil, chili sauce, and cayenne pepper and mix well. Add scallops and toss to coat. Let stand for 15 minutes.

2. Make skewers with the scallops and bacon. Thread a skewer through one end of the bacon, then add a scallop. Curve the bacon around the scallop and thread onto the skewer so it surrounds the scallop halfway. Repeat with 3 to 4 more scallops and the bacon slice.

3. Repeat with remaining scallops and bacon. Grill or broil 6" from heat source for 3–5 minutes per side, until bacon is crisp and scallops are cooked and opaque. Serve immediately.

### Bacon

*If you read labels and choose carefully, bacon can be an occasional treat. Many companies now make low-sodium bacon. In health-food stores you can often find organic bacon that has better nutrition. Also consider Canadian bacon. More like ham, this meat has less sodium, fat, and chemicals like nitrates than regular bacon.*

# Chapter 8
# **Poultry**

# Chicken Breasts with Salsa

*Whole-grain cereal provides lots of folic acid, which helps reduce homocysteine levels. It makes a nice crunchy coating on chicken breasts.*

**Serves 4**

**Calories:** 264.05
**Fat:** 4.43 grams
**Saturated fat:** 1.18 grams
**Dietary fiber:** 4.69 grams
**Sodium:** 146.85 mg
**Cholesterol:** 90.36 mg

*2 tablespoons lime juice, divided*
*1 egg white*
*1 cup whole-grain cereal, crushed*
*1 teaspoon dried thyme leaves*
*¼ teaspoon pepper*
*4 (4-ounce) boneless, skinless chicken breasts*
*1 cup Super Spicy Salsa (page 85)*
*1 jalapeño pepper, minced*

1. Preheat oven to 375°F. Line a cookie sheet with a wire rack and set aside. In small bowl, combine 1 tablespoon lime juice and egg white; beat until frothy. On shallow plate, combine crushed cereal, thyme, and pepper.

2. Dip chicken into egg white mixture, then into cereal mixture to coat. Place on prepared cookie sheet. Bake for 20–25 minutes or until chicken is thoroughly cooked and coating is crisp.

3. Meanwhile, in small saucepan combine remaining 1 tablespoon lime juice, salsa, and jalapeño pepper. Heat through, stirring occasionally. Serve with chicken.

# Sautéed Chicken with Roasted Garlic Sauce

*When roasted, garlic turns sweet and nutty. Combined with
tender sautéed chicken, this makes a memorable meal.*

**Serves 4**

**Calories:** 267.01
**Fat:** 7.78 grams
**Saturated fat:** 1.65 grams
**Dietary fiber:** 0.69 grams
**Sodium:** 158.61 mg
**Cholesterol:** 91.85 mg

*1 head Roasted Garlic (page
89)*
*⅓ cup Low-Sodium Chicken
Broth (page 120)*
*½ teaspoon dried oregano
leaves*
*4 (4-ounce) boneless, skinless
chicken breasts*
*¼ cup flour*
*⅛ teaspoon salt*
*⅛ teaspoon pepper*
*¼ teaspoon paprika*
*2 tablespoons olive oil*

1. Squeeze garlic cloves from the skins and combine in small saucepan with chicken broth and oregano leaves.

2. On shallow plate, combine flour, salt, pepper, and paprika. Dip chicken into this mixture to coat.

3. In large skillet, heat 2 tablespoons olive oil. At the same time, place the saucepan with the garlic mixture over medium heat. Add the chicken to the hot olive oil; cook for 5 minutes without moving. Then carefully turn chicken and cook for 4–7 minutes longer until chicken is thoroughly cooked.

4. Stir garlic sauce with wire whisk until blended. Serve with the chicken.

## Chicken and Cholesterol

*Chicken is fairly high in cholesterol, but it's very low in saturated fat. The American Heart Association has boneless, skinless chicken breasts on its approved foods list, so you don't have to worry. If you are susceptible to cholesterol in food, reduce the serving size to 3 ounces per person.*

# Asian Chicken Stir-Fry

*Yellow summer squash is a thin-skinned squash
like zucchini. It has a mild, sweet flavor.*

**Serves 4**

**Calories:** 252.42
**Fat:** 12.42 grams
**Saturated fat:** 2.06 grams
**Dietary fiber:** 3.36 grams
**Sodium:** 202.04 mg
**Cholesterol:** 41.11 mg

2 (5-ounce) boneless, skinless
  chicken breasts
½ cup Low-Sodium Chicken
  Broth (page 120)
1 tablespoon low-sodium soy
  sauce
1 tablespoon cornstarch
1 tablespoon sherry
2 tablespoons peanut oil
1 onion, sliced
3 cloves garlic, minced
1 tablespoon grated ginger
  root
1 cup snow peas
½ cup canned sliced water
  chestnuts, drained
1 yellow summer squash,
  sliced
¼ cup chopped unsalted
  peanuts

1. Cut chicken into strips and set aside. In small bowl, combine chicken broth, soy sauce, cornstarch, and sherry and set aside.

2. In large skillet or wok, heat peanut oil over medium-high heat. Add chicken; stir-fry until almost cooked, about 3–4 minutes. Remove to plate. Add onion, garlic, and ginger root to skillet; stir-fry for 4 minutes longer. Then add snow peas, water chestnuts, and squash; stir-fry for 2 minutes longer.

3. Stir chicken broth mixture and add to skillet along with chicken. Stir-fry for 3–4 minutes longer or until chicken is thoroughly cooked and sauce is thickened and bubbly. Sprinkle with peanuts and serve immediately.

# Chicken Stir-Fry with Napa Cabbage

*The combination of cabbage, bell pepper, and edamame is delicious and very healthy.*

**Serves 4**

**Calories:** 307.21
**Fat:** 14.90 grams
**Saturated fat:** 2.47 grams
**Dietary fiber:** 5.25 grams
**Sodium:** 214.61 mg
**Cholesterol:** 45.57 mg

2 (5-ounce) boneless, skinless
    chicken breasts
2 tablespoons cornstarch
2 tablespoons lemon juice
1 tablespoon low-sodium soy
    sauce
1 cup Low-Sodium Chicken
    Broth (page 120)
2 tablespoons peanut oil
4 cups shredded Napa
    cabbage
4 green onions, sliced
1 green bell pepper, sliced
1½ cups frozen edamame,
    thawed

1. Cut chicken into 1" pieces. In small bowl, combine cornstarch, lemon juice, soy sauce, and chicken broth. Add chicken and let stand for 15 minutes.

2. Heat oil in large skillet or wok. Drain chicken, reserving marinade. Add chicken to skillet; stir-fry until almost cooked, about 4 minutes. Remove chicken to a plate.

3. Add cabbage and green onions to skillet; stir fry until cabbage wilts, about 4 minutes. Add bell pepper and edamame; stir-fry for 3–5 minutes longer until hot.

4. Stir marinade and add to skillet along with chicken. Stir-fry until sauce bubbles and thickens and chicken is thoroughly cooked. Serve over hot cooked brown rice.

## Stir-Frying

*Stir-frying is one of the healthiest ways to cook. Once all the ingredients are prepared, the method takes 10 minutes or less. But all of the food must be prepared before the actual cooking begins. There is no time to chop or slice vegetables once the wok is hot and you start to stir-fry.*

# Chicken Breasts with Mashed Beans

*For a pretty presentation, divide the beans among*
*plates and top with a sautéed chicken breast.*

**Serves 6**

**Calories:** 316.30
**Fat:** 10.55 grams
**Saturated fat:** 2.56 grams
**Dietary fiber:** 2.99 grams
**Sodium:** 133.71 mg
**Cholesterol:** 97.34 mg

*3 tablespoons olive oil,*
*divided*
*1 onion, chopped*
*3 cloves garlic, minced*
*1 (14-ounce) can low-sodium*
*cannellini beans*
*½ cup chopped flat-leaf*
*parsley*
*½ teaspoon dried oregano*
*leaves*
*1 teaspoon dried basil leaves*
*¼ cup grated Parmesan*
*cheese*
*3 tablespoons flour*
*¼ teaspoon white pepper*
*6 (4-ounce) boneless, skinless*
*chicken breasts*

1. In medium saucepan, heat 1 tablespoon olive oil and add onion and garlic. Cook and stir until tender, about 5 minutes. Drain beans, rinse, and drain again.

2. Add to saucepan along with parsley, oregano, and basil. Cook until hot, stirring frequently, about 5 minutes. Using a potato masher, mash the bean mixture. Turn heat to very low.

3. On shallow plate, combine Parmesan, flour, and pepper and mix well. Coat chicken on both sides with cheese mixture. In large skillet, heat remaining 2 tablespoons olive oil over medium heat.

4. Add chicken to skillet; cook for 5 minutes without moving. Carefully turn chicken and cook for 4–6 minutes until thoroughly cooked. Serve with mashed beans.

# Chicken Spicy Thai Style

*Peanut butter thickens the sauce and adds rich flavor
to this easy stir-fry without adding any cholesterol.*

**Serves 4**

**Calories:** 300.35
**Fat:** 16.70 grams
**Saturated fat:** 3.20 grams
**Dietary fiber:** 2.16 grams
**Sodium:** 309.32 mg
**Cholesterol:** 51.56 mg

*2 tablespoons lime juice*
*1 tablespoon low-sodium soy
    sauce*
*½ cup Low-Sodium Chicken
    Broth (page 120)*
*¼ cup dry white wine*
*¼ cup natural peanut butter*
*2 tablespoons peanut oil*
*1 onion, chopped*
*4 cloves garlic, minced*
*3 (4-ounce) boneless, skinless
    chicken breasts, sliced*
*4 cups shredded Napa
    cabbage*
*1 cup shredded carrots*

1. In small bowl, combine lime juice, soy sauce, chicken broth, wine, and peanut butter and mix with wire whisk until blended. Set aside.

2. In wok or large skillet, heat peanut oil over medium-high heat. Add onion and garlic; stir-fry until crisp-tender, about 4 minutes. Add chicken; stir-fry until almost cooked, about 3 minutes. Add cabbage and carrots; stir-fry until cabbage begins to wilt, about 3–4 minutes longer.

3. Remove food from wok and return wok to heat. Add peanut butter mixture and bring to a simmer. Return chicken and vegetables to wok; stir fry until sauce bubbles and thickens and chicken is thoroughly cooked, about 3–4 minutes. Serve immediately.

### Natural Peanut Butter

*Whenever possible, use natural peanut butter, not the regular kind found on store shelves. Read labels carefully. You'll notice that most regular peanut butter contains hydrogenated vegetable oil, which is a source of trans fat. The oil will separate out of the natural peanut butter as it stands; just stir it back in before using.*

# Chicken Breasts with New Potatoes

*This easy one-dish meal has the best combination of flavors. Mustard
adds a nice bit of spice to tender chicken and crisp potatoes.*

**Serves 6**

**Calories:** 395.92
**Fat:** 9.57 grams
**Saturated fat:** 1.85 grams
**Dietary fiber:** 5.21 grams
**Sodium:** 142.98 mg
**Cholesterol:** 61.23 mg

*12 small new red potatoes*
*2 tablespoons olive oil*
*⅛ teaspoon white pepper*
*4 cloves garlic, minced*
*1 teaspoon dried oregano
    leaves*
*2 tablespoons Dijon mustard*
*4 (4-ounce) boneless, skinless
    chicken breasts*
*1 cup cherry tomatoes*

1.  Preheat oven to 400°F. Line a roasting pan with parchment paper and set aside. Scrub potatoes and cut each in half. Place in prepared pan.

2.  In small bowl, combine oil, pepper, garlic, oregano, and mustard and mix well. Drizzle half of this mixture over the potatoes and toss to coat. Roast for 20 minutes.

3.  Cut chicken breasts into quarters. Remove pan from oven and add chicken to potato mixture. Using a spatula, mix potatoes and chicken together. Drizzle with remaining oil mixture. Return to oven and roast for 15 minutes longer.

4.  Add tomatoes to pan. Roast for 5–10 minutes longer, or until potatoes are tender and browned and chicken is thoroughly cooked.

# Chicken Poached in Tomato Sauce

*Tarragon is a mild, licorice-tasting herb that pairs
beautifully with chicken and tomatoes.*

1. In medium saucepan, combine rice and water and bring to a boil over high heat. Reduce heat to low, cover, and simmer for 30–40 minutes or until rice is tender.

2. Meanwhile, in large saucepan heat olive oil over medium heat. Add onion and garlic; cook and stir for 4 minutes until crisp-tender. Add tomatoes, tarragon, wine, tomato paste, chicken broth, salt, and pepper, and bring to a simmer, stirring frequently.

3. Add chicken and bring back to a simmer. Cover pan, reduce heat to low, and poach chicken for 15–20 minutes or until thoroughly cooked. Serve over hot cooked rice.

## Tomato Paste

*If you don't use a whole can of tomato paste, you can freeze the rest for another use. Freeze the tomato paste in 1-tablespoon portions on a cookie sheet, then package into a freezer bag, label, and freeze for up to 3 months. To use, let stand at room temperature for 15 minutes, then use in recipe.*

**Serves 4**

**Calories:** 285.33
**Fat:** 9.22 grams
**Saturated fat:** 1.70 grams
**Dietary fiber:** 2.49 grams
**Sodium:** 129.66 mg
**Cholesterol:** 61.80 mg

1 cup brown rice
2 cups water
2 tablespoons olive oil
1 onion, chopped
3 cloves garlic, minced
2 cups chopped plum
    tomatoes
½ teaspoon dried tarragon
¼ cup dry red wine
3 tablespoons no-salt tomato
    paste
1 cup Low-Sodium Chicken
    Broth (page 120)
⅛ teaspoon salt
⅛ teaspoon pepper
3 (5-ounce) boneless, skinless
    chicken thighs, sliced

# Hazelnut-Crusted Chicken Breasts

*This super-quick dish is perfect for a last-minute dinner.
Serve with a spinach salad and some crisp breadsticks.*

**Serves 2**

**Calories:** 276.64
**Fat:** 16.02 grams
**Saturated fat:** 1.88 grams
**Dietary fiber:** 1.46 grams
**Sodium:** 266.25 mg
**Cholesterol:** 65.77 mg

*2 (4-ounce) boneless, skinless
    chicken breasts*
*Pinch salt*
*Pinch pepper*
*1 tablespoon Dijon mustard*
*1 egg white*
*⅓ cup chopped hazelnuts*
*1 tablespoon olive oil*

1. Place chicken between two sheets of waxed paper. Pound, starting at center of chicken, until ¼" thick. Sprinkle chicken with salt and pepper. Spread each side of chicken with some of the mustard.

2. In small bowl, beat egg white until foamy. Dip chicken into egg white, then into hazelnuts, pressing to coat both sides.

3. In skillet, heat olive oil over medium heat. Add chicken; cook for 3 minutes without moving. Then carefully turn and cook for 1–3 minutes on second side until chicken is thoroughly cooked and nuts are toasted. Serve immediately.

### Dijon Mustard

*Dijon mustard is not the same as the yellow mustard you put on hot dogs. To be called 'Dijon' it has to be made from the recipe created in Dijon, France, using brown or black mustard seeds. The flavor is much stronger than yellow mustard. It is high in potassium, calcium, and niacin, and has little or no fat or cholesterol.*

# Hot-and-Spicy Peanut Thighs

*Serve this easy and spicy recipe with Whole-Grain
Cornbread (page 56) and Citrus Shimmer (page 239).*

1. Preheat oven to 350°F. Spray a roasting pan with nonstick cooking spray and set aside. Pound chicken slightly, to ⅓" thickness.

2. In shallow bowl, combine barbecue sauce and chili powder and mix well. Dip chicken into sauce, then dip one side into peanuts. Place, peanut side up, in prepared pan.

3. Bake for 30–40 minutes, or until chicken is thoroughly cooked and nuts are browned. Serve immediately.

## Coating for Poultry

*When you're baking poultry that has a nut or breadcrumb coating, it's usually best to coat only the top side of the meat. The coating underneath can become mushy and fall off because of the moisture in the chicken. If you want to coat both sides, it's best to pan-fry or sauté the chicken, or bake it on a wire rack.*

**Serves 4**

**Calories:** 327.41
**Fat:** 19.55 grams
**Saturated fat:** 4.22 grams
**Dietary fiber:** 2.08 grams
**Sodium:** 129.88 mg
**Cholesterol:** 94.26 mg

*4 (4-ounce) chicken thighs*
*½ cup low-sodium barbecue
    sauce*
*2 teaspoons chili powder*
*½ cup chopped unsalted
    peanuts*

# Turkey with Prunes

*Prunes are high in a soluble fiber called pectin, which absorbs cholesterol in your intestines even better than oat bran does.*

**Serves 6**

**Calories:** 327.80
**Fat:** 15.34 grams
**Saturated fat:** 2.04 grams
**Dietary fiber:** 1.28 grams
**Sodium:** 92.23 mg
**Cholesterol:** 57.71 mg

*3 tablespoons olive oil*
*1 onion, chopped*
*3 cloves garlic, minced*
*1 cup finely chopped pitted prunes*
*⅛ teaspoon salt*
*⅛ teaspoon pepper*
*½ cup chopped hazelnuts*
*6 (3-ounce) turkey cutlets*
*2 tablespoons flour*
*½ cup Low-Sodium Chicken Broth (page 120)*
*¼ cup dry white wine*
*½ teaspoon dried thyme leaves*
*1 tablespoon lemon juice*

1. In small saucepan, heat 1 tablespoon olive oil over medium heat. Add onion and garlic; cook and stir until crisp-tender, about 4 minutes. Add prunes and sprinkle with salt and pepper. Cook for 3–4 minutes or until prunes begin to plump. Add nuts and remove from heat. Let cool for 20 minutes.

2. Arrange turkey cutlets on work surface. Divide prune mixture among the cutlets. Roll up, securing with kitchen twine or toothpicks. Dredge filled cutlets in flour.

3. Heat remaining 2 tablespoons olive oil in large skillet. Brown turkey, turning to cook evenly, for about 4–5 minutes. Then add broth, wine, and thyme leaves to skillet. Cover and braise cutlets for 6–8 minutes or until turkey is tender and thoroughly cooked. Add lemon juice and serve immediately.

# Sesame-Crusted Chicken

*Nutty and crunchy sesame seeds make a delicious coating on tender chicken in this simple recipe.*

**Serves 4**

**Calories:** 363.65
**Fat:** 20.83 grams
**Saturated fat:** 4.15 grams
**Dietary fiber:** 2.24 grams
**Sodium:** 250.28 mg
**Cholesterol:** 99.28 mg

*2 tablespoons low-sodium soy sauce*
*2 cloves garlic, minced*
*1 tablespoon grated ginger root*
*1 tablespoon brown sugar*
*1 teaspoon sesame oil*
*4 (4-ounce) boneless, skinless chicken breasts*
*½ cup sesame seeds*
*3 tablespoons olive oil*
*1 tablespoon butter*

1. In large food storage heavy-duty plastic bag, combine soy sauce, garlic, ginger root, brown sugar, and sesame oil and mix well. Add chicken; seal bag, and squish to coat chicken with marinade. Place in bowl and refrigerate for 8 hours.

2. When ready to eat, remove chicken from marinade; discard marinade. Dip chicken in sesame seeds to coat on all sides.

3. Heat olive oil and butter in large skillet over medium heat. Add chicken and cook for 5 minutes. Carefully turn chicken and cook for 3–6 minutes on second side or until chicken is thoroughly cooked and sesame seeds are toasted. Serve immediately.

## Sesame Seeds

*Sesame seeds are high in an antioxidant called lignan, which can lower cholesterol along with reducing blood pressure. These tiny, nutty seeds are also high in monounsaturated fats, which can raise HDL cholesterol levels. Because they are high in fat they can go rancid easily; store them, tightly covered, in the refrigerator.*

# Texts BBQ Chicken Thighs

*Make a double batch of this fabulous barbecue sauce all by itself in your slow cooker and freeze it in ¼-cup portions to use anytime.*

**Serves 6**

**Calories:** 236.53 mg
**Fat:** 9.30 grams
**Saturated fat:** 1.79 grams
**Dietary fiber:** 1.76 grams
**Sodium:** 277.24 mg
**Cholesterol:** 94.12 mg

*2 tablespoons olive oil*
*1 onion, chopped*
*4 cloves garlic, minced*
*1 jalapeño pepper, minced*
*¼ cup orange juice*
*1 tablespoon low-sodium soy sauce*
*2 tablespoons apple-cider vinegar*
*2 tablespoons brown sugar*
*2 tablespoons Dijon mustard*
*1 (14-ounce) can crushed tomatoes, undrained*
*½ teaspoon cumin*
*1 tablespoon chili powder*
*¼ teaspoon pepper*
*6 (4-ounce) boneless, skinless chicken thighs*
*3 tablespoons cornstarch*
*¼ cup water*

1. In a small skillet, heat olive oil over medium heat. Add onion and garlic; cook and stir until crisp-tender, about 4 minutes. Place in 3–4 quart slow cooker and add jalapeño, orange juice, soy sauce, vinegar, brown sugar, mustard, tomatoes, cumin, chili powder, and pepper.

2. Add chicken to the sauce, pushing chicken into the sauce to completely cover. Cover and cook on low for 8–10 hours or until chicken is thoroughly cooked.

3. In small bowl, combine cornstarch and water; stir until smooth. Add to slow cooker and stir. Cook on high for 15–20 minutes longer until sauce is thickened.

### Chicken Thighs

*Many people may consider chicken thighs too fatty. Though chicken thighs do contain more fat than skinless chicken breasts, they still only have 11 grams of fat per 4-ounce serving. That is less fat than one would find in the same size serving of beef, lamb, or pork.*

# Turkey Cutlets Florentine

*The word* Florentine *on a menu means spinach. This deep-green leaf is full of antioxidants and fiber. And it's delicious, too!*

**Serves 6**

**Calories:** 258.57
**Fat:** 9.19 grams
**Saturated fat:** 2.15 grams
**Dietary fiber:** 2.09 grams
**Sodium:** 236.98
**Cholesterol:** 83.31 mg

*1 egg white, beaten*
*½ cup dry breadcrumbs*
*⅛ teaspoon white pepper*
*2 tablespoons grated*
  *Parmesan cheese*
*6 (4-ounce) turkey cutlets*
*2 tablespoons olive oil*
*2 cloves minced garlic*
*2 (8-ounce) bags fresh baby*
  *spinach*
*⅛ teaspoon ground nutmeg*
*⅓ cup shredded Jarlsberg*
  *cheese*

1. In shallow bowl, place egg white and beat until foamy. On shallow plate, combine breadcrumbs, pepper, and Parmesan and mix well.

2. Place turkey cutlets between waxed paper and pound to ⅛" thickness if necessary. Dip cutlets into egg white, then into breadcrumb mixture to coat.

3. In large saucepan, heat olive oil over medium-high heat. Add turkey; cook for 4 minutes. Carefully turn and cook for 4–6 minutes longer, until thoroughly cooked. Remove to serving plate and cover with foil to keep warm.

4. Add garlic to drippings remaining in pan; cook and stir for 1 minute. Then add spinach and nutmeg; cook and stir until spinach wilts, about 4–5 minutes. Add the Jarlsberg, top with the turkey, cover, and remove from heat. Let stand for 2 minutes to melt cheese, then serve.

## Cheeses

*You can use low-fat or nonfat cheeses, but they really don't have much flavor. Try using smaller amounts of very sharply flavored cheeses instead. Use extra-sharp Cheddar instead of Colby; Gruyère instead of Swiss, and Cotija instead of Parmesan. Grating or shredding cheese will also enhance the flavor and let you use less.*

# Tomatoes with Chicken Mousse

*Serve this elegant dish for a ladies' lunch along with a fruit salad and Lite Creamy Cheesecake (page 296) for dessert.*

**Serves 4**

**Calories:** 169.29
**Fat:** 7.01 grams
**Saturated fat:** 1.41 grams
**Dietary fiber:** 2.54 grams
**Sodium:** 167.31 mg
**Cholesterol:** 30.98 mg

*1 cup diced cooked chicken*
*¼ cup minced red onion*
*1 tablespoon chopped fresh chives*
*1 tablespoon fresh rosemary, minced*
*⅓ cup low-fat yogurt*
*¼ cup low-fat mayonnaise*
*1 tablespoon lime juice*
*½ cup chopped celery*
*4 large ripe tomatoes*

1. In blender or food processor, combine all ingredients except celery and tomatoes. Blend or process until smooth. Stir in celery.

2. Cut the tops off the tomatoes and scoop out the insides, leaving a ⅓" shell. Turn upside down on paper towels and let drain for 10 minutes.

3. Fill tomatoes with the chicken mixture and top each with the tomato top. Cover and chill for 2–3 hours before serving.

## Celery

*Raw celery is an excellent food to add to your diet. It has almost no calories, and researchers at the University of Chicago found that if you eat two stalks per day, you can reduce total cholesterol levels by almost 20 percent. The vegetable contains a substance called butyl phthalide, which may reduce cholesterol levels*

# Chicken Paillards with Mushrooms

*Cremini mushrooms are baby portobellos.*
*They are a creamy color, with brown caps.*

1. Place chicken breasts between two sheets of waxed paper and pound until ¼" thick. On shallow plate, combine flour, salt, pepper, and marjoram. Dredge chicken in flour mixture to coat.

2. In large skillet, heat olive oil over medium heat. Add chicken; sauté on first side for 3 minutes, then carefully turn and cook for 1 minute longer. Remove to platter and cover to keep warm.

3. Add shallots and mushrooms to skillet; cook and stir for 4–5 minutes until tender. Meanwhile, in small bowl combine broth, wine, Worcestershire sauce, and cornstarch, and mix well. Add to mushroom mixture and bring to a boil.

4. Return chicken to skillet; cook until chicken is hot and sauce bubbles and thickens. Serve immediately over brown rice, couscous, or pasta.

### Paillard

Paillard *is a French word that literally means "bawdy." In cooking, it means to pound chicken, veal, or beef to ¼" thickness, to tenderize the meat so it cooks very quickly. To pound, place the meat between two sheets of waxed paper and pound with a meat mallet, starting from the center of the meat, to desired thickness.*

**Serves 4**

---

**Calories:** 270.13
**Fat:** 8.25 grams
**Saturated fat:** 1.71 grams
**Dietary fiber:** 1.01 grams
**Sodium:** 167.63 mg
**Cholesterol:** 79.63 mg

4 (3-ounce) chicken breasts
3 tablespoons flour
⅛ teaspoon salt
⅛ teaspoon cayenne pepper
½ teaspoon dried marjoram
   leaves
2 tablespoons olive oil
4 shallots, minced
1 cup sliced button
   mushrooms
1 cup sliced cremini
   mushrooms
½ cup Low-Sodium Chicken
   Broth (page 120)
¼ cup dry white wine
1 teaspoon Worcestershire
   sauce
1 tablespoon cornstarch

# Turkey Cutlets Parmesan

*This classic dish is usually smothered in cheese, with deep-fried breaded turkey. This lighter version is just as delicious.*

**Serves 6**

**Calories:** 275.49
**Fat:** 10.98 grams
**Saturated fat:** 3.43 grams
**Dietary fiber:** 1.55 grams
**Sodium:** 229.86 mg
**Cholesterol:** 88.13 mg

*1 egg white*
*¼ cup dry breadcrumbs*
*⅛ teaspoon pepper*
*4 tablespoons grated Parmesan cheese, divided*
*6 (4-ounce) turkey cutlets*
*2 tablespoons olive oil*
*1 (15-ounce) can no-salt tomato sauce*
*1 teaspoon dried Italian seasoning*
*½ cup finely shredded part-skim mozzarella cheese*

1. Preheat oven to 350°F. Spray a 2-quart baking dish with nonstick cooking spray and set aside.

2. In shallow bowl, beat egg white until foamy. On plate, combine breadcrumbs, pepper, and 2 tablespoons Parmesan. Dip the turkey cutlets into the egg white, then into the breadcrumb mixture, turning to coat.

3. In large saucepan, heat olive oil over medium heat. Add turkey cutlets; brown on both sides, about 2–3 minutes per side. Place in prepared baking dish. Add tomato sauce and Italian seasoning to saucepan; bring to a boil.

4. Pour sauce over cutlets in baking pan and top with mozzarella cheese and remaining 2 tablespoons Parmesan. Bake for 25–35 minutes or until sauce bubbles and cheese melts and begins to brown. Serve with pasta, if desired.

# Turkey Breast with Dried Fruit

*This is a good choice for smaller families celebrating Thanksgiving.
The sauce is delicious over mashed potatoes or steamed brown rice.*

1. Sprinkle turkey with salt, pepper, and flour. In large saucepan, heat olive oil and butter over medium heat. Add turkey and cook until browned, about 5 minutes. Turn turkey.

2. Add all fruit to saucepan along with broth and wine. Cover and bring to a simmer. Reduce heat to medium low and simmer for 55–65 minutes or until turkey is thoroughly cooked. Serve turkey with fruit and sauce.

### Keep the Skin

*Keeping the skin on chicken and turkey while it's baking ensures that the flesh will be moist and doesn't transfer much fat to the flesh. Just remove the skin and discard after cooking. The poultry will be much more flavorful and tender, and the fat content will be virtually the same as skinless.*

**Serves 6**

**Calories:** 293.15
**Fat:** 6.01 grams
**Saturated fat:** 1.94 grams
**Dietary fiber:** 1.89 grams
**Sodium:** 127.28 mg
**Cholesterol:** 78.37 mg

1½ pounds bone-in turkey breast
⅛ teaspoon salt
⅛ teaspoon pepper
1 tablespoon flour
1 tablespoon olive oil
1 tablespoon butter or plant sterol margarine
½ cup chopped prunes
½ cup chopped dried apricots
2 Granny Smith apples, peeled and chopped
1 cup Low-Sodium Chicken Broth (page 120)
¼ cup Madeira wine

# Turkey Curry with Fruit

*This simple dish is fancy enough for company. Serve it with*
*brown-rice pilaf and some toasted whole wheat French bread.*

**Serves 6**

**Calories:** 371.52
**Fat:** 11.15 grams
**Saturated fat:** 2.80 grams
**Dietary fiber:** 3.22 grams
**Sodium:** 121.35 mg
**Cholesterol:** 78.24 mg

*6 (4-ounce) turkey cutlets*
*1 tablespoon flour*
*1 tablespoon plus 1 teaspoon*
*   curry powder, divided*
*1 tablespoon olive oil*
*2 pears, chopped*
*1 apple, chopped*
*½ cup raisins*
*1 tablespoon sugar*
*⅛ teaspoon salt*
*⅓ cup apricot jam*

1. Preheat oven to 350°F. Spray a cookie sheet with sides with nonstick cooking spray. Arrange cutlets on prepared cookie sheet. In small bowl, combine flour, 1 tablespoon curry powder, and olive oil and mix well. Spread evenly over cutlets.

2. In medium bowl, combine pears, apple, raisins, sugar, salt, 1 teaspoon curry powder, and apricot jam, and mix well. Divide this mixture over the turkey cutlets.

3. Bake for 35–45 minutes or until turkey is thoroughly cooked and fruit is hot and caramelized. Serve immediately.

### Raisins

*The sweet and chewy fruit children love, can be a good ally in the fight against cholesterol. Studies have shown that consuming raisins on a daily basis can help lower cholesterol levels. Eating just 3 ounces of raisins a day caused statistically significant reductions in total cholesterol and LDL cholesterol.*

# Chicken Pesto

*Pesto can be made with any nut. Hazelnuts are especially good at lowering LDL cholesterol, and they're delicious in this green sauce.*

1. Bring a large pot of salted water to a boil. In blender or food processor, combine basil, hazelnuts, and garlic. Blend or process until very finely chopped. Add olive oil and water; blend until a paste forms. Then blend in Parmesan cheese; set aside.

2. In large skillet, bring chicken broth to a simmer over medium heat. Cut chicken into strips and add to broth. Cook for 4 minutes, then add the pasta to the boiling water.

3. Cook pasta for 3–4 minutes according to package directions, until al dente. Drain and add to chicken mixture; cook and stir for 1 minute until chicken is thoroughly cooked. Add basil mixture, remove from heat, and stir until a sauce forms. Serve immediately.

## Herbs

*Fresh herbs should be part of a healthy diet, simply because their wonderful tastes and aromas will let you reduce salt and fat without feeling deprived. Fresh herbs like basil, thyme, and oregano are also easy to grow in a pot on your windowsill. You can substitute dried herbs for fresh in a 1:3 ratio. For every tablespoon of fresh, use a teaspoon of dried.*

**Serves 6**

**Calories:** 373.68
**Fat:** 11.06 grams
**Saturated fat:** 2.01 grams
**Dietary fiber:** 2.18 grams
**Sodium:** 108.92 mg
**Cholesterol:** 38.04 mg

*1 cup packed fresh basil leaves*
*¼ cup toasted chopped hazelnuts*
*2 cloves garlic, chopped*
*2 tablespoons olive oil*
*1 tablespoons water*
*¼ cup grated Parmesan cheese*
*½ cup Low-Sodium Chicken Broth (page 120)*
*12 ounces boneless, skinless chicken breasts*
*1 (12-ounce) package angel hair pasta*

# Cold Chicken with Cherry Tomato Sauce

*This is nice for a hot summer day. Prepare the chicken early in the day, then quickly make the sauce, slice the chicken, and serve.*

**Serves 3**

**Calories:** 227.58
**Fat:** 8.63 grams
**Saturated fat:** 2.57 grams
**Dietary fiber:** 1.86 grams
**Sodium:** 198.32 mg
**Cholesterol:** 73.64 mg

*2 teaspoons fresh thyme leaves*
*½ cup Low-Sodium Chicken Broth (page 120)*
*12 ounces boneless, skinless chicken breasts*
*1 tablespoon olive oil*
*3 cloves garlic, minced*
*2 cups cherry tomatoes*
*½ cup no-salt tomato juice*
*½ cup chopped fresh basil*
*¼ cup low-fat sour cream*
*⅛ teaspoon white pepper*

1. In large saucepan, combine thyme and chicken broth; bring to a simmer over medium heat. Add chicken and reduce heat to low. Cover and poach for 7–9 minutes or until chicken is thoroughly cooked.

2. Place chicken in a casserole dish just large enough to hold the chicken. Pour poaching liquid over, then cover and refrigerate for at least 8 hours.

3. When ready to eat, heat olive oil in large skillet. Add garlic; cook and stir for 1 minute. Then stir in cherry tomatoes; cook and stir until the tomatoes pop, about 4–6 minutes. Add tomato juice, basil, sour cream, and pepper; stir, and heat briefly.

4. Slice the chicken and fan out on serving plate. Top with tomato mixture and serve immediately.

# Chapter 9
## Beef Entrees

# Filet Mignon with Capers

*Capers are so salty you don't need to add any additional salt.*
*This elegant recipe is perfect for a romantic dinner for two.*

**Serves 2**

**Calories:** 244.62
**Fat:** 12.13 grams
**Saturated fat:** 4.01 grams
**Dietary fiber:** 0.50 grams
**Sodium:** 360.50 mg
**Cholesterol:** 65.45 mg

*2 (3-ounce) filet mignon*
 *steaks*
*⅛ teaspoon pepper*
*1 tablespoon grapeseed oil*
*2 cloves garlic, minced*
*2 tablespoons tiny capers,*
 *rinsed*
*⅓ cup dry red wine*
*2 teaspoons mustard*

1. Trim excess fat from the steaks and sprinkle with pepper. Heat grape-seed oil in medium saucepan over medium-high heat. Add steaks and cook until they can be moved and the bottom is browned, about 4–5 minutes. Carefully turn steaks and add garlic to the pan.

2. Cook steaks 4 minutes longer for medium rare, 5 minutes longer for medium, and 6 minutes longer for medium-well done. Remove steaks from pan and cover with foil to keep warm.

3. Drain capers and add to drippings in skillet along with wine. Bring to a boil, scraping pan to loosen drippings. Boil for 1 minute to reduce slightly. Then turn off the heat, whisk in the mustard, and serve sauce with steaks.

## Capers

*Capers are the flower bud of a shrub that grows in the Mediterranean. The little rounds are related to the cabbage family. They are usually pickled in a very strong vinegar brine or packed in salt. The salt-packed capers have better flavor, but they can be difficult to find. Be sure that you rinse the capers thoroughly before using.*

# Filet Mignon with Vegetables

*This is a wonderful dish for entertaining. The roasted
vegetables are tender and sweet, and the meat is juicy.*

1. Preheat oven to 425°F. Place carrots, onions, and potatoes in large roasting pan and drizzle with olive oil; toss to coat. Spread in an even layer. Roast for 15 minutes, then remove from oven.

2. Top with filet mignon; sprinkle the meat with salt and pepper. Pour wine over meat and vegetables.

3. Return to oven; roast for 20–30 minutes longer until beef registers 150°F for medium. Remove from oven, tent with foil, and let stand for 5 minutes, then carve to serve.

**Serves 8–10**

---

**Calories:** 442.64
**Fat:** 11.83 grams
**Saturated fat:** 3.77 grams
**Dietary fiber:** 6.06 grams
**Sodium:** 140.70 mg
**Cholesterol:** 70.55 mg

1 (16-ounce) package baby
   carrots, halved lengthwise
1 (8-ounce) package frozen
   pearl onions
16 new potatoes, halved
2 tablespoons olive oil
2 pounds filet mignon
⅛ teaspoon salt
⅛ teaspoon white pepper
½ cup dry red wine

# Beef with Mushroom Kabobs

*Serve these kabobs with cooked brown rice, a tomato and spinach salad,
and Strawberry-Mango Meringue Pie (page 292) for dessert.*

1. In medium glass bowl, combine wine, olive oil, salt, pepper, basil leaves, and garlic, and mix well. Cut steak into 1½" cubes and add to wine mixture. Stir to coat, cover, and refrigerate for 1 hour.

2. When ready to cook, prepare and preheat grill. Drain steak, reserving marinade. Trim mushroom stems and discard; brush mushrooms with lemon juice. Thread steak and mushrooms onto metal skewers.

3. Grill for 7–10 minutes, turning once and brushing with marinade, until beef is deep golden brown and mushrooms are tender. Discard remaining marinade.

**Serves 4**

---

**Calories:** 215.70
**Fat:** 7.08 grams
**Saturated fat:** 2.39 grams
**Dietary fiber:** 1.42 grams
**Sodium:** 101.33 mg
**Cholesterol:** 78.63 mg

¼ cup dry red wine
1 tablespoon olive oil
⅛ teaspoon salt
⅛ teaspoon cayenne pepper
1 tablespoon dried basil leaves
2 cloves garlic, minced
1 pound beef sirloin steak
½ pound button mushrooms
½ pound cremini mushrooms
1 tablespoon lemon juice

# Spicy Rib Eye in Red Sauce

*This is one way to stretch a steak to serve six people. It's full of flavor and easy, too.*

**Serves 6**

**Calories:** 267.81
**Fat:** 10.22 grams
**Saturated fat:** 3.27 grams
**Dietary fiber:** 2.91 grams
**Sodium:** 138.71 mg
**Cholesterol:** 77.35 mg

1¼ pounds rib eye steak
⅛ teaspoon salt
⅛ teaspoon cayenne pepper
1 tablespoon olive oil
1 onion, chopped
3 cloves garlic, minced
⅓ cup dry red wine
1 tablespoon chili powder
½ teaspoon crushed red
    pepper flakes
½ teaspoon coriander seed
1 (20-ounce) can no-salt
    crushed tomatoes

1. Trim excess fat from steak and sprinkle with salt and pepper. Heat a skillet over medium-high heat and add olive oil. Add steak to pan; cook without moving until steak is browned, about 4–6 minutes. Turn steak and cook for 2–3 minutes on second side, until medium rare. Remove to plate.

2. Add onion and garlic to drippings remaining in skillet. Cook and stir until tender, about 4 minutes. Add wine, chili powder, red pepper flakes, coriander, and tomatoes and bring to a simmer. Reduce heat to low and simmer for 15 minutes until sauce is reduced and thickened.

3. Thinly slice the steak against the grain and add to the sauce. Cook and stir for 2–3 minutes or until steak is hot and tender and sauce is blended. Serve immediately over brown rice, couscous, quinoa, or pasta.

# Sirloin Meatballs in Sauce

*Cooking meatballs in a sauce keeps them moist and tender.*
*Serve this with hot cooked pasta or brown rice.*

1. In small saucepan, heat olive oil over medium heat. Add garlic and onion; cook and stir until tender, about 5 minutes. Remove from heat and place in large mixing bowl.

2. Add egg whites, breadcrumbs, Parmesan, fennel, oregano, Worcestershire sauce, pepper, and pepper flakes and mix well. Add sirloin; mix gently but thoroughly until combined. Form into 12 meatballs.

3. In large nonstick saucepan, place Spaghetti Sauce and bring to a simmer. Carefully add meatballs to sauce. Return to a simmer, partially cover, and simmer for 15–25 minutes or until meatballs are thoroughly cooked.

## Baking Meatballs

*You can also bake these meatballs and freeze them plain to use in other recipes like Meatball Pizza (page 178). Place meatballs on a cookie sheet. Bake at 375°F for 15–25 minutes or until meatballs are browned and cooked through. Cool for 30 minutes, then chill until cold. Freeze individually, then pack into freezer bags. To thaw, let stand in refrigerator overnight.*

---

Serves 6; serving
size 2 meatballs

**Calories:** 367.93
**Fat:** 13.56 grams
**Saturated fat:** 3.91 grams
**Dietary fiber:** 5.58 grams
**Sodium:** 305.47 mg
**Cholesterol:** 61.12 mg

*1 tablespoon olive oil*
*3 cloves garlic, minced*
*½ cup minced onion*
*2 egg whites*
*½ cup dry breadcrumbs*
*¼ cup grated Parmesan cheese*
*½ teaspoon crushed fennel seeds*
*½ teaspoon dried oregano leaves*
*2 teaspoons Worcestershire sauce*
*⅛ teaspoon pepper*
*⅛ teaspoon crushed red pepper flakes*
*1 pound 95% lean ground sirloin*
*1 recipe Spaghetti Sauce (page 207)*

# Steak with Mushroom Sauce

*A rich mushroom sauce adds great flavor to tender marinated steak. This is a recipe for company!*

**Serves 6**

**Calories:** 262.45
**Fat:** 16.09 grams
**Saturated fat:** 6.42 grams
**Dietary fiber:** 0.72 grams
**Sodium:** 114.22 mg
**Cholesterol:** 53.86 mg

*1 to 1¼ pounds flank steak*
*2 tablespoons red wine*
*1 tablespoon olive oil*
*1 tablespoon butter*
*1 onion, minced*
*1 (8-ounce) package sliced*
*mushrooms*
*2 tablespoons flour*
*1½ cups Low-Sodium Beef*
*Broth (page 119)*
*¼ teaspoon ground coriander*
*2 teaspoons Worcestershire*
*sauce*
*⅛ teaspoon pepper*

1. In glass dish, combine flank steak, red wine, and olive oil. Cover and marinate for at least 8 hours.

2. When ready to eat, prepare and preheat grill. Drain steak, reserving marinade.

3. In large skillet, melt butter over medium heat. Add onion and mushrooms; cook and stir until liquid evaporates, about 8–9 minutes. Stir in flour; cook and stir for 2 minutes. Add beef broth and marinade from beef and bring to a boil. Stir in coriander, Worcestershire sauce, and pepper; reduce heat to low and simmer while cooking steak.

4. Cook steak 6" from medium coals for 7–10 minutes, turning once, until steak reaches desired doneness. Remove from heat, cover, and let stand for 10 minutes. Slice thinly against the grain and serve with mushroom sauce.

# Asian Beef Kabobs

*Make sure that the wasabi powder is completely mixed with the olive oil before proceeding with the recipe, so the strong taste is evenly distributed.*

1. In small bowl, combine olive oil and wasabi powder; mix well. Add soy sauce and lemon juice and mix well.

2. Thread peppers, mushrooms, zucchini, and steak on metal skewers. Brush with the marinade and let stand for 10 minutes.

3. Prepare and preheat grill. Grill skewers 6" from medium coals for 7–10 minutes, turning once and brushing with wasabi mixture several times, until beef reaches desired doneness and vegetables are crisp-tender. Serve immediately. Discard any remaining marinade.

### Cremini Mushrooms

*Cremini mushrooms are baby portobellos. These light-brown fungi have more flavor than button mushrooms. Because mushrooms don't synthesize sugars, they are very low in carbohydrates. They are a good source of fiber and niacin. They are fat-free and cholesterol-free and have a nice amount of fiber per serving.*

---

**Serves 4**

**Calories:** 254.80
**Fat:** 9.55 grams
**Saturated fat:** 2.76 grams
**Dietary fiber:** 3.43 grams
**Sodium:** 217.78 mg
**Cholesterol:** 81.36 mg

*2 tablespoons olive oil*
*1 teaspoon wasabi powder*
*1 tablespoon low-sodium soy sauce*
*1 tablespoon lemon juice*
*2 red bell peppers, sliced*
*1 (8-ounce) package cremini mushrooms*
*1 zucchini, sliced ½" thick*
*1 pound beef sirloin steak, cubed*

# Flank Steak with Mango Salsa

*Meat and fruit is a wonderful combination; the sweetness of the fruit complements the tender richness of the meat.*

**Serves 4**

**Calories:** 352.36
**Fat:** 13.71 grams
**Saturated fat:** 4.37 grams
**Dietary fiber:** 2.42 grams
**Sodium:** 151.61 mg
**Cholesterol:** 58.51 mg

*2 mangoes, peeled*
*½ cup minced red onion*
*1 tablespoon grated fresh*
    *ginger root*
*2 tablespoons lime juice*
*⅛ teaspoon salt*
*2 tablespoons honey*
*2 jalapeño peppers, minced*
*1 pound flank steak*
*¼ cup dry red wine*
*2 tablespoons olive oil*

1. Chop mangoes and combine in small bowl with onion, ginger root, lime juice, salt, honey, and jalapeño peppers. Stir, cover, and refrigerate while steak marinates.

2. Pierce flank steak with fork and combine in glass dish with red wine and olive oil. Cover and marinate in refrigerator for 6–8 hours.

3. When ready to eat, prepare and preheat grill. Remove flank steak from marinade; discard marinade. Grill for 5–7 minutes on each side, turning once, until the steak reaches desired doneness.

4. Let steak stand, covered with foil, for 10 minutes, then slice very thinly across the grain. Serve with Mango Salsa.

# Whole-Grain Meatloaf

*Save some of this meatloaf to use in Grilled Meatloaf Sandwiches (page 282).*

1. Preheat oven to 325°F. Spray a 9" × 5" loaf pan with nonstick cooking spray and set aside. In large saucepan, heat olive oil over medium heat. Add onion, garlic, and mushrooms; cook and stir until tender, about 6 minutes. Place in large mixing bowl, sprinkle with pepper and marjoram, and let stand for 15 minutes.

2. Add egg, egg white, chili sauce, milk, and Worcestershire sauce, and mix well. Make crumbs from the oatmeal bread and add to onion mixture.

3. Add all of the meat and work gently with your hands just until combined. Press into prepared loaf pan. Top with ketchup. Bake for 60–75 minutes, or until internal temperature registers 165°F. Remove from oven, cover with foil, and let stand for 10 minutes before slicing.

## Meatloaf Secrets

*There are a few tricks to making the best meatloaf. First, combine all the other ingredients and mix well, then add the meat last. The less the meat is handled, the more tender the meatloaf will be. Then, when it's done baking, remove from the oven, cover with foil, and let sit for 10 minutes to let the juices redistribute.*

**Serves 8**

**Calories:** 325.29
**Fat:** 15.51 grams
**Saturated fat:** 4.70 grams
**Dietary fiber:** 2.18 grams
**Sodium:** 184.45 mg
**Cholesterol:** 90.46 mg

1 tablespoon olive oil
1 onion, finely chopped
3 cloves garlic, minced
1 cup minced mushrooms
⅛ teaspoon pepper
1 teaspoon dried marjoram
 leaves
1 egg
1 egg white
½ cup chili sauce
¼ cup milk
1 tablespoon Worcestershire
 sauce
4 slices Whole-Grain Oatmeal
 Bread (page 63)
8 ounces 85% lean ground
 beef
8 ounces ground turkey
8 ounces ground pork
3 tablespoons ketchup

# Steak-and-Pepper Kabobs

*Serve these kabobs with a rice pilaf and a mixed fruit salad.*

**Serves 4**

**Calories:** 205.53
**Fat:** 6.23 grams
**Saturated fat:** 2.24 grams
**Dietary fiber:** 3.03 grams
**Sodium:** 133.03 mg
**Cholesterol:** 58.54 mg

*2 tablespoons brown sugar*
*½ teaspoon garlic powder*
*⅛ teaspoon cayenne pepper*
*¼ teaspoon onion salt*
*½ teaspoon chili powder*
*⅛ teaspoon ground cloves*
*1 (1-pound) sirloin steak, cut
   in 1" cubes*
*2 red bell peppers, cut in
   strips*
*2 green bell peppers, cut in
   strips*

1. In small bowl, combine brown sugar, garlic powder, cayenne pepper, onion salt, chili powder, and clove, and mix well. Toss sirloin steak with brown sugar mixture. Place in glass dish and cover; refrigerate for 2 hours.

2. When ready to cook, prepare and preheat grill. Thread steak cubes and pepper strips on metal skewers. Grill 6" from medium coals for 5–8 minutes, turning once, until steak reaches desired doneness and peppers are crisp-tender. Serve immediately.

## Dry Rubs

*A dry rub adds flavor and moistness to meat and also makes it easier for the meat to caramelize on the grill because there is less moisture to dilute the sugars. You can create rubs with any types of flavoring or seasoning you'd like. Make a large batch and store in a tightly covered jar in a cool place for up to 3 months.*

# Beef-and-Pumpkin Quinoa Pilaf

*This hearty pilaf is delicious for a cold winter evening. Serve it with a spinach salad and some Seeded Breadsticks (page 77).*

1. In large saucepan, heat olive oil over medium heat. Add steak; cook and stir until browned, about 5 minutes. Add onion; cook and stir for 3 minutes longer. Add quinoa and stir.

2. Pour in the beef broth; bring to a simmer. Cover and simmer for 10 minutes. Then add pumpkin; cook and stir until hot, about 4 minutes. Stir in Parmesan, parsley, sage leaves, and nutmeg. Stir, pour into serving dish, and top with pumpkin seeds. Serve immediately.

### Pumpkins

*Pumpkins are excellent sources of beta-carotene, vitamin C, and potassium. They can also help fight arterosclerosis, or hardening of the arteries, which can lead to heart attacks. Pumpkin seeds are also a good source of zinc and unsaturated fatty acids.*

---

**Serves 6**

**Calories:** 317.83
**Fat:** 10.72 grams
**Saturated fat:** 3.21 grams
**Dietary fiber:** 3.15 grams
**Sodium:** 119.79 mg
**Cholesterol:** 49.03 mg

*1 tablespoon olive oil*
*1 pound sirloin steak, cubed*
*1 onion, chopped*
*1 cup quinoa*
*2½ cups Low-Sodium Beef Broth (page 119)*
*1 cup canned solid-pack pumpkin*
*¼ cup grated Parmesan cheese*
*½ cup chopped flat-leaf parsley*
*4 chopped fresh sage leaves*
*⅛ teaspoon nutmeg*
*½ cup toasted no-salt pumpkin seeds*

# Corned-Beef Hash

*Serve this delicious hash on toasted Hearty Grain French Bread (page 74), topped with scrambled eggs made with egg substitute.*

**Serves 6**

**Calories:** 283.21
**Fat:** 11.97 grams
**Saturated fat:** 3.09 grams
**Dietary fiber:** 4.88 grams
**Sodium:** 472.63 mg
**Cholesterol:** 37.02 mg

*2 tablespoons olive oil*
*2 onions, chopped*
*4 cloves garlic, minced*
*8 fingerling potatoes, chopped*
*4 carrots, chopped*
*¼ cup water*
*½ pound deli corned beef, diced*
*⅛ teaspoon ground cloves*
*⅛ teaspoon white pepper*
*3 tablespoons low-sodium chili sauce*

1. Place olive oil in large saucepan; heat over medium heat. Add onion and garlic; cook and stir for 3 minutes. Add potatoes and carrots; cook and stir until potatoes are partially cooked, about 5 minutes.

2. Add water, corned beef, cloves, pepper, and chili sauce. Stir well, then cover, reduce heat to low, and simmer for 10–15 minutes or until blended and potatoes are cooked. Serve immediately.

## Corned Beef

*Corned beef is a very high-sodium food, made of brisket that has been pickled, or "corned" in a mixture of water, vinegar, sugars, and salt. When you use it, use a small amount (about an ounce per person), mainly for flavor. Adding lots of vegetables helps reduce the sodium count and makes this treat more healthy.*

# Stuffed Meatloaf

*A savory mushroom and bread filling adds great
flavor and texture to this hearty meatloaf.*

**Serves 8**

**Calories:** 362.10
**Fat:** 17.28 grams
**Saturated fat:** 5.65 grams
**Dietary fiber:** 3.44 grams
**Sodium:** 258.17 mg
**Cholesterol:** 94.27 mg

*1 tablespoon butter*
*1 onion, chopped*
*1 (8-ounce) package sliced
   mushrooms*
*½ (10-ounce) package frozen
   spinach, thawed and
   drained*
*2 tablespoons chopped fresh
   parsley*
*1 recipe Whole-Grain
   Meatloaf (page 173),
   uncooked*
*2 tablespoons ketchup*
*2 tablespoons mustard*

1. Preheat oven to 350°F. Spray a 9" × 5" loaf pan with nonstick cooking spray and set aside. In medium saucepan, melt butter over medium heat. Add onion and mushrooms; cook and stir for 3 minutes. Then add spinach; cook until the vegetables are tender and the liquid evaporates.

2. Remove from heat and stir in parsley. Press half of the meatloaf mixture into prepared pan. Top with mushroom mixture, keeping mixture away from sides of pan. Top with remaining meatloaf mixture.

3. In small bowl, combine ketchup and mustard and mix well. Spoon over meatloaf. Bake for 55–65 minutes or until internal temperature registers 165°F. Let stand for 10 minutes, then cut into slices.

# Meatball Pizza

Serves 6

**Calories:** 437.80
**Fat:** 15.85 grams
**Saturated fat:** 6.29 grams
**Dietary fiber:** 4.88 grams
**Sodium:** 432.76 mg
**Cholesterol:** 61.04 mg

*1 Whole-Grain Pizza Crust
    (page 69), prebaked*
*1 tablespoon olive oil*
*1 onion, chopped*
*1 green bell pepper, chopped*
*½ cup shredded carrots*
*1 (6-ounce) can no-salt
    tomato paste*
*2 tablespoons mustard*
*¼ cup water*
*12 plain Sirloin Meatballs
    (page 169), baked*
*1 cup shredded extra-sharp
    Cheddar cheese*
*½ cup shredded part-skim
    mozzarella cheese*

*Your own homemade pizza is always going to taste better than delivery!*

1. Preheat oven to 400°F. In medium saucepan, heat olive oil over medium heat. Add onion, bell pepper, and carrots; cook and stir until crisp-tender, about 5 minutes. Add tomato paste, mustard, and water and bring to a simmer. Simmer, stirring frequently, for 5 minutes.

2. Spread the sauce over the pizza crust. Cut the meatballs in half and arrange on the pizza. Sprinkle with Cheddar and mozzarella cheeses.

3. Bake for 20–30 minutes or until crust is golden brown, pizza is hot, and cheese is melted and bubbling. Let stand for 5 minutes, then serve.

## Pizza Variations

*Once you have the basic recipe down, it's very easy to make your own pizzas. Use lots of vegetables for added flavor, fiber, and nutrition, and to reduce the amount of meat you need. You can use deli-sliced roast beef, cooked chicken, Canadian bacon, or ham to top your pizza, or just use vegetables and cheese.*

# Cowboy Steak with Chimichurri Sauce

*Chimichurri Sauce is a condiment from
Argentina usually served with grilled meats.*

1. In blender or food processor, combine parsley, oregano, olive oil, lemon juice, sherry vinegar, garlic, salt, and pepper; blend or process until smooth. Pour into small bowl, cover, and refrigerate until ready to use.

2. Pierce flank steak all over with a fork. Place in large heavy-duty zip-close freezer bag and add red wine and olive oil. Seal bag and squish to mix. Place in pan and refrigerate for 8–12 hours.

3. When ready to eat, prepare and preheat grill. Grill steak for 6–10 minutes, turning once, until desired doneness. Remove from grill and let stand, covered, for 10 minutes. Slice thinly against the grain and serve with the Chimichurri Sauce.

---

**Serves 4–6**

**Calories:** 244.50
**Fat:** 18.59 grams
**Saturated fat:** 5.20 grams
**Dietary fiber:** 0.41 grams
**Sodium:** 117.31 mg
**Cholesterol:** 38.34 mg

1 cup chopped parsley
¼ cup minced fresh oregano
  leaves
¼ cup extra-virgin olive oil
2 tablespoons lemon juice
3 tablespoons sherry vinegar
6 cloves garlic, minced
⅛ teaspoon salt
¼ teaspoon pepper
1 pound flank steak
2 tablespoons red wine
2 tablespoons olive oil

# Beef-Risotto–Stuffed Peppers

*You can use any leftover cooked rice dish in this simple recipe. Just add some chopped cooked roast beef from the deli, an egg, and some cheese.*

**Serves 4**

**Calories:** 331.74
**Fat:** 12.15 grams
**Saturated fat:** 3.20 grams
**Dietary fiber:** 6.87 grams
**Sodium:** 130.25 mg
**Cholesterol:** 70.97 mg

1 tablespoon olive oil
1 onion, chopped
2 cups Beef Risotto (page 181)
1 egg
1 egg white
1 tomato, chopped
2 slices Whole-Grain Oatmeal
　　Bread (page 63)
4 bell peppers
1 cup Spaghetti Sauce
　　(page 207)
¼ cup water

1. Preheat oven to 350°F. Spray a 9"-square baking pan with nonstick cooking spray and set aside. In medium saucepan, heat olive oil over medium heat. Add onion; cook and stir until tender, about 5 minutes. Remove from heat and stir in risotto, egg, egg white, and tomato and mix well.

2. Make crumbs from the bread and add to the risotto mixture. Cut off the pepper tops and remove membranes and seeds. Stuff with risotto mixture.

3. Place stuffed peppers in prepared baking dish. In small bowl, combine Spaghetti Sauce and water; pour over and around peppers. Cover with foil and bake for 45–55 minutes or until peppers are tender. Serve immediately.

### Peppers for Stuffing

*For stuffing, choose bell peppers that are short and wide, preferably those that will stand upright unaided. Reserve the tops; after stuffing the peppers, you can put the tops back on. For a nice presentation, think about using four different colors of peppers in this dish; choose red, green, yellow, and orange.*

# Beef Risotto

*This elegant recipe is perfect for a spring dinner. It is a last-minute recipe, so don't start it until after your guests have arrived.*

1. In medium saucepan, combine water and broth; heat over low heat until warm; keep on heat.

2. In large saucepan, heat olive oil over medium heat. Add beef; cook and stir until browned. Remove from pan with slotted spoon and set aside. Add onion and garlic to pan; cook and stir until crisp-tender, about 4 minutes.

3. Add rice; cook and stir for 2 minutes. Add the broth mixture, a cup at a time, stirring until the liquid is absorbed, about 15 minutes. When there is 1 cup broth remaining, return the beef to the pot and add the steak sauce, pepper, and asparagus. Cook and stir until rice is tender, beef is cooked, and asparagus is tender, about 5 minutes. Stir in Parmesan and butter and serve immediately.

**Serves 6**

**Calories:** 365.04
**Fat:** 11.67 grams
**Saturated fat:** 4.09 grams
**Dietary fiber:** 3.47 grams
**Sodium:** 138.81 mg
**Cholesterol:** 36.20 mg

*2 cups water*
*2 cups Low-Sodium Beef Broth (page 119)*
*2 tablespoons olive oil*
*½ pound sirloin steak, chopped*
*1 onion, minced*
*2 cloves garlic, minced*
*1½ cups Arborio rice*
*2 tablespoons steak sauce*
*¼ teaspoon pepper*
*1 pound asparagus, cut into 2" pieces*
*¼ cup grated Parmesan cheese*
*1 tablespoon butter*

# Whole-Wheat Spaghetti and Meatballs

*This simple recipe is full of vitamins C and A. Serve it with toasted
Hearty-Grain French Bread (page 74) and some red wine.*

**Serves 6–8**

**Calories:** 386.78
**Fat:** 12.34 grams
**Saturated fat:** 4.08 grams
**Dietary fiber:** 7.47 grams
**Sodium:** 444.23 mg
**Cholesterol:** 51.34 mg

*1 recipe Sirloin Meatballs in
Sauce (page 169)*
*1 (8-ounce) can no-salt
tomato sauce*
*½ cup grated carrots*
*1 (16-ounce) package whole-
wheat spaghetti*
*½ cup grated Parmesan
cheese, divided*

1. Bring a large pot of water to a boil. Prepare the Sirloin Meatballs in Sauce, adding tomato sauce and grated carrots to the sauce. Simmer until meatballs are cooked.

2. Cook spaghetti in water according to package directions or until almost al dente. Drain spaghetti, reserving ¼ cup cooking water. Add spaghetti to meatballs in sauce along with ¼ cup of the cheese. Simmer, stirring gently, for 5–6 minutes or until pasta is al dente, adding reserved cooking water if necessary for desired sauce consistency. Sprinkle with the remaining ¼ cup Parmesan cheese and serve immediately.

### Whole-Wheat Spaghetti

*Whole-wheat spaghetti has a much stronger taste than regular pasta. It should be served with strongly flavored sauces until your family is used to the taste. You can also gradually switch to whole-wheat pastas by starting out using just a third whole-wheat pasta (and the other two-thirds plain) and increasing the proportion of whole wheat each time you serve it.*

# Wasabi-Roasted Filet Mignon

*Wasabi is like horseradish, but its flavor is much more intense.*
*It's served with sushi and other Japanese meals.*

**Serves 12**

**Calories:** 298.15
**Fat:** 24.00 grams
**Saturated fat:** 8.99 grams
**Dietary fiber:** 0.13 grams
**Sodium:** 143.07 mg
**Cholesterol:** 68.57 mg

1 (3-pound) filet mignon
    roast
¼ teaspoon pepper
1 teaspoon powdered wasabi
2 tablespoons sesame oil
2 tablespoons soy sauce

1. Preheat oven to 400°F. If the roast has a thin end and a thick end, fold the thin end under so the roast is about the same thickness. Place on roasting pan.

2. In small bowl, combine pepper, wasabi, oil, and soy sauce, and mix well. Brush half over roast. Roast the beef for 30 minutes, then remove and brush with remaining wasabi mixture. Return to oven for 5–10 minutes longer or until meat thermometer registers at least 145°F for medium rare.

3. Remove from oven, cover, and let stand for 15 minutes before slicing to serve.

### Filet Mignon

*Filet mignon is one of the most expensive cuts of steak, but it is almost 100-percent edible with no waste. The cut is very tender, but not the most flavorful, so it is often cooked with very intense ingredients, like wasabi and jalapeño peppers. Slice it into very thin slices against the grain to serve.*

# Beef Rollups with Pesto

*This recipe is perfect for entertaining. You can make the rollups ahead of time;*
*don't dredge or brown them until about an hour before you'd like to eat.*

**Serves 6**

**Calories:** 290.23
**Fat:** 18.73 grams
**Saturated fat:** 3.90 grams
**Dietary fiber:** 1.03 grams
**Sodium:** 95.79 mg
**Cholesterol:** 63.60 mg

½ cup packed basil leaves
½ cup packed baby spinach
    leaves
3 cloves garlic, minced
⅓ cup toasted chopped
    hazelnuts
⅛ teaspoon white pepper
2 tablespoons grated
    Parmesan cheese
2 tablespoons olive oil
2 tablespoons water
3 tablespoons flour
½ teaspoon paprika
6 (4-ounce) top round steaks,
    ¼" thick
2 oil-packed sun-dried
    tomatoes, minced
1 tablespoon canola oil
1 cup Low-Sodium Beef Broth
    (page 119)

1. In blender or food processor, combine basil, spinach, garlic, hazelnuts, and white pepper, and blend or process until finely chopped. Add Parmesan and blend again. Add olive oil and blend until a paste forms, then add water and blend.

2. On shallow plate, combine flour, and paprika and mix well. Place beef between sheets of waxed paper and pound until ⅛" thick. Spread pesto on one side of the pounded beef and sprinkle with tomatoes. Roll up, fastening closed with toothpicks.

3. Dredge rollups in flour mixture. Heat canola oil in large saucepan and brown rollups on all sides, about 5 minutes total. Pour beef broth into pan and bring to a simmer. Cover, reduce heat to low, and simmer for 40–50 minutes or until beef is tender.

# Chapter 10
## Pork Entrees

# Thin Pork Chops with Mushrooms and Herbs

*Serve this quick and easy dish with Buttermilk Mashed Potatoes (page 254) and Snow Peas with Shallots (page 252).*

**Serves 4**

**Calories:** 238.91
**Fat:** 14.92 grams
**Saturated fat:** 3.97 grams
**Dietary fiber:** 0.43 grams
**Sodium:** 392.89 mg
**Cholesterol:** 43.68 mg

*3 tablespoons flour*
*¼ teaspoon salt*
*⅛ teaspoon white pepper*
*1 teaspoon dried thyme leaves*
*4 (3-ounce) boneless pork chops*
*2 tablespoons olive oil*
*2 shallots, minced*
*1 cup sliced cremini mushrooms*
*1 tablespoon fresh rosemary leaves, minced*
*¼ cup dry sherry*

1. On shallow plate, combine flour, salt, pepper, and thyme leaves and mix well. Place pork between two sheets of waxed paper and pound until ½" thick. Dredge pork chops in mixture, shaking off excess.

2. Heat olive oil in large skillet over medium heat. Add pork chops; brown on first side without moving, about 4 minutes.

3. Turn pork and add shallots and mushrooms to the pan. Cook for 3 minutes, then remove pork from pan. Stir vegetables, scraping pan to remove drippings.

4. Add rosemary and sherry to pan and bring to a boil. Return pork to skillet, lower heat, and simmer pork for 2–4 minutes longer until pork is very light pink. Serve immediately.

### Pounding Meat

*Many meat dishes start by pounding the meat before it's seasoned and cooked. This reduces the cooking time and tenderizes the meat by breaking the fibers. It also makes the portion size look bigger, which is helpful for reducing saturated fat and cholesterol intake. Don't pound too hard, and use a meat mallet or rolling pin.*

# Pork Chops with Mustard Sauce

*Spreading the meat with a yogurt-and-mustard mixture before grilling
helps keep the meat moist and tender and adds great flavor.*

1. Prepare and preheat grill. In small bowl, combine 1 tablespoon mustard, yogurt, and pepper and mix well. Spread mixture on both sides of pork chops; set aside for 15 minutes.

2. In small saucepan, heat olive oil over medium heat. Add onion; cook and stir until tender, about 5 minutes. Add flour; cook and stir until combined and bubbly. Add broth, wine, and remaining 1 tablespoon mustard; bring to a boil, stirring with wire whisk, until sauce is slightly thickened.

3. Grill the chops for 4–6 minutes on each side, turning once, until pork is just slightly pink in the center. Serve with the sauce.

**Serves 4**

**Calories:** 284.17
**Fat:** 17.76 grams
**Saturated fat:** 4.69 grams
**Dietary fiber:** 0.47 grams
**Sodium:** 141.49 mg
**Cholesterol:** 60.00 mg

*2 tablespoons Dijon mustard,
 divided*
*2 tablespoons plain yogurt*
*⅛ teaspoon pepper*
*4 (3-ounce) bone-in pork
 chops*
*2 tablespoons olive oil*
*1 onion, chopped*
*1 tablespoon flour*
*1 cup Low-Sodium Chicken
 Broth (page 120)*
*¼ cup dry white wine*

# BBQ Pork Chops

**Serves 8**

**Calories:** 276.23
**Fat:** 11.80 grams
**Saturated fat:** 3.53 grams
**Dietary fiber:** 3.32 grams
**Sodium:** 417.98 mg
**Cholesterol:** 43.68 mg

2 tablespoons olive oil
1 onion, chopped
4 cloves garlic, minced
1 (14-ounce) can no-salt
   crushed tomatoes,
   undrained
1 cup low-sodium chili sauce
1 tablespoon lemon juice
2 tablespoons mustard
¼ cup brown sugar
2 tablespoons molasses
½ teaspoon cumin
1 teaspoon dried thyme
   leaves
⅛ teaspoon ground cloves
8 (3-ounce) boneless pork
   chops

*You can make lots of this excellent barbecue sauce and freeze it in 1-cup portions to use throughout the summer on everything from ribs to chicken.*

1. In large pot, heat olive oil over medium heat. Add onion and garlic; cook and stir for 3–4 minutes until crisp-tender. Add tomatoes, chili sauce, lemon juice, mustard, sugar, molasses, cumin, thyme, and cloves. Bring to a simmer, then reduce heat, cover, and simmer for 2 hours.

2. When ready to cook, prepare and preheat grill. Spray grill rack with nonstick cooking spray and add pork chops. Grill until the chops can be easily moved, about 4 minutes. Turn and brush with sauce. Cook for 3–5 minutes longer or until chops are just pink, turning again and brushing with more sauce. Serve with sauce that hasn't been used to brush the pork.

### BBQ Sauce on the Grill

*Most BBQ sauces should be added to the meat during the last part of grilling time. Since these sauces are usually high in sugar, they can burn easily on the high heat of the grill. Brush sauces onto the meat when they are almost fully cooked. The purpose of the sauce is to provide a glaze and add a layer of flavor.*

# Whole-Grain Sausage Pizza

*This rich pizza is very nutritious and filling. Serve it
with a green salad and some fresh corn on the cob.*

1. Preheat oven to 400°F. Crumble pork sausage into saucepan and place
   over medium heat. Cook until sausage is browned, stirring frequently.
   Remove pork from saucepan and drain excess fat, but do not wipe
   saucepan.

2. Add onion, mushrooms, and bell pepper to saucepan; cook, stirring
   to loosen drippings, for 3–4 minutes or until crisp-tender. Add tomato
   sauce, tomatoes, dried Italian seasoning, and pork sausage; cook and
   stir for 2 minutes.

3. Place pizza crust on cookie sheet and top with pork mixture. Sprinkle
   with cheeses. Bake for 20–25 minutes or until pizza is hot and cheese
   is melted and beginning to brown. Let stand for 5 minutes, then serve.

**Serves 6–8**

**Calories:** 325.25
**Fat:** 11.91 grams
**Saturated fat:** 4.17 grams
**Dietary fiber:** 4.46 grams
**Sodium:** 349.87 mg
**Cholesterol:** 37.63 mg

*8 ounces pork sausage*
*1 onion, chopped*
*1 (8-ounce) package sliced
    mushrooms*
*1 green bell pepper, chopped*
*1 (8-ounce) can low-sodium
    tomato sauce*
*2 tomatoes, chopped*
*1 teaspoon dried Italian
    seasoning*
*1 Whole-Grain Pizza Crust
    (page 69), prebaked*
*1 cup shredded part-skim
    mozzarella cheese*
*3 tablespoons grated
    Parmesan cheese*

# Pork Chops with Cabbage

*Cabbage is the ideal accompaniment to pork. It's tangy and sweet
and becomes very tender when cooked in the slow cooker.*

**Serves 6**

**Calories:** 242.86
**Fat:** 10.57 grams
**Saturated fat:** 3.37 grams
**Dietary fiber:** 2.72 grams
**Sodium:** 364.80 mg
**Cholesterol:** 43.68 mg

*1 red onion, chopped*
*4 cloves garlic, minced*
*3 cups chopped red cabbage*
*3 cups chopped green
    cabbage*
*1 apple, chopped*
*6 (3-ounce) boneless pork
    chops*
*⅛ teaspoon white pepper*
*1 tablespoon olive oil*
*¼ cup brown sugar*
*¼ cup apple cider vinegar*
*1 tablespoon mustard*

1. In 4- to 5-quart slow cooker, combine onion, garlic, cabbages, and apple and mix well.

2. Trim pork chops of any excess fat and sprinkle with pepper. Heat olive oil in large saucepan over medium heat. Brown chops on just one side, about 3 minutes. Add to slow cooker with vegetables.

3. In small bowl, combine brown sugar, vinegar, and mustard and mix well. Pour into slow cooker. Cover and cook on low for 7–8 hours or until pork and cabbage are tender. Serve immediately.

### Cabbage and Nutrition

*Cabbage is a member of the cruciferous vegetable family, which also includes cauliflower and broccoli. These vegetables have phytochemicals called indoles which may help protect heart health. Cabbage is high in vitamin C, fiber, and folate. Red cabbage has more vitamin C and fiber than green cabbage.*

# Pork Quesadillas

*You can serve these toasty sandwiches with some salsa for dipping.*

1. In medium bowl, combine sour cream, cheese, pork tenderloin, avocado, and jalapeño pepper and mix gently.

2. Divide mixture among half the tortillas, placing the remaining half of tortillas on top to make sandwiches. Heat griddle and brush with olive oil. Place quesadillas on the griddle; cover and grill for 2–3 minutes on each side until tortillas are crisp and cheese is melted. Cut into quarters and serve.

**Serves 6**

**Calories:** 315.36
**Fat:** 16.67 grams
**Saturated fat:** 5.55 grams
**Dietary fiber:** 4.65 grams
**Sodium:** 161.17 mg
**Cholesterol:** 43.36 mg

⅓ cup low-fat sour cream
1 cup shredded part-skim
   mozzarella cheese
1 cup chopped Mustard Pork
   Tenderloin (below)
1 avocado, chopped
1 jalapeño pepper, minced
10 (6-inch) corn tortillas
2 tablespoons olive oil

# Mustard Pork Tenderloin

*Mustard and low-fat sour cream coats pork tenderloin to keep in moisture while it slowly roasts to perfection.*

1. In glass baking dish, combine red wine, sugar, and olive oil. Add pork tenderloin; turn to coat. Cover and refrigerate for 8 hours.

2. Preheat oven to 325°F. Let pork stand at room temperature for 20 minutes. Roast for 30 minutes, basting occasionally with the marinade.

3. In small bowl, combine sour cream, mustard, and chives. Spread over the tenderloin. Continue roasting for 25–35 minutes or until pork registers 160°F. Let stand for 5 minutes, then slice to serve.

**Serves 6**

**Calories:** 209.84
**Fat:** 9.08 grams
**Saturated fat:** 2.98 grams
**Dietary fiber:** 0.25 grams
**Sodium:** 147.13 mg
**Cholesterol:** 83.83 mg

2 tablespoons red wine
1 tablespoon sugar
1 tablespoon olive oil
1¼ pounds pork tenderloin
¼ cup low-fat sour cream
3 tablespoons Dijon mustard
1 tablespoon minced fresh
   chives

# Canadian-Bacon Risotto

*Risotto has a reputation of being difficult to make, but it's not.*
*Just add the warm broth gradually and keep stirring!*

**Serves 6**

**Calories:** 379.72
**Fat:** 9.41 grams
**Saturated fat:** 3.17 grams
**Dietary fiber:** 2.65 grams
**Sodium:** 292.55 mg
**Cholesterol:** 26.94 mg

*2 cups water*
*3 cups Low-Sodium Chicken Broth (page XX)*
*1 tablespoon olive oil*
*1 chopped onion*
*3 cloves garlic, minced*
*1 (8-ounce) package sliced mushrooms*
*½ teaspoon dried oregano leaves*
*1 teaspoon dried basil leaves*
*2 cups Arborio rice*
*⅛ teaspoon white pepper*
*1 cup chopped Canadian bacon*
*¼ cup shredded Parmesan cheese*
*1 tablespoon butter*

1. In medium saucepan, combine water and broth; heat over low heat until warm; keep on heat.

2. In large saucepan, heat olive oil over medium heat. Add onion, garlic, and mushrooms to pan; cook and stir until crisp-tender, about 4 minutes. Add oregano and basil.

3. Add rice; cook and stir for 2 minutes. Add the broth mixture, a cup at a time, stirring until the liquid is absorbed, about 15 minutes. When there is 1 cup broth remaining, add pepper and Canadian bacon along with the last cup of broth. Cook and stir until rice is tender, about 5 minutes.

4. Stir in Parmesan and butter and serve immediately.

### Canadian Bacon

*In the United States, Canadian bacon is simply lean bacon, or smoked back bacon. But in Canada, it's a specific cut of ham called Canadian peameal. It's a lean cut of cured pork. It used to be rolled in ground yellow peas, which extended the shelf life; now it's rolled in ground corn. You can order the real Canadian peameal bacon online.*

# Western Omelet

*This classic omelet can be made with a jalapeño or habanero pepper thrown in if you like it really spicy.*

**Serves 4**

**Calories:** 216.81
**Fat:** 13.12 grams
**Saturated fat:** 5.15 grams
**Dietary fiber:** 1.02 grams
**Sodium:** 477.02 mg
**Cholesterol:** 81.19 mg

1 tablespoon olive oil
½ cup chopped onion
3 cloves garlic, minced
½ cup chopped green bell pepper
½ cup chopped red bell pepper
3 ounces chopped ham
1 egg
8 egg whites
¼ teaspoon cayenne pepper
1 teaspoon chili powder
¼ cup skim milk
⅛ teaspoon pepper

1. In large nonstick skillet, heat olive oil over medium heat. Add onion, garlic, and bell peppers; cook and stir until crisp-tender, about 4 minutes. Add ham; cook and stir until ham is hot.

2. In large bowl, combine egg, egg whites, cayenne pepper, chili powder, milk, and pepper and mix well. Pour into skillet with vegetables and ham.

3. Cook, running a spatula around the edges to let uncooked mixture flow underneath, until eggs are set and bottom is golden brown. Fold omelet over on itself and slide onto plate, serve.

## Cayenne Pepper

*The capsaicin in chile peppers, which gives them their spicy heat, fights inflammation in your body with a compound called substance P. These little red peppers can also prevent blood clots by helping your body dissolve fibrin, which is used in the formation of blood clots. Add it to recipes and sprinkle it on your food at the table.*

# Pork Loin with Cranberry BBQ Sauce

**Serves 12**

**Calories:** 275.13
**Fat:** 12.34 grams
**Saturated fat:** 4.45 grams
**Dietary fiber:** 0.52 grams
**Sodium:** 95.07 mg
**Cholesterol:** 82.88 mg

1 (3-pound) lean pork loin
    roast
¾ cup low-sodium ketchup
3 tablespoons apple cider
    vinegar
3 tablespoons spicy brown
    mustard
2 tablespoons brown sugar
3 cloves garlic
1 onion, minced
½ cup chopped fresh
    cranberries
¼ cup water
⅛ teaspoon pepper

*You can use this barbecue sauce on any other meat as well—
and use it on the grill as well as on meat roasted in the oven.*

1. Preheat oven to 350°F. Trim excess fat from pork roast and place in roasting pan. Roast for 45 minutes.

2. Meanwhile, combine ketchup, vinegar, mustard, brown sugar, garlic, onion, cranberries, water, and pepper in small saucepan and bring to a boil. Simmer for 5 minutes, then remove from heat.

3. Remove pork from oven and baste with sauce. Continue roasting, basting every 5 minutes with sauce, for another 40–50 minutes or until pork registers 155°F on a meat thermometer. Let rest for 5 minutes.

4. While pork is resting, simmer remaining sauce for 2 minutes. Slice pork and serve with sauce.

### The Other White Meat

*There has been a very effective advertising campaign about pork being "the other white meat." While pork is considered a red meat, changes in breeding over the last fifteen years have resulted in leaner pork that has 25 percent less saturated fat. The tenderloin, with little internal marbling, actually does have as much fat and cholesterol as chicken.*

# Pork Scallops with Spinach

*A simple creamed spinach tops tender pork
scallops in this easy recipe for dinner.*

1. Preheat oven to 350°F. On plate, combine 3 tablespoons flour, salt, and pepper and mix well. Pound pork scallops, if necessary, to ⅛" thickness.

2. Heat olive oil in nonstick pan over medium-high heat. Dredge pork in flour mixture and sauté in pan, turning once, until just browned, about 1 minute per side. Remove to a baking dish.

3. Add onion to pan; cook and stir for 3 minutes. Drain spinach well and add to pan; cook and stir until liquid evaporates. Add flour and celery seed; cook and stir for 1 minute.

4. Stir in light cream; cook and stir until thickened, about 3 minutes. Remove from heat and add ricotta cheese and half of the breadcrumbs.

5. Divide spinach mixture on top of pork in baking dish. Top with remaining breadcrumbs and Romano. Bake for 10–15 minutes or until pork is tender and thoroughly cooked. Serve immediately.

**Serves 6**

**Calories:** 298.66
**Fat:** 12.60 grams
**Saturated fat:** 4.08 grams
**Dietary fiber:** 2.51 grams
**Sodium:** 303.25 mg
**Cholesterol:** 80.88 mg

*3 tablespoons flour*
*⅛ teaspoon salt*
*⅛ teaspoon pepper*
*6 (3-ounce) pork scallops*
*2 tablespoons olive oil*
*1 onion, chopped*
*1 (10-ounce) package frozen
    chopped spinach, thawed*
*1 tablespoon flour*
*½ teaspoon celery seed*
*⅓ cup nonfat light cream*
*⅓ cup part-skim ricotta
    cheese*
*½ cup dried breadcrumbs,
    divided*
*2 tablespoons grated
    Romano cheese*

# Pork Scallops Françoise

*This fresh and simple recipe takes just minutes to make.*
*Use the best ingredients you can find for the perfect meal.*

**Serves 4**

**Calories:** 224.74
**Fat:** 11.25 mg
**Saturated fat:** 4.04 mg
**Dietary fiber:** 0.18 grams
**Sodium:** 158.05 mg
**Cholesterol:** 80.87 mg

*3 tablespoons flour*
*⅛ teaspoon salt*
*⅛ teaspoon pepper*
*1 egg white, slightly beaten*
*4 (3-ounce) pork scallops*
*1 tablespoon olive oil*
*1 tablespoon butter*
*3 cloves garlic, minced*
*2 tablespoons lemon juice*
*2 tablespoons chopped fresh*
   *parsley*

1. On plate, combine flour, salt, and pepper. Place egg white in shallow bowl. If necessary, pound scallops until they are ⅛" thick. Dip scallops into flour, then into egg whites.

2. Heat olive oil and butter in nonstick skillet. Add garlic; cook for 1 minute. Then add coated pork; brown for 2–3 minutes per side. Add lemon juice; cook for 2–3 minutes or until pork is cooked and tender. Sprinkle with parsley and serve immediately.

## Parsley

*Parsley, like most greens, does have a good amount of antioxidants, those molecules that help prevent cholesterol oxidation in your body. Be sure to use flat-leaf parsley, which has more flavor than curly-leaf. Parsley also adds great eye appeal to your food, especially when sprinkled over light-colored ingredients.*

# Pork Tenderloin with Apples

*Pork and apples are a natural combination. Serve this delicious entrée with a Quinoa Pepper Pilaf (page 211) and Red-Lettuce Jicama Salad (page 227).*

1. Trim excess fat from pork and sprinkle with salt, pepper, and flour. Heat olive oil in large saucepan and brown pork on all sides, about 5 minutes total.

2. Add onion, garlic, apples, and wine to saucepan, and bring to a simmer. Reduce heat to low, cover, and simmer for 20 minutes. Add rosemary, uncover, and simmer for 5–10 minutes longer or until pork registers 155°F. Let stand for 5 minutes off the heat, then serve.

## Pork's Vitamins

*Pork is an excellent source of many vitamins and minerals including iron, magnesium, phosphorous, potassium, thiamin, riboflavin, niacin, vitamin B12, and vitamin B6. In fact, pork rivals milk as the best source of riboflavin, a vitamin that promotes the growth and repair of tissues and maintains the health of skin and eyes.*

**Serves 6**

**Calories:** 243.96
**Fat:** 9.42 grams
**Saturated fat:** 2.34 grams
**Dietary fiber:** 1.59 grams
**Sodium:** 100.07 mg
**Cholesterol:** 71.02 mg

*1½ pounds pork tenderloin*
*⅛ teaspoon salt*
*⅛ teaspoon pepper*
*2 tablespoons flour*
*2 tablespoons olive oil*
*1 onion, chopped*
*4 cloves garlic, minced*
*2 apples, thinly sliced*
*½ cup dry white wine*
*1 tablespoon chopped fresh rosemary*

# Chops with Mint and Garlic

*This recipe tastes best cooked on the grill; the wood smoke adds another layer of flavor to this simple dish.*

**Serves 4**

**Calories:** 251.09
**Fat:** 17.56 grams
**Saturated fat:** 4.97 grams
**Dietary fiber:** 0.24 grams
**Sodium:** 242.71 mg
**Cholesterol:** 58.24 mg

*3 tablespoons minced fresh mint*
*1 tablespoon minced garlic*
*2 tablespoons olive oil*
*1 tablespoon lemon juice*
*4 (4-ounce) pork chops*
*⅛ teaspoon salt*
*⅛ teaspoon white pepper*

1. Prepare and preheat grill. In small bowl, combine mint, garlic, olive oil, and lemon juice and mix well.

2. Sprinkle pork chops with salt and pepper. Brush with sauce and place on grill. Grill 6" from medium coals for 5–6 minutes per side until internal temperatures reach 155ºF, brushing with mint sauce. Discard any remaining mint sauce. Let chops stand for 5 minutes, then serve.

### Pork Chops: Boneless or Bone-In?

*It's mostly personal choice and availability that dictates whether you buy boneless or bone-in pork chops. The boneless chops are generally a bit more expensive, while the bone provides more flavor. If you are going to pound pork chops to make them thinner, choose boneless chops for the best results.*

# Fruit-Stuffed Pork Tenderloin

*Perfect for entertaining, you can make this recipe ahead of time.*
*Stuff the pork mixture, then brown and bake it just before serving.*

1. Trim excess fat from meat. Cut tenderloin lengthwise, cutting to, but not through, the other side. Open up the meat and place on work surface, cut side up. Lightly pound with a rolling pin or meat mallet until about ½" thick.

2. In small saucepan, combine wine, prunes, apricots, and onion. Simmer for 10 minutes or until fruit is soft and wine is absorbed. Place this mixture in the center of the pork tenderloin. Roll the pork around the fruit mixture, using a toothpick to secure.

3. Sprinkle pork with flour, salt, and pepper. In ovenproof saucepan, heat olive oil. Add pork; brown on all sides, turning frequently, about 5–6 minutes. Add broth and thyme to saucepan. Bake for 25–35 minutes or until internal temperature registers 155°F. Let pork stand for 5 minutes, remove toothpicks, and slice to serve.

**Serves 6**

**Calories:** 249.06
**Fat:** 9.82 grams
**Saturated fat:** 2.41 grams
**Dietary fiber:** 1.45 grams
**Sodium:** 102.85 mg
**Cholesterol:** 72.51 mg

*1½ pounds pork tenderloin*
*¼ cup dry white wine*
*6 prunes, chopped*
*5 dried apricots, chopped*
*1 onion, chopped*
*2 tablespoons flour*
*⅛ teaspoon salt*
*⅛ teaspoon pepper*
*2 tablespoons olive oil*
*½ cup Low-Sodium Chicken Broth (page 120)*
*1 teaspoon dried thyme leaves*

# Risotto with Ham and Pineapple

*This risotto is fresh and delicious, reminiscent of Hawaii!*
*Serve it with a green salad and some sherbet for dessert.*

**Serves 4–6**

**Calories:** 369.77
**Fat:** 8.92 grams
**Saturated fat:** 3.17 grams
**Dietary fiber:** 3.15 grams
**Sodium:** 390.26 mg
**Cholesterol:** 26.81 mg

*2 cups water*
*2 cups Low-Fat Chicken Broth*
*(page 120)*
*1 tablespoon olive oil*
*1 tablespoon butter*
*1 onion, chopped*
*3 cloves garlic, minced*
*½ teaspoon dried thyme*
*leaves*
*1 red bell pepper, chopped*
*1½ cups Arborio rice*
*1 cup chopped ham*
*1 (20-ounce) can pineapple*
*tidbits, drained*
*⅛ teaspoon pepper*
*¼ cup grated Parmesan*
*cheese*

1. In medium saucepan, combine water and chicken broth and bring to a simmer over low heat. Keep warm. In large saucepan, heat olive oil and butter over medium heat. Add onion and garlic; cook and stir for 3 minutes. Add thyme, bell pepper, and rice; cook and stir for 4 minutes.

2. Start adding the broth, 1 cup at a time, stirring frequently. When 1 cup broth remains to be added, add ham, pineapple, and pepper to risotto. Add last cup of broth; cook and stir until rice is tender and creamy and liquid is absorbed. Stir in Parmesan, cover, let stand for 5 minutes, then serve.

## Pineapple

*Pineapple is another delicious weapon in the war against too much cholesterol. It contains micronutrients that can break up blood clots in your arteries. It also has a good amount of manganese. A manganese deficiency could be a factor in abnormal blood cholesterol levels. The fruit also contains Vitamin C, potassium, and fiber; eat up!*

# Pork Skewers with Cherry Tomatoes

*Cherry tomatoes, when grilled, burst with flavor in your mouth. Serve these kabobs with a rice pilaf.*

1. Prepare and preheat grill. Thread pork, cherry tomatoes, and onion on metal skewers. In small bowl, combine olive oil, lemon juice, pepper, parsley, and oregano leaves. Brush skewers with olive oil mixture.

2. Grill skewers 6" from medium coals for 8–10 minutes, turning and brushing occasionally with marinade, until pork registers 155°F. Sprinkle with Parmesan, let stand to melt, and serve.

## Parmesan: Shredded or Grated?

*There is quite a difference in the amounts when Parmesan cheese is shredded as opposed to grated. Shredded cheese is in strips, and the total amount will be less. Grated is very finely shredded cheese, and you'll end up eating more of it. They both will give about the same flavor and taste. Be sure to read packages carefully if you buy cheese already shredded.*

**Serves 4**

**Calories:** 240.01
**Fat:** 10.48 grams
**Saturated fat:** 3.50 grams
**Dietary fiber:** 1.76 grams
**Sodium:** 177.18 mg
**Cholesterol:** 78.34 mg

¾ pound pork tenderloin, cubed
24 cherry tomatoes
1 onion, cut into eighths
2 tablespoons olive oil
1 tablespoon lemon juice
⅛ teaspoon pepper
2 tablespoons chopped flat-leaf parsley
1 tablespoon fresh oregano leaves
¼ cup shredded Parmesan cheese

# Herb-Crusted Pork Tenderloin

*Pork tenderloin is a cut with very little fat that is tender and delicious.*
*Save some to use in Pork-and-Slaw Sandwiches (page 276).*

**Serves 8**

**Calories:** 199.58
**Fat:** 9.77 grams
**Saturated fat:** 2.63 grams
**Dietary fiber:** 0.30 grams
**Sodium:** 139.95 mg
**Cholesterol:** 74.84 mg

*⅓ cup chopped flat-leaf parsley*
*4 fresh sage leaves, chopped*
*¼ cup dried breadcrumbs*
*2 tablespoons fresh thyme leaves*
*1 tablespoon mustard*
*1 tablespoon olive oil*
*2 (1-pound) pork tenderloins*
*⅛ teaspoon salt*
*⅛ teaspoon pepper*
*2 tablespoons olive oil*

1. Preheat oven to 400°F. On shallow plate, combine parsley, sage, breadcrumbs, and thyme leaves and mix until combined. Add mustard and olive oil; toss until combined. Set aside.

2. Sprinkle tenderloins with salt and pepper. Heat 2 tablespoons olive oil in heavy ovenproof saucepan over medium high heat. Sear tenderloins on all sides, about 2 minutes a side, until golden brown.

3. Remove pan from heat. Carefully press herb mixture onto top and sides of tenderloins. Roast for 15–20 minutes or until internal temperature registers 155°F. Let pork stand for 5 minutes, then serve.

# Prosciutto Fruit Omelet

*Ham and fruit are a classic combination. You can peel
the apple or not, as you wish; unpeeled, it has more fiber.*

**Serves 4**

**Calories:** 221.48
**Fat:** 12.35 grams
**Saturated fat:** 4.99 grams
**Dietary fiber:** 1.27 grams
**Sodium:** 551.41 mg
**Cholesterol:** 80.91 mg

1. Trim off excess fat from prosciutto and discard. Thinly slice the prosciutto and combine with the mozzarella and Parmesan cheeses. Set
aside.

2. In large bowl, combine egg, egg whites, sour cream, and pepper and mix
well. In large nonstick saucepan, heat olive oil over medium heat; add
apples and stir until apples are tender. Pour in egg mixture.

3. Cook, running spatula around edges to let uncooked mixture flow
underneath, until eggs are almost set and bottom is golden brown.

4. Sprinkle with cheese and ham mixture and cook for 2–3 minutes longer. Cover, remove from heat, and let stand for 2 minutes. Fold omelet
over on itself and slide onto plate to serve.

*¼ pound thinly sliced
prosciutto
½ cup shredded part-skim
mozzarella cheese
2 tablespoons grated
Parmesan cheese
1 egg
8 egg whites
¼ cup low-fat sour cream
⅛ teaspoon pepper
1 tablespoon olive oil
1 apple, chopped*

### Prosciutto

*Prosciutto is an Italian ham that has been dry-cured and smoked. It's
usually available at the deli counter and is very thinly sliced. The best
prosciutto is cured for at least two years. This ham is usually very highly
marbled. Even though purists would shudder, you can cut off the visible
fat and discard it to reduce the fat content.*

# Asian Pork Stir-Fry

*Serve this delicious and spicy stir-fry over hot cooked brown rice, with chopsticks.*

**Serves 6**

**Calories:** 214.75
**Fat:** 9.01 grams
**Saturated fat:** 1.81 grams
**Dietary fiber:** 2.93 grams
**Sodium:** 147.48 mg
**Cholesterol:** 49.90 mg

*1 tablespoon low-sodium soy
    sauce*
*2 tablespoons honey*
*2 tablespoons water*
*½ teaspoon wasabi powder*
*1 tablespoon cornstarch*
*2 tablespoons canola oil*
*3 cloves garlic, minced*
*1 tablespoon minced ginger
    root*
*1 pound pork tenderloin,
    sliced*
*1 red bell pepper, chopped*
*1 (8-ounce) package cremini
    mushrooms, sliced*
*2 zucchini, sliced*
*8 ounces snow peas*

1. In small bowl, combine soy sauce, honey, water, wasabi powder, and cornstarch and mix thoroughly with wire whisk. Set aside. Prepare the meat and all of the vegetables.

2. In large wok or large skillet, heat canola oil over medium-high heat. Add garlic and ginger; stir-fry for 2 minutes. Then add pork tenderloin slices; stir-fry for 3–4 minutes. Remove pork from wok.

3. Add bell pepper, mushrooms, zucchini, and snow peas to wok and stir-fry until crisp-tender, about 4 minutes. Return meat to wok. Stir soy sauce mixture and pour into wok. Stir-fry for 2–4 minutes or until sauce boils and thickens. Serve immediately.

# Chapter 11
## Vegetarian Entrees

# Savory French Toast

*French toast doesn't have to be sweet! This version
is delicious topped with spicy tomato sauce.*

**Serves 4–6**

**Calories:** 342.51
**Fat:** 14.56 grams
**Saturated fat:** 6.14 grams
**Dietary fiber:** 3.98 grams
**Sodium:** 198.74 mg
**Cholesterol:** 65.18 mg

1 tablespoon olive oil
1 tablespoon butter
1 onion, chopped
4 (1-inch thick) slices Light
    Whole-Grain Bread (page
    70)
1 cup shredded Jarlsberg
    cheese
1 egg
1 egg white
⅓ cup buttermilk
1 teaspoon dried thyme
    leaves
½ teaspoon hot sauce
1 cup Spaghetti Sauce (page
    207)

1. In large saucepan, combine olive oil and butter over medium heat. Add onion; cook and stir until tender, about 5 minutes. Continue cooking until onion begins to turn golden, about 5–8 minutes longer. Remove onion from pan and place in small bowl. Remove pan from heat.

2. Let onion cool for 15 minutes. Meanwhile, cut a pocket in the center of each slice of bread. Add Jarlsberg to the onion mixture and mix. Stuff this into the bread pockets.

3. In shallow bowl, combine egg, egg whites, buttermilk, thyme, and hot sauce, and beat well. Dip stuffed bread into egg mixture, turning to coat.

4. Return saucepan to heat. Sauté the stuffed bread, turning once, about 4–5 minutes on each side until golden brown. Serve with the warmed Spaghetti Sauce.

# Spaghetti Sauce

*Grated carrots add nutrition and fiber to this rich sauce,*
*and help reduce the problem of sauce separation.*

1. In large saucepan, heat olive oil over medium heat. Add onion and garlic; cook and stir until crisp-tender, about 4 minutes. Add celery and mushrooms; cook and stir for 2–3 minutes longer.

2. Add tomato paste; let paste brown a bit without stirring (this adds flavor to the sauce). Then add remaining ingredients and stir gently but thoroughly.

3. Bring sauce to a simmer, then reduce heat to low and partially cover. Simmer for 60–70 minutes, stirring occasionally, until sauce is blended and thickened. Serve over hot cooked pasta, couscous, or rice.

### Freezing Spaghetti Sauce

*Spaghetti sauce freezes beautifully, and it can be used in all sorts of casseroles and soups in addition to just serving it over spaghetti. To freeze, portion 4 cups into a hard-sided freezer container, leaving about 1" of head space for expansion. Seal, label, and freeze for up to 3 months. To thaw, let stand in fridge overnight, then heat in saucepan.*

Yields 6 cups; serving size 1 cup

**Calories:** 155.73
**Fat:** 5.11 grams
**Saturated fat:** 0.72 grams
**Dietary fiber:** 4.96 grams
**Sodium:** 84.74 mg
**Cholesterol:** 0.0 grams

*2 tablespoons olive oil*
*1 onion, chopped*
*4 cloves garlic, minced*
*1 cup chopped celery*
*1 (8-ounce) package sliced mushrooms*
*1 (6-ounce) can no-salt tomato paste*
*2 (14-ounce) cans no-salt diced tomatoes, undrained*
*1 tablespoon dried Italian seasoning*
*½ cup grated carrots*
*⅛ teaspoon white pepper*
*½ cup dry red wine*
*½ cup water*

# Rice-and-Vegetable Casserole

*Vegetables are layered with a rice-and-egg mixture*
*in this easy and delicious vegetarian entrée.*

**Serves 8**

**Calories:** 276.42
**Fat:** 10.87 grams
**Saturated fat:** 5.35 grams
**Dietary fiber:** 3.25 grams
**Sodium:** 175.20 mg
**Cholesterol:** 49.67 mg

*1 tablespoon olive oil*
*2 onions, chopped*
*1 (8-ounce) package sliced*
*    mushrooms*
*2 red bell peppers, chopped*
*1 jalapeño pepper, minced*
*4 cups cooked brown rice*
*1½ cups milk*
*1 egg*
*2 egg whites*
*½ cup low-fat sour cream*
*1 cup shredded part-skim*
*    mozzarella cheese*
*½ cup shredded Colby cheese*

1. Preheat oven to 350°F. Spray a 13" × 9" baking pan with nonstick cook-ing spray and set aside.

2. In large saucepan, heat olive oil. Add onions and mushrooms; cook and stir for 3 minutes. Then add bell peppers and jalapeño pepper; cook and stir for 3–4 minutes longer until vegetables are crisp-tender.

3. In large bowl, combine rice, milk, egg, egg whites, sour cream, moz-zarella cheese, and Colby cheese. Layer half of this mixture in the pre-pared baking pan. Top with vegetables, then top with remaining rice mixture. Bake for 50–65 minutes or until casserole is bubbling, set, and beginning to brown. Let stand for 5 minutes, then cut into squares to serve.

# Potato Soufflé

*This soufflé isn't as light as others; it's more like a potato puff.
Serve it with a fruit salad for a nice lunch.*

1. Preheat oven to 450°F. Peel and thinly slice potatoes, adding to a pot of cold water as you work. Bring potatoes to a boil over high heat, reduce heat, and simmer until tender, about 12–15 minutes.

2. Drain potatoes and return to hot pot; shake for 1 minute. Add olive oil, nutmeg, salt, and pepper and mash until smooth. Beat in the half-and-half and Parmesan.

3. In large bowl, combine egg whites with cream of tartar and beat until stiff peaks form. Stir a dollop of the egg whites into the potato mixture and stir. Then fold in remaining egg whites.

4. Spray the bottom of a 2-quart casserole with nonstick cooking spray. Spoon potato mixture into casserole. Bake for 20 minutes, then reduce heat to 375°F and bake for another 12–17 minutes or until soufflé is golden brown and puffed.

5. While soufflé is baking, combine tomatoes and basil in small bowl and mix gently. Serve immediately with tomato mixture for topping the soufflé.

## Cooking Potatoes

*When you are cooking with potatoes, be sure to place them in cold water to cover as they are being peeled or chopped. Potatoes can turn brown very quickly, and this slows the process. Do not overcook potatoes; cook them just until they are tender when pierced with a knife. Drain well and shake in the hot pot to remove excess moisture.*

---

**Serves 4**

**Calories:** 224.39
**Fat:** 9.11 grams
**Saturated fat:** 2.24 grams
**Dietary fiber:** 2.79 grams
**Sodium:** 260.97 mg
**Cholesterol:** 6.51 mg

*2 Yukon Gold potatoes*
*1 tablespoon olive oil*
*⅛ teaspoon nutmeg*
*¼ teaspoon onion salt*
*⅛ teaspoon cayenne pepper*
*⅓ cup fat-free half-and-half*
*¼ cup grated Parmesan cheese*
*4 egg whites*
*¼ teaspoon cream of tartar*
*1 cup chopped grape tomatoes*
*¼ cup chopped fresh basil*

# Corn-and-Chili Pancakes

**Serves 6**

**Calories:** 252.62
**Fat:** 9.20 grams
**Saturated fat:** 3.03 grams
**Dietary fiber:** 2.17 grams
**Sodium:** 287.01 mg
**Cholesterol:** 10.91 mg

½ cup buttermilk
1 tablespoon olive oil
½ cup egg substitute
½ cup grated extra-sharp
 Cheddar cheese
1 jalapeño pepper, minced
2 ears sweet corn
½ cup cornmeal
1 cup all-purpose flour
1½ teaspoons baking powder
½ teaspoon baking soda
1 tablespoon sugar
1 tablespoon chili powder
1 tablespoon peanut oil
1 tablespoon butter

*Top these spicy pancakes with some nonfat sour cream and
Super Spicy Salsa (page XX), or some warmed maple syrup.*

1. In large bowl, combine buttermilk, olive oil, egg substitute, Cheddar, and jalapeño pepper and mix well.

2. Cut the kernels off the sweet corn and add to buttermilk mixture along with cornmeal, flour, baking powder, baking soda, sugar, and chili powder; mix until combined. Let stand for 10 minutes.

3. Heat griddle or frying pan over medium heat. Brush with the butter, then add the batter, ¼ cup at a time. Cook until bubbles form and start to break and sides look dry, about 3–4 minutes. Carefully flip pancakes and cook until light golden brown on second side, about 2–3 minutes. Serve immediately.

# Quinoa Pepper Pilaf

*You can use this pilaf to stuff vegetables from tomatoes to zucchini, or serve it as a side dish.*

**Serves 6**

**Calories:** 241.29
**Fat:** 8.16 grams
**Saturated fat:** 1.14 grams
**Dietary fiber:** 4.21 grams
**Sodium:** 199.17 mg
**Cholesterol:** 0.98 mg

*2 tablespoons olive oil*
*2 Italian frying peppers, chopped*
*1 green bell pepper, chopped*
*1 red bell pepper, chopped*
*1 onion, chopped*
*4 garlic cloves, minced*
*¼ cup chopped sun-dried tomatoes*
*⅛ teaspoon salt*
*⅛ teaspoon white pepper*
*1¼ cups quinoa*
*2½ cups low-sodium vegetable broth*

1. In large saucepan, heat olive oil over medium heat. Add frying peppers, green bell pepper, red bell pepper, onion, and garlic; cook and stir until crisp-tender, about 4 minutes. Add sun-dried tomatoes, salt, pepper, and quinoa; cook and stir for 2 minutes.

2. Pour in 1½ cups broth and bring to a simmer. Reduce heat to medium low and cook, stirring frequently, until the broth is absorbed, about 7 minutes. Add remaining broth and cook, stirring frequently, until quinoa is tender. Cover and remove from heat; let stand for 5 minutes. Fluff with a fork and serve.

## Quinoa

*Quinoa (pronounced keen-wah) is an ancient grain tin cultivation for at least 5,000 years. It is high in fiber and protein, chewy and delicious. Quinoa is an unusual grain. It provides complete protein, so it does not need to be combined with another grain or legume for the vegetarian. The grain is also gluten-free.*

# Roasted Garlic Soufflé

*This unusual recipe is delicious for a light lunch
on the porch, served with a baby spinach salad.*

**Serves 4**

**Calories:** 223.79
**Fat:** 14.23 grams
**Saturated fat:** 3.92 grams
**Dietary fiber:** 0.40 grams
**Sodium:** 253.37 mg
**Cholesterol:** 79.32 mg

1 head Roasted Garlic (page
    89)
2 tablespoons olive oil
1 cup finely chopped cooked
    turkey breast
¼ cup grated Parmesan
    cheese
⅛ teaspoon pepper
1 egg
¼ cup low-fat sour cream
6 egg whites
¼ teaspoon cream of tartar
¼ cup chopped flat-leaf
    parsley

1. Preheat oven to 375°F. Grease the bottom of a 2-quart soufflé dish with peanut oil and set aside. Squeeze the garlic from the papery skins. Discard skins, and in medium bowl, combine olive oil with the garlic. Add turkey, cheese, pepper, egg, and sour cream, and mix well.

2. In large bowl, combine egg whites with cream of tartar. Beat until stiff peaks form. Stir a spoonful of egg whites into the turkey mixture and stir well. Then fold in remaining egg whites. Fold in parsley.

3. Spoon mixture into prepared soufflé dish. Bake for 40–50 minutes or until the soufflé is puffed and golden. Serve immediately.

# Risotto with Artichokes

*If you can't find frozen artichoke hearts, you can substitute canned,
but the sodium content will be higher. Rinse the artichokes
before using to reduce the amount of sodium.*

**Serves 6**

**Calories:** 317.17
**Fat:** 8.90 grams
**Saturated fat:** 2.86 grams
**Dietary fiber:** 4.25 grams
**Sodium:** 223.71 mg
**Cholesterol:** 9.25 mg

2 cups water
2½ cups low-sodium
 vegetable broth
2 tablespoons olive oil
4 shallots, minced
3 cloves garlic, minced
1 (10-ounce) box frozen
 artichoke hearts, thawed
1½ cups Arborio rice
⅛ teaspoon pepper
¼ cup grated Parmesan
 cheese
1 tablespoon butter
½ cup chopped fresh basil
 leaves

1. In medium saucepan, combine water and broth; heat over low heat until warm; keep on heat.

2. In large saucepan, heat olive oil over medium heat. Add shallots and garlic; cook and stir until crisp-tender, about 4 minutes. Add artichokes; cook and stir for 3 minutes.

3. Add rice; cook and stir for 2 minutes. Add the broth mixture, a cup at a time, stirring until the liquid is absorbed, about 20–25 minutes. Stir in pepper, Parmesan, butter, and basil; cover and let stand for 5 minutes off the heat. Serve immediately.

### Arborio Rice

*Arborio rice is a short-grain rice that contains a lot of starch. When cooked in broth and stirred, the rice releases much of that starch, which combines with the liquid to form a creamy sauce. If you can't find true Arborio rice, long-grain or medium-grain rice will work just as well. The risotto just won't be quite as creamy.*

## Crisp Polenta with Tomato Sauce

*Crisp and crunchy polenta is served with hot pasta sauce in this simple recipe.*

**Serves 8**

**Calories:** 229.70
**Fat:** 8.43 grams
**Saturated fat:** 4.20 grams
**Dietary fiber:** 3.46 grams
**Sodium:** 260.08 mg
**Cholesterol:** 17.91 mg

*1 recipe Cheese Polenta (page 257)*
*1 cup shredded part-skim mozzarella cheese*
*3 cups Spaghetti Sauce (page 207), heated*

1. Prepare polenta as directed, except when done, pour onto a greased cookie sheet; spread to a ½"-thick rectangle, about 9" × 15". Cover and chill until very firm, about 2 hours.

2. Preheat broiler. Cut polenta into fifteen 3" squares. Place on broiler pan; broil for 4–6 minutes or until golden brown. Carefully turn polenta and broil for 3–5 minutes or until golden brown.

3. Remove from oven and sprinkle with mozzarella cheese. Top each with a dollop of the hot Spaghetti Sauce, and serve immediately.

## Quinoa-Stuffed Peppers

*Stuffed peppers are an excellent vegetarian dish.*
*You could add more vegetables to the pilaf if you'd like.*

**Serves 6**

**Calories:** 406.04
**Fat:** 15.40 grams
**Saturated fat:** 4.69 grams
**Dietary fiber:** 9.31 grams
**Sodium:** 468.06 mg
**Cholesterol:** 17.54 mg

*1 recipe Quinoa Pepper Pilaf (page 211)*
*½ cup chopped flat-leaf parsley*
*1 cup shredded Havarti cheese*
*6 large red bell peppers*
*2 cups Spaghetti Sauce (page 207)*

1. Preheat oven to 350°F. Prepare pilaf and fluff. Stir in parsley and Havarti. Cut tops from peppers and remove seeds and membranes.

2. Spray 9" × 13" baking dish with nonstick cooking spray. Place a layer of Spaghetti Sauce in the dish. Stuff peppers with pilaf and arrange on sauce. Pour remaining sauce over and around peppers.

3. Bake for 50–60 minutes or until peppers are tender. Serve immediately.

# Ratatouille

*This rich vegetable stew can be served over brown rice,
pasta, or couscous, either hot or cold.*

1. In large saucepan, heat olive oil over medium heat. Add onion and garlic; cook and stir until crisp-tender, about 3 minutes. Add bell peppers; cook and stir until crisp-tender, about 3 minutes.

2. Sprinkle eggplant with salt, pepper, and flour. Add to saucepan; cook and stir until eggplant begins to soften. Add remaining ingredients except parsley; cover, and simmer for 30–35 minutes or until vegetables are soft and mixture is blended. Sprinkle with parsley and serve.

### Eggplant

*Eggplant is very low in calories and sodium and has a fairly high fiber content, about 2 grams per cup. It has lots of minerals, but a low vitamin content. It does contain the phytochemical monoterpene, which may help prevent cancer. To reduce bitterness, choose smaller eggplants that are firm and heavy for their size.*

**Serves 6**

**Calories:** 124.26
**Fat:** 7.10 grams
**Saturated fat:** 1.02 grams
**Dietary fiber:** 4.47 grams
**Sodium:** 187.22 mg
**Cholesterol:** 0.0 mg

3 tablespoons olive oil
2 onions, chopped
4 cloves garlic, minced
1 green bell pepper, sliced
1 yellow bell pepper, sliced
1 eggplant, peeled and cubed
¼ teaspoon salt
⅛ teaspoon pepper
2 tablespoons flour
2 zucchini, sliced
1 tablespoon red-wine vinegar
2 tablespoons capers, rinsed
¼ cup chopped flat-leaf parsley

# Pumpkin Soufflé

*This beautiful little entrée is wonderful for entertaining.*
*Serve it with a crisp green salad and some breadsticks.*

**Serves 4**

**Calories:** 118.83
**Fat:** 5.74 grams
**Saturated fat:** 1.56 grams
**Dietary fiber:** 3.02 grams
**Sodium:** 183.15 mg
**Cholesterol:** 55.20 mg

*1 tablespoon olive oil*
*1 onion, chopped*
*4 cloves garlic, minced*
*1 (13-ounce) can solid-pack pumpkin*
*1 egg yolk*
*2 teaspoons chopped fresh thyme*
*4 egg whites*
*⅛ teaspoon salt*
*¼ teaspoon cream of tartar*
*2 tablespoons grated Parmesan cheese*

1. Preheat oven to 425°F. Grease the bottom of a 1-quart soufflé dish with peanut oil and set aside. In small saucepan, heat olive oil over medium heat. Add onion and garlic; cook and stir until tender, about 5 minutes.

2. Place in large bowl and let cool for 10 minutes. Blend in pumpkin, egg yolk, and thyme until smooth.

3. In medium bowl, combine egg whites, salt, and cream of tartar and beat until stiff peaks form. Stir a spoonful of the beaten egg whites into pumpkin mixture, then fold in remaining egg whites along with the Parmesan cheese. Pour into prepared soufflé dish.

4. Bake for 15 minutes, then reduce heat to 350°F and bake for another 20–25 minutes or until soufflé is puffed and golden brown. Serve immediately.

# Spaghetti with Creamy Tomato Sauce

*You can serve this simple and flavorful recipe to just about anybody!*

**Serves 6–8**

**Calories:** 354.63
**Fat:** 6.65 grams
**Saturated fat:** 1.90 grams
**Dietary fiber:** 3.90 grams
**Sodium:** 188.68 mg
**Cholesterol:** 6.26 mg

*1 recipe Spaghetti Sauce
   (page 207)*
*½ cup fat-free half-and-half*
*1 (16-ounce) package whole-
   grain pasta*
*½ cup grated Parmesan
   cheese*

1. Bring large pot of water to a boil. Prepare Spaghetti Sauce as directed. During last 5 minutes of cooking time, stir in light cream and stir to blend.

2. Cook pasta in boiling water according to package directions until al dente. Drain and add to Spaghetti Sauce; cook and stir for 1 minute to let the pasta absorb some of the sauce. Sprinkle with Parmesan and serve immediately.

### Tomatoes

*Tomatoes are an excellent heart-healthy food, high in vitamins C and A and with no fat or cholesterol. They are usually sold unripe in the super-market. Let them stand at room temperature for 1–2 days until they give to slight pressure. Don't store tomatoes in the refrigerator; their texture will become mealy.*

# Peanut-Butter-Banana Skewered Sammies

**Serves 4–6**

**Calories:** 376.36
**Fat:** 18.67 grams
**Saturated fat:** 5.57 grams
**Dietary fiber:** 5.27 grams
**Sodium:** 77.44 mg
**Cholesterol:** 23.30 mg

½ cup natural no-salt peanut
 butter
8 slices Honey-Wheat Sesame
 Bread (page 66)
2 bananas
2 tablespoons lime juice
2 tablespoons butter or
 margarine, softened

*You can find low-fat and no-salt peanut butters on the market. Natural peanut butters are a good choice because they don't contain trans fat.*

1. Spread peanut butter on one side of each slice of bread. Slice bananas, and as you work, sprinkle with lime juice. Make sandwiches by putting the bananas on the peanut butter and combining slices.

2. Butter the outsides of the sandwiches. Heat grill and cook sandwiches until bread is crisp and golden brown. Remove from grill, cut into quarters, and skewer on wood or metal skewers. Serve immediately.

### Dual-Contact Grill

*The indoor grill (one brand name is George Foreman Grills) is a wonderful appliance that can help reduce fat intake. The grills are slanted with ridges, so fat runs off, especially when grilling sandwiches, burgers, and meat. Read the directions carefully and be sure to clean the grill very well after each use.*

# Cheese-and-Veggie Stuffed Artichokes

*This is a delicious main dish for a hot summer day.*
*Serve with iced green tea and some fruit sorbet for dessert.*

1. In medium bowl, combine Havarti, Parmesan, yogurt, mayonnaise, lemon juice, scallions, and capers and mix well. Stir in carrots, tomatoes, and salt, and set aside.

2. Cut off the top inch of the artichokes. Cut off the sharp tip of each leaf. Pull off the tough outer leaves and discard. Rub cut edges with lemon wedges. Cut artichokes in half lengthwise.

3. Bring a large pot of salted water to a boil and add lemon wedges. Add artichokes and simmer for 20–25 minutes or until a leaf pulls out easily from the artichoke. Cool, then carefully remove choke with spoon.

4. Stuff artichokes with the cheese mixture, place on serving plate, cover, and chill for 2–4 hours before serving.

## Artichoke Health Benefits

*Artichokes contain a phytochemical called cynarin, which studies show may help the liver regenerate. Since the liver is essential to processing and removing cholesterol from the body, it's critical to your health. Artichokes are nutrient-dense, providing potassium, fiber, vitamin C, and folate. They are low in fat and contain no cholesterol.*

**Serves 4**

**Calories:** 266.61
**Fat:** 14.24 grams
**Saturated fat:** 6.47 grams
**Dietary fiber:** 8.11 grams
**Sodium:** 413.37 mg
**Cholesterol:** 29.43 mg

*1 cup shredded Havarti cheese*
*2 tablespoons grated Parmesan cheese*
*¼ cup plain yogurt*
*¼ cup low-fat mayonnaise*
*1 tablespoon lemon juice*
*2 scallions, chopped*
*1 tablespoon capers*
*1 cup grated carrots*
*1 cup grape tomatoes*
*⅛ teaspoon salt*
*4 globe artichokes*
*1 lemon, cut into wedges*

# Quinoa with Spinach and Artichokes

*Since quinoa provides complete protein, you don't need
any other grain in this hearty vegetarian main dish.*

**Serves 6**

**Calories:** 226.63
**Fat:** 7.41 grams
**Saturated fat:** 1.07 grams
**Dietary fiber:** 6.55 grams
**Sodium:** 206.13 mg
**Cholesterol:** 0.50 mg

2 tablespoons olive oil
1 onion, chopped
4 cloves garlic, minced
1 (10-ounce) package frozen
    spinach, thawed and
    drained
1 (10-ounce) package frozen
    artichoke hearts, thawed
    and drained
1 cup quinoa
2½ cups low-sodium
    vegetable broth
2 tablespoons lemon juice
⅛ teaspoon pepper
1 teaspoon fresh oregano
    leaves

1. In large saucepan, combine olive oil, onion, and garlic over medium heat; cook and stir until tender, about 5 minutes. Add spinach and artichokes; cook and stir until most of the liquid evaporates.

2. Stir in quinoa, then add vegetable broth. Bring to a simmer, then reduce heat to low. Cover and cook for 8 minutes, then uncover and cook, stirring, until quinoa is tender, about 4–5 minutes longer.

3. Stir in lemon juice, pepper, and oregano leaves and serve immediately.

### Quinoa and Whole Grains

*Studies have found that postmenopausal women who ate whole grains like quinoa slowed progression of plaque buildup in the arteries. Quinoa also is a good source of those important antioxidants that help reduce inflammation, including one with the tongue-twister name of superoxide dismutase. It's also a good source of folate and magnesium.*

# Chickpeas in Lettuce Wraps

*This fabulous creamy and flavorful spread can also be spread on toasted bread or used as an appetizer dip.*

1. Drain the chickpeas; rinse, and drain again. Place half in a blender or food processor. Add olive oil, lemon juice, garlic, and mint. Blend or process until smooth.

2. Place in medium bowl and stir in remaining chickpeas and red onion; stir until combined.

3. To make sandwiches, place lettuce leaves on work surface. Divide chickpea mixture among leaves and top with tomatoes and bell pepper. Roll up, folding in sides, to enclose filling. Serve immediately.

### Chickpeas

*Chickpeas, also known as garbanzo beans, are a round legume with a nutty flavor and tender texture. One cup of cooked beans provides more than 10 grams of fiber. Eating high-fiber foods reduces cholesterol and helps prevent heart disease. The beans are also very high in folate, the molecule that reduces homocysteine levels.*

---

**Serves 6–8**

**Calories:** 148.96
**Fat:** 6.56 grams
**Saturated fat:** 0.87 grams
**Dietary fiber:** 4.98 grams
**Sodium:** 6.80 grams
**Cholesterol:** 0.0 grams

*1 (15-ounce) can no-salt chickpeas*
*3 tablespoons olive oil*
*3 tablespoons lemon juice*
*3 cloves garlic, minced*
*1 tablespoon chopped fresh mint*
*½ cup diced red onion*
*8 lettuce leaves*
*1 cup chopped tomatoes*
*1 cup chopped yellow bell pepper*

# Spanish Omelet

*If you remove the seeds from the jalapeño, the sauce*
*will be milder. Like it hot? Leave the seeds in.*

**Serves 4**

**Calories:** 219.98
**Fat:** 14.03 grams
**Saturated fat:** 4.95 grams
**Dietary fiber:** 2.12 grams
**Sodium:** 316.92 mg
**Cholesterol:** 70.96 mg

*2 tablespoons olive oil,*
*divided*
*1 onion, minced*
*2 cloves garlic, minced*
*1 stalk celery, chopped*
*½ cup chopped red bell*
*pepper*
*1 jalapeño pepper, minced*
*½ teaspoon dried oregano*
*2 tomatoes, chopped*
*⅛ teaspoon salt*
*⅛ teaspoon pepper*
*1 egg*
*8 egg whites*
*¼ cup skim milk*
*2 tablespoons low-fat sour*
*cream*
*½ cup grated extra-sharp*
*Cheddar cheese*

1. For the sauce, in a small saucepan heat 1 tablespoon olive oil over medium heat. Add onion, garlic, celery, bell pepper, and jalapeño pepper; cook and stir for 4 minutes until crisp-tender. Add oregano, tomatoes, salt, and pepper, and bring to a simmer. Reduce heat to low and simmer for 5 minutes.

2. In large bowl, combine egg, egg whites, skim milk, and sour cream and beat until combined. Heat 1 tablespoon olive oil in nonstick skillet and add egg mixture. Cook, moving spatula around pan and lifting to let uncooked mixture flow underneath, until eggs are set but still moist.

3. Sprinkle with Cheddar and top with half of the tomato sauce. Cover and cook for 2–4 minutes longer, until bottom of omelet is golden brown. Fold over, slide onto serving plate, top with remaining tomato sauce, and serve.

# Spinach-Ricotta Omelet

*Yes, you can have an omelet! Even though egg yolks are high in cholesterol, just one in this omelet adds some body and flavor while still keeping cholesterol low.*

1. Press spinach between layers of paper towel to remove all excess moisture. Set aside. In small bowl, combine ricotta with Parmesan cheese and nutmeg; set aside.

2. In medium bowl, beat egg whites until a soft foam forms. In small bowl, combine egg yolk with milk and pepper and beat well.

3. Heat a nonstick skillet over medium heat. Add olive oil, then add spinach and onion; cook and stir until onion is crisp-tender, about 4 minutes. Meanwhile, fold egg-yolk mixture into beaten egg whites. Add egg mixture to skillet; cook, running spatula around edges to let uncooked mixture flow underneath, until eggs are set but still moist.

4. Spoon ricotta mixture on top of eggs; cover pan, and let cook for 2 minutes. Then fold omelet and serve immediately.

## Omelet Variety

*You can add just about any cooked vegetable or meat to omelets, and you can vary the cheese as well. Just make sure that the vegetables and meats are well drained so they don't water down the omelet. These lower-cholesterol omelets made with more egg white than egg yolk are quite fragile.*

---

**Serves 4**

**Calories:** 162.81
**Fat:** 8.74 grams
**Saturated fat:** 3.23 grams
**Dietary fiber:** 2.34 grams
**Sodium:** 245.82 mg
**Cholesterol:** 66.00 mg

*1 (10-ounce) package frozen chopped spinach, thawed and drained*
*½ cup part-skim ricotta cheese*
*2 tablespoons grated Parmesan cheese*
*⅛ teaspoon nutmeg*
*7 egg whites*
*1 egg yolk*
*¼ cup milk*
*⅛ teaspoon pepper*
*1 tablespoon olive oil*
*¼ cup finely chopped onion*

# Sour-Cream-and-Herb Omelet

*The combination of hot omelet with cold sour cream topping
is really delicious. Use any fresh herbs you like.*

**Serves 4**

**Calories:** 243.49
**Fat:** 15.62 grams
**Saturated fat:** 6.42 grams
**Dietary fiber:** 0.02 grams
**Sodium:** 354.41 mg
**Cholesterol:** 27.24 mg

*1 tablespoon olive oil*
*2 shallots, minced*
*1 clove garlic, minced*
*2 cups egg substitute*
*¼ cup skim milk*
*¼ cup low-fat sour cream*
*1 teaspoon grated lemon zest*
*1 teaspoon fresh thyme
    leaves*
*⅛ teaspoon pepper*
*⅔ cup shredded extra-sharp
    Cheddar cheese*

1. In a large nonstick skillet, heat olive oil over medium heat. Add shallots and garlic; stir-fry for 2 minutes, until fragrant.

2. In medium bowl, combine egg substitute and milk and beat well. Add to saucepan; cook, running a spatula around the edges, and lifting the edges to let uncooked mixture flow underneath. Cook until eggs are set and bottom is golden brown, about 4–6 minutes.

3. Meanwhile, in small bowl combine sour cream, lemon zest, thyme, and pepper and mix well. Sprinkle omelet with Cheddar, cover pan, and remove from heat. Let stand for 3 minutes, then cut into pieces and serve with the sour-cream mixture.

### Shallots

*Shallots have a mild onion flavor and are quite delicate. They grow in clusters called offsets, like garlic, but they are much larger, with copper-colored skin. They can be difficult to peel; you can blanch them in boiling water for 30 seconds and the peel will slip right off. Mince them finely and cook in a bit of oil before adding to recipes.*

# Chapter 12
# **Salads**

# Fennel-and-Orange Salad

*Fennel has a mild licorice taste. This salad is a refreshing side dish with pork, ham, or fish. Serve it thoroughly chilled.*

**Serves 4**

**Calories:** 193.25
**Fat:** 13.54 grams
**Saturated fat:** 1.66 grams
**Dietary fiber:** 4.67 grams
**Sodium:** 148.69 mg
**Cholesterol:** 0.00 mg

*2 fresh oranges*
*1 fennel bulb*
*4 scallions, trimmed and finely chopped*
*3 tablespoons olive oil*
*1 teaspoon fennel seeds, crushed*
*2 tablespoons lemon juice*
*1 tablespoon mustard*
*⅛ teaspoon white pepper*
*1 jalapeño pepper, minced, if desired*
*4 cups baby spinach leaves*
*¼ cup sliced almonds, toasted*

1. Peel the oranges, and slice them thinly crosswise. Set aside. Trim the fennel and remove the outer layer. Using a mandoline or vegetable peeler, shave the fennel into thin ribbons.

2. In small bowl, combine scallions, oil, fennel seeds, lemon juice, mustard, pepper, and jalapeño, if using. Whisk thoroughly until combined.

3. Arrange spinach leaves on chilled salad plates. Top with the orange slices and fennel. Drizzle with dressing, sprinkle with almonds, and serve immediately.

### Mustard

*Typically, prepared mustards are high in sodium, about 170 mg per tablespoon. You can find low-sodium varieties in health-food stores and co-ops, or you can make your own. Combine ¼ cup mustard seeds with ⅓ cup water, 2 teaspoons whole-wheat flour, 3 tablespoons white vinegar, and 2 tablespoons brown sugar. Stir well and refrigerate for at least 4 days before using.*

## Roasted Baby-Beet Salad

*This is very pretty salad; the red of the beets contrasts with the white yogurt and green romaine leaves. You can garnish the salad with chopped toasted walnuts.*

1. Preheat oven to 350°F. Wash the beets and scrub gently; cut off stem and root ends. Wrap them in aluminum foil and place on cookie sheet; roast for 30 to 40 minutes, or until tender. Let cool. Slip the beets from their skins and thinly slice.

2. In a small bowl, toss beets with oil and vinegar, sprinkle with salt, pepper, and dill. In large serving bowl, toss beets with romaine and onions. Spoon dollop of yogurt on each salad and serve immediately.

**Serves 4**

**Calories:** 111.96
**Fat:** 7.45 grams
**Saturated fat:** 1.27 grams
**Dietary fiber:** 2.34 grams
**Sodium:** 203.24 mg
**Cholesterol:** 1.84 mg

*8 baby beets*
*2 tablespoons olive oil*
*2 tablespoons white-wine vinegar*
*¼ teaspoon salt*
*⅛ teaspoon white pepper*
*½ teaspoon dried dill weed*
*½ sweet onion, sliced*
*4 cups torn romaine leaves*
*½ cup low-fat yogurt*

## Red-Lettuce Jicama Salad

*Jicama is a tropical tuber, the root of a legume. It is slightly sweet and very crisp, and almost always eaten raw.*

In a large salad bowl, combine jicama with lettuce, radicchio, and red onion and toss gently. Drizzle with vinaigrette and serve immediately.

**Serves 4**

**Calories:** 204.85
**Fat:** 16.30 grams
**Saturated fat:** 2.24 grams
**Dietary fiber:** 5.08 grams
**Sodium:** 97.81 mg
**Cholesterol:** 0.0 mg

*½ pound jicama*
*1 head red lettuce, shredded*
*1 head radicchio, thinly sliced*
*½ red onion, thinly sliced*
*½ cup Balsamic Vinaigrette (page 243)*

# Arugula Salad with Marinated Mushrooms

*This salad has a nice tang. The marinated mushrooms can also be used in other salads or as a garnish for grilled hamburgers or chicken.*

**Serves 6**

**Calories:** 213.16
**Fat:** 17.25 grams
**Saturated fat:** 4.62 grams
**Dietary fiber:** 2.35 grams
**Sodium:** 360.96 mg
**Cholesterol:** 14.67 mg

*3 tablespoons red-wine vinegar*
*1 teaspoon lemon juice*
*1 tablespoon fresh rosemary, chopped*
*1 teaspoon chopped fresh thyme leaves*
*⅓ cup extra-virgin olive oil*
*¼ teaspoon salt*
*⅛ teaspoon white pepper*
*2 cups sliced button mushrooms*
*1 cup sliced cremini mushrooms*
*2 red bell peppers, sliced*
*3 cups torn arugula*
*3 cups torn romaine lettuce*
*¼ cup grated Parmesan cheese*

1. In a large bowl, combine vinegar, lemon juice, rosemary, thyme, olive oil, salt, and pepper. Add button and cremini mushrooms and stir well; cover and refrigerate for 2 hours.

2. Add the peppers, arugula, and romaine lettuce and toss well. Sprinkle with Parmesan and serve.

### Preparing Mushrooms

*Do not wash mushrooms before using. They are like sponges and will absorb lots of water. Just brush them with a soft brush or wipe with a damp paper towel. Commercial mushrooms are grown in sterilized soil, so don't worry about the dirt on them. Be sure to slice mushrooms just before using them so they don't turn brown.*

# New Potato Salad

*The secret to this recipe is to combine the dressing with the potatoes while they are still hot so they absorb the wonderful flavors.*

1. Rinse potatoes to clean and slice into ½" pieces. Place in a large pot and cover with cold water. Bring to a boil over high heat. Reduce the heat to medium and cook for 8–12 minutes, or until just tender when pierced with fork.

2. Meanwhile, whisk together vinegar, sugar, olive oil, yogurt, salt, pepper, mustard, and dill in a large bowl. Add the drained, hot potatoes and toss carefully to coat. Add onion, celery, and bell pepper and mix gently. Serve immediately, or cover and chill for 2–4 hours.

### New Potatoes

*These young potatoes have a delicious, waxy consistency and a mild flavor. Leaving the tender skins on adds to the flavor and nutrition, and the colorful skins add interest to mashed potatoes or potato salad. Varieties include red, creamery, fingerling, or purple. They are perishable, so buy only the amount you are going to use.*

**Serves 6**

**Calories:** 244.05
**Fat:** 9.75 grams
**Saturated fat:** 1.52 grams
**Dietary fiber:** 3.85 grams
**Sodium:** 98.18 mg
**Cholesterol:** 1.23 mg

*2 pounds new potatoes*
*¼ cup apple cider vinegar*
*1 teaspoon sugar*
*¼ cup olive oil*
*½ cup plain yogurt*
*¼ teaspoon salt*
*⅛ teaspoon pepper*
*2 tablespoons mustard*
*1 teaspoon fresh dill weed*
*½ cup finely chopped sweet onion*
*2 stalks celery, chopped*
*1 red bell pepper, chopped*

# Cucumber-Mango Salad

*The combination of cucumbers and mangoes is delicious and
very fresh. This salad is the ideal complement to grilled fish.*

## Serves 4

**Calories:** 119.80
**Fat:** 1.13 grams
**Saturated fat:** 0.48 grams
**Dietary fiber:** 3.15 grams
**Sodium:** 43.06 mg
**Cholesterol:** 2.45 mg

½ cup plain yogurt
¼ cup buttermilk
2 tablespoons lemon juice
1 tablespoon honey
2 tablespoons chopped fresh
  dill
½ cup finely chopped red
  onion
2 cucumbers
2 ripe mangoes

1. In large bowl, combine yogurt, buttermilk, lemon juice, honey, dill, and onion and mix well with wire whisk.

2. Peel cucumbers and cut in half lengthwise; using a spoon, scoop out the seeds. Cut into ¼" slices and add to yogurt mixture.

3. Peel mangoes and, standing them on end, slice down around the pit to remove the flesh. Cut into cubes and add to yogurt mixture; toss gently and serve, or chill for 2–3 hours before serving.

# Wheat-Berry Salad

*Wheat berries are actually the whole grain. You can find them
in the bulk section of health-food stores and co-ops.*

## Serves 6

**Calories:** 300.99
**Fat:** 10.66 grams
**Saturated fat:** 1.59 grams
**Dietary fiber:** 8.75 grams
**Sodium:** 137.01 mg
**Cholesterol:** 1.23 mg

1 cup wheat berries
3 cups water
2 cups broccoli florets
¼ cup olive oil
3 tablespoons mustard
½ cup plain yogurt
2 tablespoons lemon juice
⅛ teaspoon pepper
½ cup dried cranberries
4 green onions, chopped

1. Rinse the wheat berries and drain. Combine in large saucepan with water over high heat. Bring to a boil, then cover, reduce heat to low, and simmer for about 55–65 minutes or until berries are tender. Add broccoli florets to pan, cover, and simmer for another 5 minutes to steam the broccoli. Drain well if necessary.

2. In large bowl, combine olive oil, mustard, yogurt, lemon juice, and pepper and mix well. Add wheat berries, broccoli, cranberries, and green onions and mix gently. Cover and refrigerate for 3–4 hours before serving.

# Pasta Salad with Crunchy Vegetables

*Any fresh vegetables that are typically eaten raw would be delicious in this flavorful salad; you could add mushrooms, other bell peppers, or zucchini.*

1. Bring a large pot of water to a boil. In large bowl, combine mayonnaise, olive oil, vinegar, garlic, oregano, parsley, and pepper and mix well with wire whisk to blend.

2. Stir in bell peppers, celery, squash, and tomatoes, and mix well. Cook pasta according to package directions until al dente. Drain and immediately add to salad in bowl. Stir gently to coat pasta with dressing. Cover and refrigerate for 4 hours before serving.

### Whole-Grain Pasta

*If you're avoiding simple carbohydrates, whole-grain pastas are a wonderful way to start eating pasta again. These pastas are readily available in the local grocery store. They have a stronger flavor than plain pastas, so you may want to mix the two kinds half-and-half at first to introduce whole grain pasta to your family.*

**Serves 8**

**Calories:** 362.47
**Fat:** 15.12 grams
**Saturated fat:** 2.21 grams
**Dietary fiber:** 1.80 grams
**Sodium:** 131.65 mg
**Cholesterol:** 0.0 mg

½ cup low-fat mayonnaise
⅓ cup olive oil
¼ cup white-wine vinegar
2 cloves garlic, minced
1 teaspoon chopped fresh oregano
¼ cup chopped flat-leaf parsley
⅛ teaspoon pepper
2 red bell peppers, chopped
4 stalks celery, chopped
1 yellow summer squash, chopped
1 pint grape tomatoes
1 (16-ounce) package whole-grain rotini pasta

# Potato-Barley Salad

*Whipped salad dressing (brand name Miracle Whip) is different from mayonnaise. It's sweeter and spicier and adds more flavor to this hearty, nutritious salad.*

**Serves 12**

**Calories:** 335.13
**Fat:** 7.76 grams
**Saturated fat:** 1.37 grams
**Dietary fiber:** 7.95 grams
**Sodium:** 130.87 mg
**Cholesterol:** 1.33 grams

*1 (5-pound) bag potatoes, cubed*
*2 tablespoons olive oil*
*1 onion, chopped*
*5 cloves garlic, minced*
*1 cup pearl barley*
*3 cups water*
*1 cup plain yogurt*
*½ cup nonfat whipped salad dressing*
*¼ cup mustard*
*¼ cup skim milk*
*1 teaspoon dried basil*
*⅛ teaspoon pepper*
*1 green bell pepper, chopped*
*1 red bell pepper, chopped*
*1 yellow bell pepper, chopped*
*1 yellow summer squash, chopped*

1. Preheat oven to 400°F. Scrub potatoes and cut into 1" cubes. Combine in large roasting pan with olive oil, onion, and garlic. Roast for 30 minutes, turn vegetables with a spatula, then roast for 30–40 minutes longer until potatoes are tender and browning on the edges.

2. Meanwhile, combine barley and water in large saucepan. Bring to a boil, then reduce heat to low, cover, and simmer for 40–50 minutes or until barley is tender. Drain if necessary.

3. Meanwhile, in large bowl combine yogurt, salad dressing, mustard, milk, basil, and pepper and mix well. Add warm potatoes and warm barley to yogurt mixture and stir to coat. Add remaining vegetables and stir to coat. Cover and refrigerate for 4–6 hours before serving.

# Broccoli Pasta Salad

*The trick of cooking the pasta and broccoli together
saves time in cooking and in cleanup.*

**Serves 8–10**

**Calories:** 346.85
**Fat:** 15.11 grams
**Saturated fat:** 2.23 grams
**Dietary fiber:** 3.59 grams
**Sodium:** 195.68 mg
**Cholesterol:** 2.93 mg

*⅓ cup balsamic vinegar*
*3 tablespoons olive oil*
*1 tablespoon walnut oil*
*½ cup low-fat mayonnaise*
*2 tablespoons Dijon mustard*
*2 tablespoons lemon juice*
*2 cloves garlic, minced*
*4 shallots, minced*
*⅛ teaspoon pepper*
*1 (16-ounce) package farfalle
pasta*
*1 head broccoli*
*½ cup walnut pieces, toasted*
*⅓ cup grated Parmesan
cheese*

1. Bring a large pot of water to a boil. Meanwhile, in large bowl combine vinegar, olive oil, walnut oil, mayonnaise, mustard, lemon juice, garlic, shallots, and pepper, and mix well.

2. Add pasta to water and stir. Meanwhile, rinse broccoli and cut off florets. When pasta has cooked for 6 minutes, add the broccoli and stir. Bring back to a boil and cook for 3–5 minutes or until pasta is tender and broccoli is crisp-tender. Drain well and add immediately to vinegar mixture.

3. Toss to coat; let stand for 10 minutes so pasta will absorb some of the dressing. Sprinkle with walnuts and Parmesan and serve.

### Cruciferous Vegetables

*All cruciferous vegetables have lots of fiber and antioxidant vitamins and may help prevent cancer. This class of vegetables includes broccoli, cabbage, cauliflower, and Brussels sprouts. You could substitute Brussels sprouts or cauliflower for the broccoli in this delicious recipe. Cook these vegetables in lots of water in an uncovered pot for best results.*

# Lentil Rice Salad

Serves 8–10

**Calories:** 333.55
**Fat:** 10.58 grams
**Saturated fat:** 1.54 grams
**Dietary fiber:** 15.38 grams
**Sodium:** 62.63 mg
**Cholesterol:** 0.0 mg

*3 tablespoons lemon juice*
*1 tablespoon white-wine vinegar*
*1 tablespoon sesame oil*
*¼ cup olive oil*
*⅓ cup low-fat mayonnaise*
*1 to 2 tablespoons curry powder*
*⅛ teaspoon pepper*
*4 green onions, sliced*
*¼ cup chopped flat-leaf parsley*
*1 (16-ounce) package lentils*
*1 cup brown rice*
*2 red bell peppers, chopped*
*½ cup red onion, chopped*

*This hearty salad is popular in France and is appearing in gourmet stores and delis in the United States. Enjoy this version for lunch on the porch.*

1. In large bowl, combine lemon juice, vinegar, sesame oil, olive oil, mayonnaise, curry powder, pepper, onions, and parsley and mix well; cover and refrigerate.

2. Pick over lentils and rinse; cover with cold water and cook according to package directions. Meanwhile, cook rice according to package directions. As soon as lentils and rice are cooked, add to mayonnaise mixture along with bell peppers and onion.

3. Stir the salad to coat all ingredients. Cover and refrigerate for 2–4 hours before serving.

# Red-Bean Salad with Taco Chips

*Low-fat taco chips are usually baked. Read labels carefully and pick a version that is low-fat and made with whole grain.*

1. In large bowl combine lime juice, sour cream, yogurt, pepper flakes, onion, and jalapeño peppers; mix well. Add bell pepper, celery, and beans and mix well. This can be chilled, well covered, until ready to eat.

2. When ready to serve, arrange lettuce on a serving platter and spoon the bean mixture over all. Sprinkle with pumpkin seeds and crushed taco chips and serve immediately.

### Beans

*Any type of bean or legume can be substituted for another. You could use kidney beans, black beans, Great Northern Beans, navy beans, black-eyed peas, pink beans, or chickpeas in this delicious salad. Beans are very high in fiber, help lower cholesterol, and have been a major protein source for populations around the world for centuries.*

**Serves 6**

**Calories:** 324.28
**Fat:** 8.60 grams
**Saturated fat:** 2.83 grams
**Dietary fiber:** 13.31 grams
**Sodium:** 204.12 mg
**Cholesterol:** 10.03 mg

¼ cup lime juice
½ cup low-fat sour cream
½ cup plain yogurt
½ teaspoon crushed red pepper flakes
1 red onion, chopped
2 jalapeño peppers, minced
1 green bell pepper, chopped
3 stalks celery, chopped
4 cups Beans for Soup (page 111)
6 cups shredded lettuce
½ cup pumpkin seeds
2 cups crushed low-fat taco chips

# Crab Edamame Salad

*Surimi is artificially flavored and colored crab meat. It actually tastes delicious, so don't be put off by that description! This excellent salad is also delicious.*

**Serves 4**

**Calories:** 387.36
**Fat:** 20.40 grams
**Saturated fat:** 2.75 grams
**Dietary fiber:** 5.20 grams
**Sodium:** 273.14
**Cholesterol:** 34.00 mg

¼ cup olive oil, divided
6 shallots, peeled and minced
2 tablespoons white-wine vinegar
2 tablespoons Dijon mustard
¼ teaspoon crushed red pepper flakes
2 tablespoons chopped flat-leaf parsley
2 (8-ounce) packages frozen surimi, thawed
1 (12-ounce) package frozen edamame
4 cups red leaf lettuce, torn
2 cups curly endive, torn

1. In small saucepan, heat 1 tablespoon olive oil over medium heat. Add shallots; cook and stir until tender, about 3–4 minutes. Remove from heat and pour into serving bowl.

2. Add remaining olive oil, vinegar, mustard, pepper flakes, and parsley and blend with wire whisk until mixed.

3. Tear thawed surimi into bite-sized pieces and add to mustard mixture. Cook edamame as directed on package, drain, and add to mustard mixture. Toss gently to coat.

4. Add lettuce and endive and toss; serve immediately. You can refrigerate the surimi mixture up to 4 hours before serving; toss with lettuce and endive just before serving.

# Apple Coleslaw

*Adding sweet and tart apples to a classic coleslaw is a delicious new twist. Serve it with some grilled salmon for a fabulous meal.*

**Serves 6**

**Calories:** 184.33
**Fat:** 10.59 grams
**Saturated fat:** 1.36 grams
**Dietary fiber:** 3.74 grams
**Sodium:** 188.36 mg
**Cholesterol:** 2.86 mg

*1 cup plain yogurt*
*¼ cup low-fat mayonnaise*
*¼ cup buttermilk*
*2 tablespoons mustard*
*2 tablespoons lemon juice*
*1 tablespoon chopped fresh tarragon leaves*
*2 Granny Smith apples, chopped*
*3 cups shredded red cabbage*
*3 cups shredded green cabbage*
*½ cup walnut pieces, toasted*

1. In large bowl, combine yogurt, mayonnaise, buttermilk, mustard, lemon juice, and tarragon leaves; mix well to blend. Add chopped apples, red cabbage, and green cabbage and mix well.

2. Cover and chill in refrigerator for 2–4 hours before serving. Sprinkle with walnuts before serving.

## Walnuts

*Walnut pieces are larger than chopped walnuts but smaller than whole. To toast walnuts, spread them evenly on a cookie sheet and bake at 350°F for 10–15 minutes, shaking pan once or twice during baking time, until nuts are fragrant and turn a deeper golden-brown color. Cool completely before using.*

# Fruity Rice Salad

*This salad can be made with any combination of fresh and canned fruits and flavored yogurt. Try it for breakfast!*

**Serves 6**

**Calories:** 186.12
**Fat:** 0.96 grams
**Saturated fat:** 0.26 grams
**Dietary fiber:** 3.54 grams
**Sodium:** 17.22 mg
**Cholesterol:** 0.86 mg

*2 tablespoons chopped fresh mint*
*1 cup low-fat strawberry yogurt*
*1 tablespoon lemon juice*
*2 tablespoons skim milk*
*1 cup cooked brown rice, chilled*
*1 cup cooked white rice, chilled*
*1 (15-ounce) can crushed pineapple, drained*
*1 banana, sliced*
*2 cups chopped strawberries*
*1 cup blueberries*

In large bowl, combine mint, yogurt, lemon juice, and skim milk and mix well. Add both types of rice and mix until combined. Then fold in remaining fruit. Cover and chill for 2–4 hours before serving.

### Health Benefits of Mint

*While mint has been enjoyed for centuries for its pleasing aroma and taste, it actually contains many health benefits as well. Mint has long been known for its ability to lessen the length and severity of stomachaches and to sooth the digestive tract. Mint teas have also been shown to help the discomfort of irritable bowel syndrome, and to slow the growth of several harmful bacteria and fungi.*

# Citus Shimmer

*Lemon-lime soda really does make this salad shimmer! It's refreshing and delicious, especially on a hot summer day.*

1. Place gelatin in large bowl. Drain pineapple and oranges, reserving juice. Measure juice and place 1½ cups in a microwave-safe glass measuring cup. Microwave on high for 1–2 minutes or until juice boils. Pour over gelatin in bowl and stir until gelatin dissolves completely.

2. Stir in yogurt until well mixed. Then add drained fruits. Gently stir in soda, then immediately pour into a 2-quart mold or casserole dish. Cover and refrigerate for 4–6 hours until firm. Cut into squares to serve.

## Gelatin

*Gelatin must be totally dissolved in hot liquid before any other ingredients are added or the salad or dessert will fail. When using a flavored gelatin, add boiling liquid and stir. To make sure the gelatin is dissolved, pick up a small amount of the mixture in a stainless spoon. Tilt the spoon; if you can't see any grains, it's ready to go.*

---

**Serves 6**

**Calories:** 145.49
**Fat:** 0.36 grams
**Saturated fat:** 0.18 grams
**Dietary fiber:** 1.25 grams
**Sodium:** 44.14 mg
**Cholesterol:** 1.13 mg

1 (6-ounce) package orange-flavored gelatin
1 (20-ounce) can pineapple tidbits
1 (15-ounce) can mandarin oranges
1 cup lemon yogurt
1 (12-ounce) can lemon-lime soda

# Black-Eyed Pea Salad

*Black-eyed peas contain pectin, another soluble fiber that
helps reduce cholesterol levels. And they're delicious!*

**Serves 6–8**

**Calories:** 174.84
**Fat:** 9.30 grams
**Saturated fat:** 2.37 grams
**Dietary fiber:** 4.37 grams
**Sodium:** 212.18 mg
**Cholesterol:** 5.10 mg

*1 (16-ounce) package dried
    black-eyed peas
8 cups cold water
1 cup plain yogurt
¼ cup olive oil
¼ cup Dijon mustard
1 teaspoon dried thyme
    leaves
¼ teaspoon salt
⅛ teaspoon pepper
2 green bell peppers,
    chopped
1 red bell pepper, chopped
1 red onion, finely chopped
½ cup crumbled goat cheese*

1. Pick over the peas and rinse; drain well, place in a large pot, cover with cold water, cover, and let stand overnight. In the morning, drain and rinse the peas and cover with cold water again. Bring to a boil, then reduce heat and simmer peas for 75–85 minutes until tender.

2. Meanwhile, in large bowl combine yogurt, olive oil, mustard, thyme, salt, and pepper and mix well. When peas are cooked, drain well and add to yogurt mixture along with peppers and red onion.

3. Toss gently to coat, then sprinkle with goat cheese. Cover and refrigerate for 4–6 hours before serving.

# Caesar Dressing

*This creamy and flavorful dressing is usually made with raw eggs. Using low-fat mayonnaise instead is a better choice for food safety reasons.*

**Yields 1 cup; serving size 2 tablespoons**

**Calories:** 152.79
**Fat:** 14.82 grams
**Saturated fat:** 2.80 grams
**Dietary fiber:** 0.02 grams
**Sodium:** 137.29 mg
**Cholesterol:** 4.55 mg

*1 garlic clove, minced*
*1 anchovy fillet*
*½ cup low-fat mayonnaise*
*¼ cup plain yogurt*
*2 tablespoons lemon juice*
*¼ cup olive oil*
*¼ teaspoon pepper*
*⅓ cup grated Parmesan cheese*

Combine garlic, anchovy, mayonnaise, yogurt, and lemon juice in blender or food processor. Blend or process until smooth. Stream in olive oil while blending or processing, until smooth. Add pepper and Parmesan and mix well; cover and refrigerate for up to 4 days.

### Caesar Salad Dressing

*Caesar Dressing is traditionally served over romaine lettuce with croutons. You can add cooked chicken, cubed ham, or salmon fillets to the salad to turn it into a main dish. The anchovy adds a salty touch and depth of flavor. It can be omitted, but the flavor of the dressing will be very mild.*

# Summer Pineapple Fruit Salad

**Serves 8**

**Calories:** 201.31
**Fat:** 3.63 grams
**Saturated fat:** 0.73 grams
**Dietary fiber:** 5.04 grams
**Sodium:** 94.22 mg
**Cholesterol:** 1.70 mg

*1 cup lemon yogurt*
*¼ cup nonfat whipped salad
    dressing*
*1 teaspoon lemon zest*
*2 tablespoons honey*
*1 teaspoon chopped fresh
    thyme*
*1 fresh pineapple*
*1 cantaloupe*
*1 honeydew melon*
*2 cups sliced strawberries*
*1 pint blueberries*
*1 cup raspberries*

*This fresh salad can even be served as dessert. For a special treat, toast some Angel Food Cake (page XX) and top it with this salad.*

1. In large bowl, combine yogurt, salad dressing, lemon zest, and honey, and mix well. Stir in thyme and set aside.

2. Twist top off pineapple and discard. Slice pineapple in half, then cut off rind. Cut into quarters, then cut out center core. Slice pineapple and add to yogurt mixture.

3. Cut cantaloupe and melon in half, scoop out seeds and discard, and peel. Cut into cubes and add to yogurt mixture along with strawberries and blueberries. Toss gently and top with raspberries. Serve immediately, or cover and refrigerate up to 4 hours.

### Fresh Fruit

*Soft fruits, like berries, are sold perfectly ripe, so should be eaten within 1–2 days. Melons are usually unripe, and can sit on the kitchen counter for a couple of days until they give when gently pressed. All fruit is very fragile, so toss it gently in the dressing. Fruit salads can be varied according to the season; use apples and pears in the fall.*

# Buttermilk Dressing

*Buttermilk is naturally thick and tastes rich, even though it's low in fat.
This classic dressing is perfect drizzled over mixed greens.*

Combine all ingredients in blender or food processor and blend or process until mixed. Cover and store in refrigerator for up to 4 days.

**Yields 1 cup; serving
size 2 tablespoons**

**Calories:** 28.37
**Fat:** 1.46 grams
**Saturated fat:** 0.31 grams
**Dietary fiber:** 0.02 grams
**Sodium:** 124.09 mg
**Cholesterol:** 0.92 mg

¾ cup buttermilk
2 tablespoons low-fat
    mayonnaise
2 tablespoons lemon juice
2 shallots, chopped
¼ teaspoon salt
1 tablespoon chopped chives
1 tablespoon chopped fresh dill
⅛ teaspoon pepper

# Balsamic Vinaigrette

*This is an incredibly versatile dressing. You can add all sorts of
different herbs to it; thyme and rosemary would be delicious.*

Whisk all ingredients together. Cover and store in refrigerator for up to
3 days. Drizzle over salad greens or use as called for in recipes.

**Serves 9; serving size
2 tablespoons**

**Calories:** 151.96
**Fat:** 16.00 grams
**Saturated fat:** 2.21 grams
**Dietary fiber:** 0.03 grams
**Sodium:** 71.49 mg
**Cholesterol:** 0.0 mg

⅔ cup extra-virgin olive oil
⅓ cup aged balsamic vinegar
1 teaspoon Worcestershire
    sauce
2 cloves garlic, minced
1 tablespoon lemon juice
1 tablespoon honey
¼ teaspoon salt
⅛ teaspoon white pepper

# Raspberry Vinaigrette

*This simple dressing is bursting with raspberry flavor. Serve it over romaine lettuce with grilled chicken and more fresh raspberries.*

**Yields 1 cup; serving size 2 tablespoons**

**Calories:** 144.88
**Fat:** 13.52 grams
**Saturated fat:** 1.87 grams
**Dietary fiber:** 0.03 grams
**Sodium:** 77.09 mg
**Cholesterol:** 0.0 mg

½ cup olive oil
¼ cup raspberry preserves
½ cup fresh raspberries
¼ cup raspberry vinegar
1 tablespoon chopped fresh
    rosemary
¼ teaspoon salt
⅛ teaspoon white pepper

Combine all ingredients in blender or food processor; blend or process until well combined. Cover and refrigerate for up to 4 days.

## Vinaigrettes

*Vinaigrettes are simply combinations of oil with an acid, like vinegar or lemon juice. They can be flavored in hundreds of different ways. Instead of the raspberry vinegar, raspberries, and rosemary, you could use tarragon vinegar, chopped green onions, and fresh tarragon. Remember to keep homemade dressings for only 4 days in the refrigerator.*

# Chapter 13
## Vegetables

# Grilled Asparagus with Lemon Sauce

*You can also roast the asparagus at 450°F for about 5–7 minutes or until tender.*

**Serves 6**

**Calories:** 108.83
**Fat:** 8.31 grams
**Saturated fat:** 1.38 grams
**Dietary fiber:** 2.40 grams
**Sodium:** 78.45 mg
**Cholesterol:** 1.23 mg

*¼ cup low-fat mayonnaise*
*¼ cup plain yogurt*
*2 tablespoons lemon juice*
*1 teaspoon grated lemon zest*
*⅛ teaspoon cayenne pepper*
*1½ pounds fresh asparagus*
*2 tablespoons olive oil*

1. Prepare and preheat grill. In small bowl, combine mayonnaise, yogurt, lemon juice, zest, and pepper and mix well; set aside.

2. Snap off the ends of the asparagus and rinse well; pat dry with kitchen towels. Toss with olive oil. Grill asparagus in a grill basket for 5–8 minutes or until crisp-tender and light golden brown. Serve with lemon sauce.

### Preparing Asparagus

*Asparagus is easy to prepare. If you hold a spear in two hands and gently bend it, it will snap at the point where the tender spear becomes tough. You can discard these ends, or save them to make cream of asparagus soup, in which the ends are used just for flavor. You don't need to peel the asparagus if you use this method.*

# Citrus-Roasted Beets

*Beets are very high in folate, which is the natural form of folic acid. Remember, this vitamin helps reduce homocysteine levels in the blood.*

1. Preheat oven to 375°F. Scrub beets and trim the stems. Place in roasting pan and drizzle with olive oil, lemon juice, and 1 tablespoon of the orange juice. Toss to coat. Sprinkle with salt and pepper. Roast for 40–50 minutes or until beets are tender when pierced with a knife.

2. Let beets cool for about 30 minutes. In small bowl, combine yogurt, remaining 2 tablespoons orange juice, mustard, and orange zest and mix well. When beets are cool enough to handle, cut off the ends and slip off the skins. Cut beets into ½"-thick slices. Arrange on platter, drizzle with yogurt mixture, and serve.

## Beets

*The bright red pigment in beets is betacyanin, which when extracted can be used as a dye or a natural food coloring. Today most cooks toss the beet tops, which just happen to be the most nutritious part of the beet! Beet greens can be cooked and served like spinach with a bit of pink twinge.*

**Serves 4**

**Calories:** 132.46
**Fat:** 7.69 grams
**Saturated fat:** 1.28 grams
**Dietary fiber:** 3.73 grams
**Sodium:** 262.93 mg
**Cholesterol:** 1.84 mg

*6 red beets*
*2 tablespoons olive oil*
*1 tablespoon lemon juice*
*3 tablespoons orange juice, divided*
*⅛ teaspoon salt*
*⅛ teaspoon white pepper*
*¼ cup plain yogurt*
*2 tablespoons mustard*
*1 teaspoon grated orange zest*

# Caramelized Spiced Carrots

*This is a simple side dish that is full of flavor. Serve it with grilled or roasted chicken, or during the holidays along with a baked ham.*

**Serves 6**

**Calories:** 62.66
**Fat:** 2.07 grams
**Saturated fat:** 1.24 grams
**Dietary fiber:** 1.72 grams
**Sodium:** 135.88 mg
**Cholesterol:** 5.08 grams

1¼ pounds baby carrots
¼ cup orange juice
⅛ teaspoon salt
⅛ teaspoon white pepper
1 teaspoon grated orange zest
1 tablespoon sugar
1 tablespoon grated ginger root
1 tablespoon butter or plant sterol margarine

1. In large saucepan, combine carrots, orange juice, salt, and pepper. Bring to a boil over high heat, then reduce heat to low, cover, and cook for 3–4 minutes or until carrots are crisp-tender.

2. Add orange zest, sugar, ginger root, and butter and bring to a boil over high heat. Cook until most of the orange juice evaporates and the carrots start to brown, stirring frequently, about 4–5 minutes. Serve immediately.

## Baby Carrots

*Since appearing on the market not so very long ago, baby carrots have overtaken regular carrots in sales. They are not technically baby carrots but a carrot variety called Imperator that is grown to be longer and sweeter than regular carrots. The carrots are then trimmed down to the baby carrot shape and size.*

# Roasted Onions

*Serve these delicious onions as a side dish to a steak, or try
them on top of a grilled turkey burger for a summer cookout.*

1. Preheat oven to 375°F. Spray a 1-quart casserole dish with nonstick cooking spray. Peel onions and slice. Arrange in prepared casserole and sprinkle with salt and pepper.

2. In small bowl, combine sugar, oil, and thyme, and mix well. Drizzle over onions. Roast for 20 minutes, then turn onions with a spatula and return to oven. Roast for 15–20 minutes longer until onions turn golden brown in spots. Serve immediately.

**Serves 4**

**Calories:** 103.26
**Fat:** 6.81 grams
**Saturated fat:** 0.95 grams
**Dietary fiber:** 1.05 grams
**Sodium:** 75.06 mg
**Cholesterol:** 0.0 mg

2 large onions
⅛ teaspoon salt
⅛ teaspoon white pepper
1 tablespoon sugar
2 tablespoons olive oil
2 teaspoons chopped fresh
    thyme

# Gingered Sugar-Snap Peas

*In the spring and summer you can find fresh sugar-snap peas
at the market. If you can't, the frozen variety works just fine.*

Rinse the peas and drain well. In large skillet, heat oil over medium heat. Add peas, garlic, and ginger root; stir-fry for 3–4 minutes or until peas are crisp-tender. Sprinkle with salt, pepper, and pistachios and serve immediately.

**Serves 4**

**Calories:** 122.75
**Fat:** 11.48 grams
**Saturated fat:** 1.51 grams
**Dietary fiber:** 1.13 grams
**Sodium:** 74.41 mg
**Cholesterol:** 0.0 mg

1 pound sugar-snap peas
2 tablespoons olive oil
3 cloves garlic, minced
1 tablespoon grated fresh
    ginger root
⅛ teaspoon salt
⅛ teaspoon pepper
¼ cup chopped pistachios

# Fried Green Tomatoes

*This classic Southern dish is a good way to use up
garden tomatoes just before the first frost.*

**Serves 8**

**Calories:** 116.06
**Fat:** 3.64 grams
**Saturated fat:** 0.47 grams
**Dietary fiber:** 1.85 grams
**Sodium:** 74.42 mg
**Cholesterol:** 26.74 mg

*4 large green tomatoes*
*1 egg*
*¼ cup buttermilk*
*½ cup cornmeal*
*½ cup all-purpose flour*
*1 teaspoon baking powder*
*⅛ teaspoon white pepper*
*¼ cup canola oil*

1. Slice tomatoes into ⅓" rounds and pat dry with paper towels. In shallow bowl, combine egg and buttermilk and whisk until blended. On plate, combine cornmeal, flour, baking powder, and pepper and mix well.

2. Place oil in heavy skillet and place over medium heat until temperature reaches 375°F. Dip tomato slices into egg mixture, then into cornmeal mixture. Fry tomatoes in hot oil, four at a time, turning once, until golden brown, about 3–6 minutes per side. Drain on paper towels and serve immediately.

## Pan-Frying

*Pan-frying is a dry-heat cooking method, as is all frying, because it removes water from the food. Frying doesn't have to add a lot of calories or fat to the food you cook, as long as the fat is at the proper temperature. A temperature of 375°F is just right; use a food thermometer. The food absorbs about 10 percent of the fat while frying.*

# Stuffed Baby Eggplants

*Baby eggplants are very tender and need little baking. You can find them in different colors; usually purple, mauve, or white.*

**Serves 4**

**Calories:** 182.53
**Fat:** 8.53 grams
**Saturated fat:** 1.66 grams
**Dietary fiber:** 6.02 grams
**Sodium:** 172.65 mg
**Cholesterol:** 2.75 mg

*8 baby eggplants*
*⅛ teaspoon salt*
*⅛ teaspoon white pepper*
*1 cloves garlic, minced*
*1 tablespoon grated lemon zest*
*¼ cup dried breadcrumbs*
*2 tablespoons grated Parmesan cheese*
*2 tablespoons olive oil*

1. Preheat oven to 450°F. Cut the eggplant in half lengthwise. Using the tines of a fork, score the cut side deeply. Place cut side up on cookie sheet.

2. In small bowl, combine salt, pepper, garlic, zest, breadcrumbs, and Parmesan and mix well. Drizzle with olive oil and toss to coat. Divide this mixture among the eggplant halves.

3. Bake for 10–15 minutes or until eggplants are tender and crumb topping is golden brown. Serve immediately.

### Eggplant

*Eggplant is a mild, oval-shaped vegetable that can be bitter and that usually has bright purple skin. Baby eggplants are usually around the size of lemons and don't have a bitter flavor. Eggplant is very low in calories and high in fiber. One cup of eggplant has about 21 calories but gives you 2.0 grams of fiber.*

## Snow Peas with Shallots

*Snow peas are completely edible, pod and all. You can usually find them fully prepped in the produce aisle.*

**Serves 4**

**Calories:** 133.38
**Fat:** 7.22 grams
**Saturated fat:** 1.02 grams
**Dietary fiber:** 4.38 grams
**Sodium:** 9.84 mg
**Cholesterol:** 0.0 mg

1 pound snow peas
2 tablespoons olive oil
4 shallots, minced
½ pound cremini mushrooms, sliced
2 tablespoons sherry vinegar
1 teaspoon lemon juice

1. Trim off ends from snow peas and pull strings, if necessary. In large saucepan, heat olive oil over medium heat. Add shallots, snow peas, and mushrooms.

2. Stir-fry for 3–5 minutes or until vegetables are crisp-tender. Stir in vinegar and lemon juice, then remove from heat and serve immediately.

## Sesame-Roasted Vegetables

*Sesame seeds add great crunch and flavor to these sweet and tender vegetables.*

**Serves 6**

**Calories:** 257.08
**Fat:** 8.95 grams
**Saturated fat:** 1.32 grams
**Dietary fiber:** 6.86 grams
**Sodium:** 51.01 mg
**Cholesterol:** 0.0 mg

2 red bell peppers, sliced
4 carrots, sliced
1½ pounds tiny fingerling potatoes, cut in half lengthwise
2 yellow summer squash, sliced
2 tablespoons olive oil
2 tablespoons honey
¼ cup sesame seeds
⅛ teaspoon white pepper

1. Preheat oven to 400°F. Place all vegetables in large roasting pan.

2. In small bowl, combine olive oil and honey and mix well. Drizzle over vegetables and toss to coat. Arrange in single layer in pan and sprinkle with sesame seeds and pepper.

3. Roast for 25–35 minutes or until vegetables are tender and sesame seeds are toasted. Serve immediately.

# Baby Peas with Water Chestnuts

*This simple side dish is the perfect complement
to grilled chicken or pork tenderloin.*

1. In medium saucepan, heat olive oil over medium heat. Add shallots; cook for 1–2 minutes until fragrant. Add water chestnuts and peas; cook and stir until hot.

2. Add cream; bring to a simmer. Cook for 2 minutes, then add Parmesan, stir, and serve immediately.

### Frozen Peas

*There are several varieties of frozen peas. The ones you want for this recipe are plain baby, or early peas. They are more tender and sweeter than regular peas. Keep a couple of packages of the frozen peas in your freezer for a super-easy side dish that's ready in minutes. The peas have better quality if they are cooked while still frozen.*

Serves 4

**Calories:** 141.42
**Fat:** 4.79 grams
**Saturated fat:** 1.19 grams
**Dietary fiber:** 4.44 grams
**Sodium:** 155.70 mg
**Cholesterol:** 3.51 grams

*1 tablespoon olive oil*
*2 shallots, minced*
*1 (8-ounce) can sliced water
    chestnuts, drained*
*2 cups frozen baby peas*
*¼ cup nonfat light cream*
*2 tablespoons grated
    Parmesan cheese*

# Buttermilk Mashed Potatoes

*These mashed potatoes taste buttery without any added butter; perfect!*

**Serves 6**

**Calories:** 201.53
**Fat:** 6.16 grams
**Saturated fat:** 1.49 grams
**Dietary fiber:** 3.49 grams
**Sodium:** 136.84 mg
**Cholesterol:** 4.34 mg

*2 pounds Yukon Gold
    potatoes*
*2 tablespoons olive oil*
*¼ cup buttermilk*
*¼ cup low-fat sour cream*
*2 tablespoons Dijon mustard*
*⅛ teaspoon white pepper*
*⅛ teaspoon salt*

1. Cut potatoes into 1" pieces. Place in large saucepan and cover with cold water. Bring to a boil over high heat, then reduce heat to medium, cover, and simmer until potatoes are tender, about 25 minutes. Drain potatoes and return to hot pot.

2. Turn heat to low and shake potatoes to dry. Add olive oil and mash with a large fork. Then add buttermilk, sour cream, mustard, pepper, and salt and mash until combined, leaving some pieces whole if desired. Serve immediately.

### Potatoes: To Peel or Not?

*Leaving the skins on potatoes adds great texture, increases the fiber count, and helps preserve the vitamin content. Plus it adds a great rustic appearance to the finished dish and it's easier! The vitamin A and potassium content of Yukon Gold potatoes is quite high, so eat them without guilt.*

## Grilled Corn with Red Peppers

*This colorful side dish is perfect for a summer cookout.*
*Serve it with grilled fish or chicken.*

1. Prepare and preheat grill. Remove husk and silk from corn. Grill corn about 6" from medium coals for 3–5 minutes, turning frequently, until corn is light brown. Cool for 10 minutes, then cut kernels from the cobs.

2. Place heavy-duty medium saucepan on the grill. Add olive oil and heat. Add onion and garlic; cook and stir until tender, about 5 minutes. Add bell pepper and corn; cook and stir for 2 minutes longer. Sprinkle with salt, pepper, and cumin, stir, and serve.

**Serves 4**

**Calories:** 179.69
**Fat:** 5.04 grams
**Saturated fat:** 0.73 grams
**Dietary fiber:** 4.45 grams
**Sodium:** 94.60 mg
**Cholesterol:** 0.0 mg

*4 ears fresh corn*
*1 tablespoon olive oil*
*1 onion, chopped*
*3 cloves garlic, minced*
*1 red bell pepper, chopped*
*⅛ teaspoon salt*
*⅛ teaspoon pepper*
*½ teaspoon cumin*

## Sautéed Fennel with Lemon

*Fennel has a licorice taste and, like most root vegetables,*
*gets sweeter the longer it's cooked.*

1. Trim fronds and ends from fennel bulbs and remove outer layer. Cut the bulb into quarters lengthwise.

2. Heat olive oil in large pan over medium heat. Add fennel and sauté, stirring occasionally, for 5 minutes. Add sliced lemon, salt, pepper, water, and lemon juice. Bring to a simmer, then cover, and simmer over low heat for 10 minutes until fennel is tender. Serve immediately.

**Serves 4**

**Calories:** 116.59
**Fat:** 7.06 grams
**Saturated fat:** 0.94 grams
**Dietary fiber:** 5.14 grams
**Sodium:** 135.07 mg
**Cholesterol:** 0.0 mg

*2 fennel bulbs*
*2 tablespoons olive oil*
*1 lemon, sliced*
*⅛ teaspoon salt*
*⅛ teaspoon pepper*
*2 tablespoons water*
*2 tablespoons lemon juice*

# Scalloped Potatoes with Aromatic Vegetables

*Layered casseroles are a great choice to serve at potlucks
or with simple meats like baked chicken or pork chops.*

**Serves 8**

**Calories:** 271.60
**Fat:** 9.04 grams
**Saturated fat:** 2.03 grams
**Dietary fiber:** 5.47 grams
**Sodium:** 211.64 mg
**Cholesterol:** 5.19 mg

*2 carrots, peeled and sliced*
*2 parsnips, peeled and sliced*
*3 russet potatoes, sliced*
*¼ cup olive oil*
*⅛ teaspoon salt*
*⅛ teaspoon white pepper*
*1 onion, finely chopped*
*4 cloves garlic, minced*
*⅓ cup grated Parmesan
    cheese*
*¾ cup dry breadcrumbs*
*1 cup milk*

1. Preheat oven to 375°F. Spray a 9" × 13" baking dish with nonstick cooking spray and set aside.

2. In large bowl, combine carrots, parsnips, and potatoes; drizzle with olive oil, sprinkle with salt and pepper, and toss to coat. Layer vegetables in prepared baking dish, sprinkling each layer with onion, garlic, Parmesan, and breadcrumbs, finishing with breadcrumbs.

3. Pour milk into casserole. Cover tightly with foil. Bake for 45 minutes, then uncover. Bake for 15–25 minutes longer or until vegetables are tender and top is browned. Serve immediately.

### Aromatic Vegetables

*Aromatic vegetables are so called because they give off a rich aroma when cooked. They include onions, garlic, celery, and carrots. They are used in most ethnic cuisines. The French* mirepoix *uses mostly onion, with celery and carrot. The Italian* soffritto *uses onion, garlic, and fennel. And the Cajun "holy trinity" includes celery, onion, and carrots.*

# Roasted-Garlic Corn

*Roasting corn concentrates the flavor and makes the vegetable extra-sweet while adding a slightly chewy texture. Yum.*

**Serves 6**

**Calories:** 147.64
**Fat:** 6.70 grams
**Saturated fat:** 0.94 grams
**Dietary fiber:** 2.23 grams
**Sodium:** 79.60 mg
**Cholesterol:** 0.0 mg

*3 cups frozen corn, thawed*
*2 tablespoons olive oil*
*2 shallots, minced*
*1 head Roasted Garlic (page 89)*
*⅛ teaspoon salt*
*⅛ teaspoon white pepper*

1. Preheat oven to 425°F. Place corn on paper towels and pat to dry. Place a Silpat liner on a 15" × 10" jelly-roll pan. Combine corn, olive oil, and shallots on pan and toss to coat. Spread in even layer.

2. Roast corn for 14–22 minutes, stirring once during cooking time, until kernels begin to turn light golden brown in spots.

3. Remove cloves from Roasted Garlic and add to corn along with salt and white pepper. Stir to mix, then serve.

# Cheese Polenta

*Polenta is a classic Italian dish that can be dressed up many ways. Add fresh herbs, sautéed onion or other vegetables, or different cheeses to this basic recipe.*

**Serves 6**

**Calories:** 171.53
**Fat:** 4.91 grams
**Saturated fat:** 2.85 grams
**Dietary fiber:** 2.13 grams
**Sodium:** 204.96 mg
**Cholesterol:** 13.71 mg

*¼ teaspoon salt*
*3 cups water*
*1 cup skim milk*
*1¼ cups yellow cornmeal*
*1 tablespoon butter or plant sterol margarine*
*¼ cup grated Parmesan cheese*
*¼ cup shredded Havarti cheese*
*½ teaspoon crushed red pepper flakes*

1. In large saucepan, combine salt and water and bring to a boil. In small bowl, combine milk with cornmeal and mix until smooth.

2. Slowly add the cornmeal mixture to the boiling water, stirring constantly with a wire whisk. Cook over medium-low heat, stirring constantly, until polenta is very thick, about 5–10 minutes. Stir in butter, cheeses, and red pepper flakes. Serve immediately.

# Chili Fries

*This recipe can be doubled; bake it on two cookie sheets, rotating the sheets in the oven halfway through the cooking time.*

**Serves 4–6**

**Calories:** 225.16
**Fat:** 4.76 grams
**Saturated fat:** 0.69 grams
**Dietary fiber:** 4.39 grams
**Sodium:** 213.81 mg
**Cholesterol:** 0.0 mg

*4 russet potatoes*
*2 tablespoons olive oil*
*2 tablespoons chili powder*
*1 tablespoon grill seasoning*
*1 teaspoon ground cumin*
*1 teaspoon paprika*
*¼ teaspoon pepper*

1. Preheat oven to 425°F. Scrub potatoes and pat dry; cut into ½" strips, leaving skin on. A few strips won't have any skin. Toss with olive oil and arrange in single layer on a large cookie sheet.

2. In small bowl, combine remaining ingredients and mix well. Sprinkle over potatoes and toss to coat. Arrange in single layer.

3. Bake for 35–45 minutes, turning once during baking time, until potatoes are deep golden brown and crisp. Serve immediately.

### Grill Seasoning

*Grill seasoning mixes usually contain pepper, garlic, salt, and a bit of sugar, along with spices like oregano and rosemary. There are quite a few different varieties, from Cajun spice to chili lime to chipotle. Read labels carefully, and choose a seasoning mix that has a low salt content for your health.*

# Veggie-Stuffed Tomatoes

*This cold side dish can also be served as a vegetarian entrée along with a fruit salad and some Seeded Breadsticks (page 77).*

**Serves 4**

**Calories:** 122.14
**Fat:** 5.75 grams
**Saturated fat:** 1.74 grams
**Dietary fiber:** 4.15 grams
**Sodium:** 194.39 mg
**Cholesterol:** 6.42 mg

*1 tablespoon olive oil*
*1 onion, chopped*
*3 cloves garlic, minced*
*1 green bell pepper, chopped*
*4 stalks celery, chopped*
*1 tablespoon chopped fresh chives*
*2 teaspoons fresh oregano leaves*
*⅛ teaspoon salt*
*⅛ teaspoon pepper*
*½ cup plain yogurt*
*1 tablespoon lime juice*
*2 tablespoons grated Parmesan cheese*
*4 large tomatoes*

1. In medium saucepan, heat olive oil over medium heat. Add onion, garlic, and green bell pepper; cook and stir until crisp-tender, about 4 minutes. Remove from heat and stir in celery, chives, oregano, salt, and pepper. Remove to medium bowl and chill until cold, about 1 hour.

2. Stir yogurt, lime juice, and Parmesan into cooled vegetable mixture. Cut tops off tomatoes and gently scoop out tomato flesh and seeds, leaving a ½" shell. Stuff with the vegetable mixture. Cover and chill for 2–3 hours before serving.

# Mashed Turnips with Greens

*This old-fashioned dish is full of vitamins and fiber. And it tastes great, too! Serve with baked chicken, cooked carrots, and Dark Dinner Rolls (page 75).*

**Serves 6**

**Calories:** 139.24
**Fat:** 9.16 grams
**Saturated fat:** 2.30 grams
**Dietary fiber:** 3.46 grams
**Sodium:** 172.43 mg
**Cholesterol:** 5.76 mg

*6 medium turnips*
*1 pound turnip greens*
*2 tablespoons olive oil*
*1 tablespoon butter*
*1 onion, chopped*
*⅓ cup milk*
*⅛ teaspoon salt*
*⅛ teaspoon pepper*
*¼ cup chopped parsley*

1. Peel the turnips and slice ½" thick. Place in cold water to cover and bring to a boil. Reduce heat and simmer for 25–30 minutes or until tender. Meanwhile, cut the tough stems out of the turnip greens and discard; cut leaves into strips, then rinse and drain.

2. In large saucepan, combine olive oil and butter over medium heat. Add onion and cook until tender, about 5 minutes. Add turnip greens and cook, turning with tongs, until greens are wilted and tender, about 5–8 minutes.

3. When turnips are tender, drain and return to hot pot. Place over low heat. Drain oil and butter from turnip greens and add to turnips; mash. Add milk, salt, and pepper and mash until desired consistency.

4. Stir in the cooked turnip greens and parsley. Serve immediately.

*Turnips*

*Turnips are low in calories and high in fiber. They are also a good source of vitamin C and folate. Look for the smallest turnips you can find so they aren't bitter or woody. Turnip greens are also a great source of vitamin C along with vitamin A, folate, and fiber. Combine these foods in one dish for a powerhouse of nutrition.*

# Baked Tomatoes with Garlic

*Baked tomatoes become tender and juicy, with an intensely sweet taste. Garlic and cheese are good companions in this easy recipe.*

**Serves 6**

**Calories:** 129.38
**Fat:** 9.15 grams
**Saturated fat:** 3.32 grams
**Dietary fiber:** 0.84 grams
**Sodium:** 159.91 mg
**Cholesterol:** 15.66 mg

4 cloves garlic, minced
3 tablespoons chopped fresh
   basil
6 tablespoons dried
   breadcrumbs
⅛ teaspoon pepper
¾ cup shredded Fontina
   cheese
2 tablespoons olive oil
6 plum tomatoes

1. Preheat oven to 400°F. In small bowl, combine garlic, basil, bread-crumbs, pepper, and Fontina and mix well. Drizzle with olive oil and toss to coat.

2. Cut tomatoes in half lengthwise. Line a cookie sheet with parchment paper and arrange tomatoes on top. Top with breadcrumb mixture.

3. Bake for 12–15 minutes or until tomatoes are tender and hot and the topping is golden brown. Serve immediately.

## Garlic and Cholesterol

*A few recent studies indicated that garlic was a wonder food that reduced cholesterol dramatically. Unfortunately, reviews of those studies indicated that although there was a reduction in three months, after another three months the reduction reversed itself. By the way, supplements are no better than raw or cooked garlic.*

# Farro Pilaf

*You could substitute spelt or quinoa for the farro to omit the soaking step.*
*Just cook the grains in water until tender, according to package directions.*

**Serves 6**

**Calories:** 224.70
**Fat:** 5.49 grams
**Saturated fat:** 0.79 grams
**Dietary fiber:** 6.69 grams
**Sodium:** 63.09 mg
**Cholesterol:** 0.0 mg

*1½ cups farro*
*2 tablespoons olive oil*
*1 onion, chopped*
*4 cloves garlic, minced*
*1 cup shredded carrots*
*¼ cup dry white wine*
*⅛ teaspoon salt*
*⅛ teaspoon pepper*

1. Wash the farro well, picking out any foreign objects like chaff. Place in large saucepan, add cold water to cover and soak for 8 hours at room temperature. Place the saucepan over high heat and bring to a boil. Reduce heat to low and simmer farro for 1½ to 2 hours, until tender but still chewy. Drain if necessary.

2. In another large saucepan, heat olive oil over medium heat. Add onion and garlic; cook and stir until crisp-tender, about 4 minutes. Add carrots, then stir in cooked and drained farro. Cook and stir for 2–3 minutes.

3. Add wine, salt, and pepper, and bring to a simmer. Simmer for 4–5 minutes or until wine is mostly absorbed. Stir and serve immediately.

## Farro

*Farro is another ancient grain, cultivated by the Egyptians. It is wheat's ancestor. The dark grains, shaped like rice, have a nutty flavor and chewy texture. It must be soaked before cooking, so plan to make any recipe using farro ahead of time. The grain is full of fiber, protein, vitamins, and minerals.*

# Chapter 14

## Sandwiches, Pizzas, and Snacks

# Mini Pork Burgers with Jalapeño Jelly

*You can serve these tiny burgers on mini hamburger buns,*
*or serve them with Super Spicy Salsa (page 85) for dipping.*

**Serves 6**

**Calories:** 211.63
**Fat:** 13.26 grams
**Saturated fat:** 4.33 grams
**Dietary fiber:** 0.68 grams
**Sodium:** 98.36 mg
**Cholesterol:** 35.72 mg

½ cup minced onion
2 cloves garlic, minced
2 tablespoons jalapeño jelly
1 egg white
½ cup dried breadcrumbs,
    divided
⅛ teaspoon crushed red
    pepper flakes
⅔ pound lean ground pork
¼ cup olive oil

1. In medium bowl, combine onion, garlic, jalapeño jelly, and egg white and mix well. Stir in ¼ cup breadcrumbs and the red pepper flakes and mix well. Add pork; work gently but thoroughly until well combined.

2. Form into 16 small patties and roll in remaining breadcrumbs. In large skillet, heat olive oil. Sauté the burgers on first side for 4 minutes or until browned. Then carefully turn and sauté for 3–6 minutes on second side until burgers are thoroughly cooked. Serve immediately.

### Jalapeños

*Jalapeños contain capsaicin, a product that has been shown to have anticancer effects. However, the amount needed to achieve this anti-cancer effect is quite high—up to twenty-four jalapeños per week. Jalapeños are also a good source of vitamin C, folate, and vitamin A.*

# Bruschetta with Roasted Garlic

*You can toast the bread or leave it plain in this easy recipe. Toasted bread has more crunch, but the plain bread will soak up more of the olive oil mixture.*

1. Remove the cloves from the garlic heads and finely chop. In small saucepan, combine garlic, olive oil, basil, oregano, salt, and red pepper flakes. Heat over low heat just until warm, about 2–4 minutes.

2. Arrange bread on serving plate. Pour garlic mixture into a small bowl and serve with the bread. Let diners spoon the garlic mixture onto the bread.

## Roasted Garlic

*If you think you don't like garlic, try roasted garlic! The heat of the oven turns this root vegetable into a totally new dish. When roasted, the garlic becomes very soft and turns brown. Its sharp flavors are eliminated and the roasted cloves taste nutty, and sweet, with a slight toasted flavor. Use them in everything from soups to appetizer spreads.*

**Serves 8**

**Calories:** 250.02
**Fat:** 10.93 grams
**Saturated fat:** 1.90 grams
**Dietary fiber:** 3.57 grams
**Sodium:** 55.23 mg
**Cholesterol:** 2.42 mg

*2 heads Roasted Garlic ( page 89)*
*¼ cup olive oil*
*1 teaspoon dried basil leaves*
*½ teaspoon dried oregano leaves*
*⅛ teaspoon salt*
*¼ teaspoon crushed red pepper flakes*
*12 slices Hearty-Grain French Bread (page 74)*

# Turkey-Tomato Hoagie Sandwiches

*These sandwiches taste like they came from a gourmet deli, but you control the nutrition!*

**Serves 4–6**

**Calories:** 366.29
**Fat:** 16.34 grams
**Saturated fat:** 6.93 grams
**Dietary fiber:** 3.69 grams
**Sodium:** 307.98 mg
**Cholesterol:** 62.59 mg

*4 Whole-Grain Hoagie Buns
    (page 76)
3 tablespoons plain yogurt
1 tablespoon olive oil
2 tablespoons Dijon mustard
1 teaspoon minced garlic
2 cups shredded lettuce
8 ounces sliced cooked deli
    turkey
2 tomatoes, sliced
4 (1-ounce) slices extra-sharp
    Cheddar cheese*

1. Cut hoagie buns in half lengthwise. Toast in a toaster oven until very light golden brown. Meanwhile, in small bowl combine yogurt, olive oil, mustard, and garlic and mix well.

2. Spread yogurt mixture on cut sides of toasted buns. Top with half of the lettuce, slices of the turkey, sliced tomatoes, Cheddar, and the rest of the lettuce. Put the buns together to form sandwiches, then cut in half crosswise and serve.

### Waldorf Salad

*The Waldorf Salad is named for the Waldorf-Astoria Hotel in New York City. This delicious salad, full of fruit and nuts, was created by the maitre d', not the chef. Originally, the recipe called for just celery, apples, and mayonnaise. Most versions now use walnuts as well as raisins. Try the salad with pears and dried cranberries!*

# Mexican Chicken Fingers

*These excellent little chicken fingers are delicious
dipped into the creamy salsa combination.*

1. In shallow bowl, combine chili powder, cumin, garlic powder, pepper, cayenne pepper, and cornmeal and mix well. Place orange juice in shallow bowl.

2. Cut chicken fingers in half crosswise. Add to orange juice and let stand for 10 minutes. Remove chicken from orange juice and toss in spice mixture.

3. In large saucepan, heat olive oil over medium heat. Add chicken; cook until browned, about 2–3 minutes. Carefully turn and cook on second side until browned, about 3–5 minutes, and chicken is thoroughly cooked.

4. In small bowl, combine salsa and sour cream and mix well. Serve with chicken fingers.

**Serves 6**

**Calories:** 189.28
**Fat:** 6.60 grams
**Saturated fat:** 2.15 grams
**Dietary fiber:** 0.80 grams
**Sodium:** 79.44 mg
**Cholesterol:** 69.74 mg

*1 tablespoon chili powder*
*1 teaspoon ground cumin*
*1 teaspoon garlic powder*
*⅛ teaspoon pepper*
*⅛ teaspoon cayenne pepper*
*3 tablespoons yellow
    cornmeal*
*¼ cup orange juice*
*1 pound chicken tenders*
*3 tablespoons olive oil*
*½ cup Super Spicy Salsa
    (page 85)*
*⅓ cup low-fat sour cream*

# Open-Faced Tomato-Basil Sandwiches

*The combination of hot bread and melted cheese with cold
seasoned tomatoes and basil is simply spectacular.*

**Serves 8**

**Calories:** 262.27
**Fat:** 11.62 grams
**Saturated fat:** 4.03 grams
**Dietary fiber:** 4.28 grams
**Sodium:** 151.05 mg
**Cholesterol:** 17.82 mg

*3 tablespoons olive oil,
    divided*
*4 tomatoes, chopped*
*¼ cup chopped fresh basil*
*1 teaspoon fresh oregano
    leaves*
*2 cloves garlic, minced*
*Pinch salt*
*⅛ teaspoon white pepper*
*12 slices Hearty-Grain French
    Bread (page 74)*
*1 cup shredded Havarti
    cheese*

1. In small bowl, combine 1 tablespoon olive oil, tomatoes, basil, oregano, and garlic and mix well. Sprinkle with salt and pepper, stir, and set aside.

2. Preheat broiler. Brush bread slices on one side with remaining olive oil. Place, oil side up, on broiler pan. Broil 6" from heat for 2–5 minutes or until bread is lightly toasted. Turn bread.

3. Sprinkle cheese on untoasted side of bread slices. Return to broiler and broil for 3–4 minutes or until cheese is melted and bubbling. Remove from broiler and immediately top each open-faced sandwich with a spoonful of the tomato mixture. Serve immediately.

### Basil

*Basil is an easy-to-grow herb that adds lots of flavor to foods, especially Italian recipes. For best flavor, make sure that you harvest the leaves before the plant bolts, or forms flowers. Rinse off the leaves, shake off excess water, and freeze the leaves in heavy-duty freezer bags. When you want to use some, just break off a small amount.*

# Waldorf-Salad Sandwiches

*This delicious sandwich has the best texture and flavor combinations. Serve it for a special luncheon.*

1. In large bowl, combine yogurt, mustard, and pepper and mix well. Stir in apples, walnuts, celery, raisins, and blueberries and mix to coat.

2. Toast the bread until light golden brown. Spread one side of each bread slice with honey. Top half the slices with a lettuce leaf, then divide fruit mixture on lettuce. Top with remaining bread slices, honey side down. Cut in half diagonally, and serve.

## Health Benefits of Walnuts

*Walnuts are excellent sources of B vitamins, magnesium, and antioxidants like vitamin E. Studies also show that a diet rich in walnuts helps reduce the risk of heart disease by improving blood vessel elasticity, plaque accumulation, and lowering LDL cholesterol. Walnuts are high in calories, though, so eat them in moderation or use them as replacements for higher fat items in your diet.*

**Serves 4–6**

**Calories:** 396.92
**Fat:** 9.32 grams
**Saturated fat:** 1.64 grams
**Dietary fiber:** 6.34 grams
**Sodium:** 165.01 mg
**Cholesterol:** 14.06 mg

½ cup plain yogurt
2 tablespoons Dijon mustard
⅛ teaspoon white pepper
2 Granny Smith apples, chopped
½ cup chopped walnuts
1 cup diced celery
½ cup golden raisins
½ cup dried blueberries
8 slices Raisin-Cinnamon Oatmeal Bread (page 67)
3 tablespoons honey
4 leaves red lettuce

# Wheat-Bread Tuna Melt

*Adding lots of vegetables to a tuna melt adds
flavor, color, texture, and lots of nutrition.*

**Serves 4–6**

**Calories:** 240.86
**Fat:** 10.66 grams
**Saturated fat:** 3.70 grams
**Dietary fiber:** 2.69 grams
**Sodium:** 309.57 mg
**Cholesterol:** 27.46 mg

1 tablespoon olive oil
½ cup chopped onion
1 clove garlic, minced
1 green bell pepper, chopped
1 (6-ounce) can solid white
    tuna, drained
½ cup chopped celery
¼ cup plain yogurt
2 tablespoons low-fat
    mayonnaise
1 tablespoon Dijon mustard
⅛ teaspoon white pepper
1 tomato
4 slices Whole-Grain Oatmeal
    Bread (page 63)
½ cup shredded Swiss cheese
¼ cup grated Parmesan
    cheese

1.  In a small saucepan, heat olive oil over medium heat. Add onion, garlic, and bell pepper; cook and stir until crisp-tender, about 4 minutes. Remove from heat and pour into medium bowl.

2.  Add tuna, celery, yogurt, mayonnaise, mustard, and pepper and mix well.

3.  Toast bread on both sides. Spread with tuna mixture. Top each sandwich with a tomato slice and sprinkle with cheeses.

4.  Preheat broiler. Broil sandwiches 6" from heat for 5–7 minutes or until sandwiches are hot and cheese melts and begins to brown. Cut in half and serve immediately.

### Melt Variety

*You can make melt sandwiches with just about any meat. Try canned or cooked cubed chicken, deli roast beef, or diced ham. Cooked shrimp makes an excellent melt sandwich, or you could just use a lot of vegetables like mushrooms, zucchini, and even shredded carrots. Vary the cheese to suit your family's tastes, too.*

# Basil-Tomato Pizza

*This simple pizza should be made in the summer,*
*or whenever fresh tomatoes and basil are available.*

**Serves 6**

**Calories:** 334.64
**Fat:** 11.54 grams
**Saturated fat:** 4.59 grams
**Dietary fiber:** 5.03 grams
**Sodium:** 303.68 mg
**Cholesterol:** 15.38 mg

*1 tablespoon olive oil*
*3 cloves garlic, minced*
*4 tomatoes*
*½ teaspoon dried oregano*
*  leaves*
*⅛ teaspoon white pepper*
*½ cup torn fresh basil leaves*
*1 Whole-Grain Pizza Crust*
*  (page 69), prebaked*
*1 cup shredded provolone*
*  cheese*

1. Preheat oven to 400°F. In small saucepan, heat olive oil over medium heat. Add garlic; cook for 2–3 minutes or until garlic is fragrant. Remove from heat and set aside.

2. Cut tomatoes in half and gently squeeze out seeds. Chop tomatoes and combine with oregano, pepper, and basil leaves in small bowl.

3. Place crust on cookie sheet or pizza stone. Brush with the garlic mixture. Top with tomato mixture, then sprinkle with cheese. Bake for 15–20 minutes or until pizza is hot and cheese melts and bubbles. Serve immediately.

# Creamy Grilled-Cheese Sandwiches

*Making a cheese spread lets you use less cheese and makes the filling very creamy.*

**Yields 1¼ cups; 6–8 servings**

**Calories:** 324.19
**Fat:** 15.70 grams
**Saturated fat:** 6.53 grams
**Dietary fiber:** 2.81 grams
**Sodium:** 329.92 mg
**Cholesterol:** 39.51 mg

1 (3-ounce) package nonfat cream cheese, softened
¼ cup Yogurt Cheese from Yogurt Cheese Balls (page 96)
1 cup shredded part-skim mozzarella cheese
1 cup shredded extra-sharp Cheddar cheese
2 tablespoons nonfat sour cream
1 teaspoon dried basil leaves
⅛ teaspoon pepper
10 slices Whole-Grain Oatmeal Bread (page 63)
2 tablespoons olive oil

1. In medium bowl, beat cream cheese until soft. Add Yogurt Cheese and mix until smooth. Add mozzarella and Cheddar cheeses and mix until blended. Then stir in sour cream, basil, and pepper and mix well.

2. Spread cheese mixture between bread slices. Spread the outside of the sandwiches with olive oil. Grill, turning once, on a covered skillet or griddle, until bread is toasted and cheese filling is melted. Cut in half and serve immediately.

## Low-Fat Sour Cream

*Low-fat and nonfat sour creams usually have additives like guar gum added for a smooth, thick texture. But this is good news! Guar gum is a soluble fiber that helps remove cholesterol from your blood. It is similar to pectin and psyllium, two soluble fibers that have been thoroughly studied in cholesterol-lowering tests.*

# "Egg" Salad Sandwich Spread

*Tofu's mild flavor can be seasoned many ways.*
*Use different spices and cheeses to vary this spread recipe.*

1. Drain tofu and drain again on paper towels, pressing to remove moisture. Set aside.

2. In medium bowl, combine remaining ingredients and stir gently to combine. Crumble tofu into bowl and mix until mixture looks like egg salad. Cover tightly and refrigerate for 2–3 hours before serving. Store, covered, in the refrigerator for 3–4 days.

### Tofu

*The best tofu to use for fake egg-salad sandwich spread is firm or extra-firm, depending on the consistency you like. Be sure to drain it very well; in fact, you can let it stand in a strainer for 30–40 minutes before using. If you don't, the excess liquid in the tofu will ruin the sandwich spread.*

**Yields 3 cups; serving size ½ cup**

**Calories:** 105.78
**Fat:** 7.17 grams
**Saturated fat:** 1.71 grams
**Dietary fiber:** 1.23 grams
**Sodium:** 235.50 mg
**Cholesterol:** 3.97 mg

½ (12-ounce) package firm tofu
⅓ cup low-fat mayonnaise
2 tablespoons plain yogurt
2 tablespoons Dijon mustard
⅛ teaspoon pepper
½ teaspoon dried oregano leaves
1 cup chopped celery
1 red bell pepper, chopped
¼ cup grated Parmesan cheese

# Spinach Artichoke Pizza

*This pizza is just full of vegetables, nutrition, fiber, and flavor!*

**Serves 8**

**Calories:** 335.56
**Fat:** 13.05 grams
**Saturated fat:** 6.06 grams
**Dietary fiber:** 5.04 grams
**Sodium:** 317.04 mg
**Cholesterol:** 27.48 mg

*1 (10-ounce) package frozen chopped spinach, thawed and drained*
*1 (9-ounce) package frozen artichoke hearts, thawed and drained*
*1 tablespoon olive oil*
*1 onion, chopped*
*3 cloves garlic, minced*
*1 red bell pepper, chopped*
*1 (8-ounce) package sliced mushrooms*
*1 cup part-skim ricotta cheese*
*¼ cup grated Parmesan cheese*
*1 cup shredded part-skim mozzarella cheese*
*½ cup shredded extra-sharp Cheddar cheese*
*1 Whole-Grain Pizza Crust (page 69)*

1. Preheat oven to 400°F. Press spinach between paper towels to remove all excess moisture. Cut artichoke hearts into small pieces.

2. In large saucepan, heat olive oil. Cook onion, garlic, red pepper, and mushrooms until crisp-tender, about 4 minutes. Add spinach; cook and stir until liquid evaporates, about 5 minutes longer. Add mushrooms; cook and stir for 2–3 minutes longer.

3. Drain vegetable mixture if necessary. Place in medium bowl and let cool for 20 minutes. Then blend in ricotta and Parmesan cheeses.

4. Spread on pizza crust. Top with mozzarella and Cheddar cheeses. Bake for 20–25 minutes or until pizza is hot and cheese is melted and begins to brown. Serve immediately.

# Moroccan Lamb Kabobs

*A flavorful mint-and-garlic marinade flavors lean tender
lamb and fresh vegetables in this simple recipe.*

1. In glass bowl, combine oil, mint, garlic, cardamom, cinnamon, pepper, and orange juice and mix well. Trim fat from lamb and cut into 1" cubes. Add to marinade, cover, and refrigerate for 2–4 hours.

2. When ready to eat, preheat broiler. Drain lamb, reserving marinade. Thread lamb, mushrooms, and peppers on metal skewers.

3. Broil skewers 6" from heat source, turning several times during cooking and brushing with reserved marinade, for 7–9 minutes or until lamb is browned and just pink inside. Discard remaining marinade. Serve immediately.

### Mint

*Mint is a very fresh-tasting, pungent herb that adds great flavor to food. It is traditionally used with lamb because the sharp taste cuts through the rich meat. You can easily grow mint in a kitchen windowsill garden or in pots. In the garden, it will rapidly spread and may take over sections, so growing it in pots is easier.*

**Serves 6**

**Calories:** 167.27
**Fat:** 7.40 grams
**Saturated fat:** 2.10 grams
**Dietary fiber:** 1.49 grams
**Sodium:** 53.38 mg
**Cholesterol:** 59.50 mg

¼ cup olive oil
½ cup chopped fresh mint
4 cloves garlic, minced
½ teaspoon ground
    cardamom
½ teaspoon cinnamon
¼ teaspoon pepper
3 tablespoons orange juice
1 pound lean lamb
1 (8-ounce) package button
    mushrooms
2 red bell peppers, sliced

# Pork-and-Slaw Sandwiches

*These hearty sandwiches hold up well because the
Ciabatta Rolls are chewy with a sturdy crust.*

**Serves 4**

**Calories:** 474.96
**Fat:** 16.35 grams
**Saturated fat:** 2.90 grams
**Dietary fiber:** 6.40 grams
**Sodium:** 367.73 mg
**Cholesterol:** 39.13 mg

*6 slices Herb-Crusted Pork
    Tenderloin (page 202)
2 cups Apple Coleslaw (page
    237)
4 Ciabatta Rolls (page 79)*

Using two forks, shred the tenderloin. Cut rolls in half. Place half of the coleslaw on the cut sides of the bread, and add the tenderloin. Top with remaining coleslaw, then remaining bun halves. Serve immediately.

# Crisp Polenta Open-Faced Sandwiches

*When polenta is chilled, then broiled, it becomes crispy and very flavorful.
Top the base with any sandwich ingredients you like.*

**Serves 8–10**

**Calories:** 176.21
**Fat:** 7.80 grams
**Saturated fat:** 4.53 grams
**Dietary fiber:** 1.93 grams
**Sodium:** 228.89 mg
**Cholesterol:** 23.95 mg

*1 recipe Cheese Polenta (page
    257)
1 cup shredded Gruyère
    cheese
¼ cup chopped fresh basil
    leaves
3 tomatoes, sliced
7 tablespoons grated
    Parmesan cheese*

1. Prepare polenta as directed, except when done, pour onto a greased cookie sheet; spread to a ½" thick rectangle, about 9" × 15". Cover and chill until very firm, about 2 hours.

2. Preheat broiler. Cut polenta into fifteen 3" squares. Place on broiler pan; broil for 4–6 minutes or until golden brown. Carefully turn polenta and broil for 3–5 minutes or until golden brown.

3. Remove from oven and sprinkle with Gruyère and basil. Top each with a slice of tomato, then Parmesan. Return to broiler and broil for 3–6 minutes or until cheese melts and sandwiches are hot. Serve immediately.

# Mini Hot-Pepper Pizzas

*English-muffin pizzas are a classic snack. Using lots of peppers adds vitamin C, fiber, and great flavor too.*

1. Preheat oven to broil. Place English muffins, split side up, on broiler pan. Broil 6" from heat source until lightly toasted, about 3–5 minutes. Remove from oven and set aside.

2. In medium skillet, heat olive oil over medium heat. Add garlic, red pepper, and jalapeño peppers. Cook and stir until tender, about 5 minutes. Sprinkle with pepper and oregano.

3. Stir ricotta into vegetable mixture; spread on the English muffin halves. Sprinkle with Parmesan. Broil 6" from heat source for 5–8 minutes or until pizzas are hot and topping bubbles and begins to brown. Let cool for 5 minutes, then serve.

### English Muffins

*English muffins are a great choice for sandwiches or a pizza base. Be sure to split the muffins with a fork to create peaks and ridges that hold ingredients and become crunchy when toasted or grilled. Whole-wheat or whole-grain English muffins are readily available. They do spoil rather quickly, so freeze them after the first day.*

**Serves 4**

**Calories:** 239.93
**Fat:** 8.87 grams
**Saturated fat:** 3.26 grams
**Dietary fiber:** 3.57 grams
**Sodium:** 351.25 mg
**Cholesterol:** 15.11 mg

*4 whole-wheat English muffins, split*
*1 tablespoon olive oil*
*2 cloves garlic, minced*
*1 red bell pepper, diced*
*2 jalapeño peppers, minced*
*⅛ teaspoon pepper*
*½ teaspoon dried oregano leaves*
*½ cup part-skim ricotta cheese*
*¼ cup grated Parmesan cheese*

# Hawaiian Pizza

*This fresh and flavorful pizza is delicious served with a green salad
and some Butterscotch Meringues (page 305) for dessert.*

**Serves 6–8**

---

**Calories:** 300.45
**Fat:** 6.94 grams
**Saturated fat:** 2.56 grams
**Dietary fiber:** 4.42 grams
**Sodium:** 365.23 mg
**Cholesterol:** 14.86 mg

*1 tablespoon olive oil*
*1 onion, chopped*
*3 cloves garlic, minced*
*1 green bell pepper, chopped*
*1 cup Spaghetti Sauce (page 207)*
*1 Whole-Grain Pizza Crust (page 69), prebaked*
*1 (20-ounce) can pineapple tidbits, drained*
*1 cup chopped Canadian bacon*
*1 cup part-skim mozzarella cheese*

1. Preheat oven to 400°F. In large saucepan, heat olive oil over medium heat. Add onion, garlic, and green pepper; cook and stir until crisp-tender, about 4 minutes. Remove from heat and mix in Spaghetti Sauce.

2. Place pizza crust on baking sheet and top with sauce mixture. Drain pineapple tidbits and pat dry between paper towels. Arrange pineapple and Canadian bacon on top of crust. Sprinkle with mozzarella.

3. Bake at 400°F for 20–30 minutes or until pizza is hot and cheese is melted and beginning to brown. Serve immediately.

# Asian Skewered Lamb

*The sugar in the marinade helps the lamb caramelize, or turn
a deep golden-brown color, that adds incredible flavor.*

**Serves 6**

**Calories:** 182.50
**Fat:** 7.58 grams
**Saturated fat:** 2.20 grams
**Dietary fiber:** 1.53 grams
**Sodium:** 85.58 mg
**Cholesterol:** 63.75 mg

*3 tablespoons olive oil*
*2 tablespoons dry sherry*
*1 tablespoon low-sodium soy
   sauce*
*1 teaspoon five-spice powder*
*1 tablespoon sugar*
*1 tablespoon grated fresh
   ginger root*
*2 cloves garlic, minced*
*1 pound lean lamb*
*½ pound sugar-snap peas*
*1 onion, cut into wedges*

1. In glass bowl, combine olive oil, sherry, soy sauce, five-spice powder, sugar, ginger root, and garlic and mix well. Trim excess fat from lamb and cut into 1" cubes. Add cubes to marinade, stir, cover, and refrigerate for 2 hours.

2. When ready to eat, preheat broiler. Drain lamb, reserving marinade. Thread lamb, sugar-snap peas, and onion wedges on metal skewers. Broil 6" from heat, turning several times and brushing with marinade, until lamb is golden brown. Discard remaining marinade. Serve immediately.

## Lamb and Cholesterol

*Lamb has about the same amount of cholesterol as chicken, beef, or pork. Be sure to trim off any visible excess fat to reduce the fat and cholesterol content. Most of the fat is on the outside, as lamb has very little marbling, or interior fat. Lamb should be served pink, or medium well done.*

# Potato Pizza

*Thinly sliced potatoes make an unusual and delicious topping on this special pizza. Serve it with a nice green salad for a simple late-night dinner.*

**Serves 6–8**

**Calories:** 370.15
**Fat:** 10.36 grams
**Saturated fat:** 4.54 grams
**Dietary fiber:** 5.97 grams
**Sodium:** 202.64 mg
**Cholesterol:** 20.07 mg

1 tablespoon olive oil
1 tablespoon butter
1 onion, finely chopped
5 cloves garlic, minced
3 Yukon Gold potatoes, thinly
    sliced
2 teaspoons fresh thyme
    leaves
⅛ teaspoon salt
⅛ teaspoon cayenne pepper
1 Whole-Grain Pizza Crust
    (page 69)
1 cup shredded Havarti
    cheese
2 tablespoons grated
    Romano cheese

1. Preheat oven to 400°F. In large saucepan, combine olive oil and butter over medium heat. When butter melts, add onion and garlic; cook and stir until crisp-tender, about 4 minutes.

2. Add potatoes. Cook, stirring occasionally, until potatoes are slightly softened. Add thyme, salt, and cayenne pepper and remove from heat.

3. Spread potato mixture on the pizza crust. Top with Havarti and Romano cheeses. Bake for 20–25 minutes or until potatoes are tender, pizza is hot, and cheeses are melted and starting to brown. Serve immediately.

# Mini Olive Pizzas

*The olives can be omitted if your family doesn't like them. Use canned sliced mushrooms instead, or just use the tomatoes and cheese.*

1. Preheat oven to broil. Split pita bread in half around the edges, creating 8 rounds. Place, rough side up, on a cookie sheet. Brush with olive oil and sprinkle with garlic. Broil 6" from heat until golden.

2. Arrange plum tomatoes on pita bread rounds and sprinkle with red pepper flakes and olives. Sprinkle with cheeses. Return to broiler; broil for 3–5 minutes or until cheese melts and begins to brown. Cut each pizza in half and serve immediately.

## Pizza Bases

*There are a lot of excellent choices for low-fat pizza bases. Pita bread, whether split or whole, makes a nice sturdy crust with a mild flavor. English muffins are another good choice, especially if they are toasted before adding toppings. And tortillas, flour or corn, flavored or plain, make a nice crisp crust with just some sauce and cheese.*

**Serves 6–8**

**Calories:** 156.74
**Fat:** 9.74 grams
**Saturated fat:** 3.70 grams
**Dietary fiber:** 1.78 grams
**Sodium:** 333.52 mg
**Cholesterol:** 15.00 mg

4 small whole-wheat pita bread rounds
2 tablespoons olive oil
2 cloves garlic, minced
4 plum tomatoes, finely chopped
¼ teaspoon crushed red pepper flakes
½ cup pitted Greek olives, chopped
1 cup grated part-skim mozzarella cheese
¼ cup grated Romano cheese

# Grilled Meatloaf Sandwiches

**Serves 6–8**

**Calories:** 364.06
**Fat:** 16.35 grams
**Saturated fat:** 5.47 grams
**Dietary fiber:** 3.48 grams
**Sodium:** 326.11 mg
**Cholesterol:** 63.86 mg

*2 tablespoons ketchup*
*2 tablespoons mustard*
*2 tablespoons grated*
*Parmesan cheese*
*4 slices Whole-Grain Meatloaf*
*(page 173), cooked and*
*chilled*
*8 slices Whole-Grain Oatmeal*
*Bread (page 63)*
*1 tomato, thinly sliced*
*½ cup shredded extra-sharp*
*Cheddar cheese*
*2 tablespoons olive oil*

*This fabulous sandwich is perfect with any
leftover meatloaf. You can also serve it cold!*

1. Preheat indoor dual-contact grill or griddle. In small bowl, combine ketchup, mustard, and Parmesan cheese. Spread on both sides of the meatloaf; place one slice of meatloaf on one slice of bread.

2. Top with tomato slices, then Cheddar cheese. Top with rest of bread slices. Brush outsides of sandwiches with olive oil. Grill sandwiches on dual-contact grill for 3–4 minutes each, or grill on a griddle, turning once, for 6–9 minutes until bread is golden brown and meatloaf is hot. Cut in half and serve immediately.

# Chapter 15
# **Desserts**

# Mango Walnut Upside-Down Cake

*You could substitute pineapple for the mango in this excellent cake.*

**Serves 12**

**Calories:** 274.81
**Fat:** 11.11 grams
**Saturated fat:** 4.47 grams
**Dietary fiber:** 1.34 grams
**Sodium:** 200.85 mg
**Cholesterol:** 33.18 mg

*2 tablespoons plus ¼ cup butter, divided*
*¼ cup dark brown sugar*
*¼ teaspoon cardamom*
*½ teaspoon cinnamon*
*1 mango, peeled and sliced*
*¼ cup vegetable oil*
*½ cup sugar*
*½ cup brown sugar*
*2 egg whites*
*1 egg*
*¼ cup yogurt*
*¼ cup orange juice*
*1 teaspoon baking powder*
*1 teaspoon baking soda*
*1½ cups flour*
*½ cup whole-wheat flour*

1. Preheat oven to 350°F. Spray a 12-cup Bundt pan with nonstick baking spray containing flour and set aside. In small microwave-safe bowl, combine 2 tablespoons butter with dark brown sugar. Microwave on high for 1 minute until butter melts; stir until smooth. Add cardamom and cinnamon.

2. Spoon this mixture into prepared pan. Arrange mango slices on top; set aside.

3. In large bowl, combine ¼ cup butter, oil, sugar, and brown sugar and beat until smooth. Add egg whites and egg and beat well. Add yogurt and orange juice, then baking powder, baking soda, flour, and whole-wheat flour. Beat for 1 minute.

4. Pour batter over mangoes in pan. Bake for 50–60 minutes or until a toothpick inserted in cake comes out clean. Let cool for 5 minutes, then invert onto serving tray. If any mango mixture remains in pan, spoon over cake. Let cool completely.

# Banana-Rum Mousse

*You can serve this mousse immediately after blending, or place it in goblets or sherbet cups and freeze before serving.*

1. In blender or food processor, combine the rum, lime juice, sugar, and bananas and blend or process until smooth.

2. Add the yogurt and blend or process until smooth, scraping down sides once during blending. Spoon into dessert glasses and serve immediately, or cover and freeze up to 8 hours before serving.

### Liqueur in Frozen Desserts

*Frozen desserts made with rum or other liqueurs will never freeze rock-hard but will keep a soft-serve consistency. If you don't want to use hard liquor, you can substitute fruit juices like pear nectar or orange juice. For a rum flavor, add ¼ teaspoon of rum extract.*

**Serves 4**

**Calories:** 164.58
**Fat:** 2.25 grams
**Saturated fat:** 1.13 grams
**Dietary fiber:** 1.80 grams
**Sodium:** 32.30 mg
**Cholesterol:** 0.72 mg

*3 tablespoons rum*
*2 tablespoons lime juice*
*2 tablespoons powdered sugar*
*2 bananas, chopped*
*1 cup vanilla frozen yogurt*
*4 sprigs fresh mint*

# Lemon Mousse

*Pear nectar is very mild, and it adds a nice bit of sweetness to this tart mousse.*

**Serves 4**

**Calories:** 151.27
**Fat:** 0.65 grams
**Saturated fat:** 0.40 grams
**Dietary fiber:** 0.33 grams
**Sodium:** 65.70 mg
**Cholesterol:** 2.27 mg

1 (0.25-ounce) envelope
    unflavored gelatin
¼ cup cold water
⅓ cup lemon juice
⅔ cup pear nectar
¼ cup sugar, divided
1 teaspoon grated lemon zest
1 cup lemon yogurt
2 pasteurized egg whites
¼ teaspoon cream of tartar

1. In microwave-safe glass measuring cup, combine gelatin and cold water; let stand for 5 minutes to soften gelatin. Stir in lemon juice, pear nectar, and 2 tablespoons sugar. Microwave on high for 1–2 minutes, stirring twice during cooking time, until sugar and gelatin completely dissolve; stir in lemon zest. Let cool for 30 minutes.

2. When gelatin mixture is cool to the touch, blend in the lemon yogurt. Then, in medium bowl, combine egg whites with cream of tartar; beat until soft peaks form. Gradually stir in remaining 2 tablespoons sugar, beating until stiff peaks form.

3. Fold gelatin mixture into egg whites until combined. Pour into serving glasses or goblets, cover, and chill until firm, about 4–6 hours.

### Pasteurized Egg Whites

*You can find pasteurized eggs in any grocery store. Be sure to carefully abide by the sell-by and use-by dates that are stamped on the package and usually on each egg. Pasteurized egg whites take longer to whip to peaks than ordinary eggs. Just keep beating them until the peaks form. Cream of tartar helps stabilize the foam.*

# Green Grapes with Lemon Sorbet

*This simple dish brings out the flavor and juicy sweetness of grapes. If you don't want to use wine, try pear nectar or white grape juice instead.*

1. Wash grapes, dry, and cut in half. Sprinkle sugar over grapes and let stand for 5 minutes. Then add wine, stirring gently until sugar dissolves. Sprinkle with orange zest, cover, and refrigerate for 1 hour.

2. When ready to serve, stir grape mixture and serve over sorbet in sherbet glasses or goblets.

**Serves 4**

**Calories:** 233.90
**Fat:** 1.61 grams
**Saturated fat:** 0.90 grams
**Dietary fiber:** 3.16 grams
**Sodium:** 35.64 mg
**Cholesterol:** 0.0 mg

*2 cups green grapes*
*2 tablespoons sugar*
*½ cup sweet white wine*
*1 teaspoon orange zest*
*2 cups lemon sorbet*

# Blueberry Cloud

*This can be made with many other fruits. Chopped strawberries, raspberries (fresh or frozen), and peaches would all be delicious.*

1. In microwave-safe glass measuring cup, combine gelatin with water; let stand for 5 minutes to let gelatin soften. Add orange juice and sugar. Microwave on high for 1–2 minutes, stirring twice during cooking time, until gelatin and sugar dissolve. Pour into blender or food processor.

2. Add berries; blend or process until smooth. Let stand until cool, about 20 minutes. Then add yogurt; process until smooth. Pour into medium bowl and fold in whipped topping. Spoon into serving dishes, cover, and freeze for at least 4 hours before serving.

**Serves 4**

**Calories:** 183.28
**Fat:** 4.72 grams
**Saturated fat:** 3.37 grams
**Dietary fiber:** 0.96 grams
**Sodium:** 49.08 mg
**Cholesterol:** 1.10 mg

*1 (0.25-ounce) envelope*
*   unflavored gelatin*
*¼ cup cold water*
*¾ cup orange juice*
*3 tablespoons sugar*
*1 cup blueberries*
*1 cup vanilla frozen yogurt*
*1 cup frozen non-fat whipped*
*   topping, thawed*

# Peach Melba Parfait

*This fresh and easy dessert can be made with many flavor combinations.*
*Try sliced pears with orange yogurt and mandarin orange segments.*

**Serves 4**

**Calories:** 153.23
**Fat:** 1.26 grams
**Saturated fat:** 0.43 grams
**Dietary fiber:** 5.48 grams
**Sodium:** 33.57 mg
**Cholesterol:** 2.27 mg

*4 ripe peaches, peeled and
 sliced
1 tablespoon lemon juice
2 tablespoons sugar
1 cup raspberry yogurt
1 pint fresh raspberries
4 sprigs fresh mint*

1. In a medium bowl, combine the peaches, lemon juice, and sugar and let stand for 10 minutes. Stir to dissolve sugar.

2. In 4 parfait or wine glasses, place some of the peach mixture. Top with a spoonful of the yogurt, then some fresh raspberries. Repeat layers, ending with raspberries. Cover and chill for 2–4 hours before serving. Garnish with mint sprig.

## Melba

*Peach Melba is a dessert invented in the 1890s to honor the opera singer Nellie Melba. She loved ice cream but didn't like its effect on her vocal cords. The chef Escoffier created Peach Melba by combining peaches and raspberries into a warm syrup served over ice cream.*

# Strawberry-Rhubarb Parfait

*Rhubarb is one of the first vegetables (yes, vegetables!)
to start growing in the spring. Combined with strawberries,
it has a wonderfully tart and refreshing flavor.*

1. In medium saucepan, combine rhubarb, apple juice, and sugar. Bring to a simmer, then reduce heat and simmer for 8–10 minutes or until rhubarb is soft.

2. Remove pan from heat and immediately stir in frozen strawberries, stirring to break up strawberries. Let stand until cool, about 30 minutes.

3. Layer rhubarb mixture and frozen yogurt in parfait glasses or goblets, starting and ending with rhubarb mixture. Cover and freeze until firm, about 8 hours.

**Serves 6**

**Calories:** 210.56
**Fat:** 4.16 grams
**Saturated fat:** 2.48 grams
**Dietary fiber:** 1.23 grams
**Sodium:** 64.41 mg
**Cholesterol:** 1.44 mg

2 stalks rhubarb, sliced
½ cup apple juice
⅓ cup sugar
1 (10-ounce) package frozen
  strawberries
3 cups frozen vanilla yogurt

# Chocolate-Butterscotch Parfaits

*The combination of creamy chocolate with airy crisp
meringues and crunchy pecans is out of this world.*

1. Prepare Silken Chocolate Mousse and refrigerate for 2 hours, until set. Prepare Butterscotch Meringues and let cool completely.

2. Break up meringues with your fingers. In six large parfait glasses, layer mousse and meringue crumbs, ending with the mousse. Sprinkle with toasted hazelnuts, cover, and chill for 2–4 hours.

3. Drizzle each parfait with 1 tablespoon butterscotch ice cream topping just before serving.

**Serves 6**

**Calories:** 365.51
**Fat:** 16.62 grams
**Saturated fat:** 8.27 grams
**Dietary fiber:** 3.01 grams
**Sodium:** 179.64 mg
**Cholesterol:** 12.09 mg

1 recipe Silken Chocolate
  Mousse (page 297)
10 Butterscotch Meringues
  (page 305)
6 tablespoons chopped
  hazelnuts, toasted
6 tablespoons butterscotch
  ice cream topping

# Apple Pear-Nut Crisp

*Leave the skins on the apples and pears for more fiber
and nutrition. You can peel them, if you'd like.*

**Serves 8**

**Calories:** 353.77
**Fat:** 9.97 grams
**Saturated fat:** 5.25 grams
**Dietary fiber:** 6.54 grams
**Sodium:** 61.78 mg
**Cholesterol:** 20.34 mg

*2 apples, sliced*
*3 pears, sliced*
*2 tablespoons lemon juice*
*¼ cup sugar*
*1 teaspoon cinnamon*
*½ teaspoon nutmeg*
*1½ cups quick-cooking*
  *oatmeal*
*½ cup flour*
*¼ cup whole-wheat flour*
*½ cup brown sugar*
*⅓ cup butter or margarine,*
  *melted*

1. Preheat oven to 350°F. Spray a 9" round cake pan with nonstick cooking spray and set aside.

2. Prepare apples and pears, sprinkling with lemon juice as you work. Combine in medium bowl with sugar, cinnamon, and nutmeg. Spoon into prepared cake pan.

3. In same bowl, combine oatmeal, flour, whole-wheat flour, and brown sugar and mix well. Add melted butter and mix until crumbly. Sprinkle over fruit in dish.

4. Bake for 35–45 minutes or until fruit bubbles and topping is browned and crisp. Let cool for 15 minutes before serving.

### Baking Fruit

*When choosing fruit for baking, pick specimens that are fairly firm and not too ripe. The baking process breaks down the cell structure of the fruit, so if you start with soft fruit, it will bake down to mush. Firm, tart apples like Granny Smith and Cortland are good choices for baking. Either Bosc or Anjou pears will work well.*

# Crepes with Poached Pears

*You can fill these crepes with anything from strawberries and yogurt to Silken Chocolate Mousse (page 297). Keep a batch in the freezer for last-minute desserts.*

1. In blender or food processor, combine egg, egg whites, milk, flour, sugar, and 1 tablespoon melted butter, and blend or process until smooth. Let stand for 15 minutes.

2. Heat a 7" nonstick skillet over medium heat. Brush with 1 tablespoon melted butter. Using a ¼-cup measure, pour 3 tablespoons batter into the skillet; immediately rotate and tilt skillet to spread batter evenly. Cook over medium heat for 1–2 minutes or until the crepe can be moved.

3. Loosen the edges of the crepe and flip; cook for 1 minute on second side, then turn out onto kitchen towels. Stack between layers of waxed or parchment paper when cool.

4. For filling, peel and chop pears and place in medium saucepan with sugar and lemon juice. Pour pear nectar over. Bring to a simmer over medium-high heat, then cook, stirring gently, until pears are very tender, about 3–5 minutes.

5. Let pears cool in liquid. When ready to serve, fold pear mixture into whipped topping. Fill crepes with this mixture and place, seam side down, on serving plates. Garnish with raspberries and sprinkle with powdered sugar.

**Serves 6**

**Calories:** 185.51
**Fat:** 5.93 grams
**Saturated fat:** 3.54 grams
**Dietary fiber:** 1.70 grams
**Sodium:** 62.39 mg
**Cholesterol:** 46.56 mg

*1 egg*
*1 egg white*
*½ cup 1% milk*
*½ cup flour*
*2 tablespoons sugar*
*2 tablespoons melted butter, divided*
*4 pears*
*¼ cup sugar*
*2 tablespoons lemon juice*
*¼ cup pear nectar*
*½ cup frozen non-dairy whipped topping, thawed*
*1 cup fresh raspberries*
*2 tablespoons powdered sugar*

# Strawberry-Mango Meringue Pie

*Meringue pie shells have absolutely no fat at all
and are the perfect foil for almost any filling.*

**Serves 8**

**Calories:** 195.15
**Fat:** 5.51 grams
**Saturated fat:** 3.40 grams
**Dietary fiber:** 1.19 grams
**Sodium:** 123.32 mg
**Cholesterol:** 17.10 mg

*1 teaspoon flour*
*3 egg whites*
*¼ teaspoon cream of tartar*
*½ cup sugar*
*1 teaspoon vanilla*
*1 (8-ounce) package low-fat
    cream cheese, softened*
*1 cup mango yogurt*
*1 cup chopped strawberries*
*2 mangoes, peeled and
    chopped*

1. Preheat oven to 300°F. Spray a 9" pie plate with nonstick cooking spray and dust with 1 teaspoon flour. In large bowl, combine egg whites and cream of tartar; beat until soft peaks form. Gradually beat in sugar until very stiff peaks form. Beat in vanilla. Spread into prepared pan, building up sides to form a shell.

2. Bake for 50–60 minutes or until shell is very light golden and dry to the touch. Turn oven off and let shell stand in oven for 1 hour. Cool completely.

3. For filling, in medium bowl beat cream cheese until fluffy. Gradually add yogurt, beating until well combined. Fold in strawberries and mangoes. Spoon into meringue pie shell, cover, and chill for 3–4 hours before serving.

### Mangoes

*It isn't difficult to prepare a mango; it just takes practice. Hold the mango upright on your work surface, then cut down the sides, avoiding the long oval pit in the center. Then hold the halves in your palm and score the fruit in a cross-hatch pattern. Turn the halves inside out and cut the cubes from the skin.*

## Chocolate Mousse Banana Meringue Pie

*This luxurious and delicious pie is low-fat, yet full of flavor. You could top it with a dollop of frozen non-dairy whipped topping for a garnish if you'd like.*

1. Follow directions to make meringue pie shell, but also beat cocoa into egg whites along with the sugar. Bake as directed in recipe. Let cool completely.

2. Make mousse as directed and chill in bowl for 4–6 hours until firm. Slice bananas, sprinkling lemon juice over slices as you work.

3. Layer mousse and sliced bananas in pie shell, beginning and ending with mousse. Cover and chill for 2–3 hours before serving.

**Serves 8**

**Calories:** 253.53
**Fat:** 9.23 grams
**Saturated fat:** 5.94 grams
**Dietary fiber:** 2.50 grams
**Sodium:** 79.66 mg
**Cholesterol:** 8.71 mg

1 recipe meringue pie shell
(page 292)
3 tablespoons cocoa powder
1 recipe Silken Chocolate
Mousse (page 297)
2 bananas, sliced
1 tablespoon lemon juice

## Grapefruit Pie

*Grapefruit is an unusual fruit to use in a pie, but it's delicious and has lots of fiber and vitamin C.*

1. Prepare crust according to directions and let cool completely. Cut one grapefruit in half and squeeze juice from one half. Peel other half and chop fruit; set aside.

2. In medium bowl, beat cream cheese until smooth; gradually add condensed milk, beating until fluffy. Add grapefruit juice and mix well; pour into crust and refrigerate.

3. Peel second grapefruit and separate into sections; remove seeds. Sprinkle chopped grapefruit over pie; arrange grapefruit sections on top. Drizzle with honey; cover and refrigerate for 4–6 hours before serving.

**Serves 8–10**

**Calories:** 349.21
**Fat:** 13.36 grams
**Saturated fat:** 5.65 grams
**Dietary fiber:** 0.96 grams
**Sodium:** 170.15 mg
**Cholesterol:** 26.74 mg

1 Loco Pie Crust (page 294),
baked
2 small red grapefruits
1 (8-ounce) package low-fat
cream cheese, softened
1 (14-ounce) can low-fat
sweetened condensed
milk
3 tablespoons honey

# Loco Pie Crust

*Yes, mayonnaise in pie crust! The egg and oil in the mayonnaise make the crust tender, while adding a nice flavor.*

**Serves 8**

**Calories:** 171.83
**Fat:** 7.35 grams
**Saturated fat:** 1.18 grams
**Dietary fiber:** 0.63 grams
**Sodium:** 65.46 mg
**Cholesterol:** 0.68 mg

½ cup plus 1 tablespoon
    mayonnaise
3 tablespoons buttermilk
1 teaspoon vinegar
1½ cups flour

1. In large bowl, combine mayonnaise, buttermilk, and vinegar and mix well. Add flour, stirring with a fork to form a ball. You may need to add more buttermilk or more flour to make a workable dough. Press dough into a ball, wrap in plastic wrap, and refrigerate for 1 hour.

2. When ready to bake, preheat oven to 400°F. Roll out dough between two sheets of waxed paper. Remove top sheet and place crust in 9" pie pan. Carefully ease off the top sheet of paper, then ease the crust into the pan and press to bottom and sides. Fold edges under and flute.

3. Either use as recipe directs, or bake for 5 minutes, then press crust down with fork if necessary. Bake for 5–8 minutes longer or until crust is light golden brown.

### Freezing Pie Crusts

*Prepared pie crusts in most regular recipes are full of fat, and solid shortenings have lots of trans fat. You can make double batches of this recipe and freeze one crust for later use. Keep the waxed paper on the crust and slip into a large freezer bag. Label, seal, and freeze for up to 3 months. Thaw by standing at room temperature for 30 minutes.*

# Fresh Peach Pie

*This delicious pie must be made with fresh peaches,*
*which come into season in the late summer and fall.*

**Serves 8**

**Calories:** 294.10
**Fat:** 16.41 grams
**Saturated fat:** 5.45 grams
**Dietary fiber:** 1.87 grams
**Sodium:** 186.80 mg
**Cholesterol:** 18.80 mg

*1½ cups graham-cracker crumbs*
*⅓ cup finely chopped walnuts*
*3 tablespoons canola oil*
*2 tablespoons butter or margarine, melted*
*1 (8-ounce) package light cream cheese, softened*
*1 cup powdered sugar*
*1 tablespoon vanilla*
*3 peaches*
*2 tablespoons lemon juice*
*1 cup Cinnamon Granola (page 24)*
*⅓ cup toasted coconut*

1.  In medium bowl, combine cracker crumbs and walnuts and mix well. Add oil and melted butter; stir with fork until crumbly. Press into bottom and up sides of 9" pie pan; place in refrigerator.

2.  In medium bowl, combine cream cheese with powdered sugar and vanilla; beat until light and fluffy. Spoon into bottom of pie crust; spread evenly.

3.  Peel peaches and slice; sprinkle with lemon juice. Arrange over cream cheese filling in pie crust. Top with granola and coconut; cover and chill for at least 4 hours before serving.

## Graham Crackers

*There are several varieties of graham crackers available; you can find them in honey varieties, whole-grain varieties, and low-sodium varieties. About 14 crackers, crushed, equal 1 cup of crumbs. To crush the crackers, place in a large zip-close bag, seal (leaving a small opening), and pound with a rolling pin or meat mallet until crumbs are fine.*

# Lite Creamy Cheesecake

*The secret to this cheesecake is to make sure that the cottage cheese is completely smooth before proceeding with the recipe.*

**Serves 12**

**Calories:** 254.77
**Fat:** 9.11 grams
**Saturated fat:** 4.07 grams
**Dietary fiber:** 0.49 grams
**Sodium:** 206.98 mg
**Cholesterol:** 37.05 mg

1½ cups crushed gingersnap
crumbs
⅓ cup finely chopped walnuts
2 tablespoons butter or
margarine, melted
2 tablespoons orange juice
1½ cups nonfat cottage
cheese
1 cup sugar
¼ cup orange juice
2 tablespoons lemon juice
1 (8-ounce) package light
cream cheese, softened
1 (3-ounce) package nonfat
cream cheese, softened
1 cup nonfat sour cream
1 egg
3 egg whites
¼ cup cornstarch
1 tablespoon vanilla

1. Preheat oven to 350°F. In medium bowl, combine gingersnap crumbs, walnuts, butter, and 2 tablespoons orange juice; mix until even. Press into bottom and up sides of 9" springform pan; set aside in refrigerator.

2. In blender or food processor, combine cottage cheese, sugar, ¼ cup orange juice, and lemon juice; blend or process until very smooth. Scrape down sides and blend or process again.

3. In large mixing bowl, combine both packages of cream cheese and beat until smooth. Add sour cream; beat again until smooth. Add egg and beat well, then add cottage cheese mixture and beat well. Stir in egg whites, cornstarch, and vanilla and beat until smooth.

4. Pour cheese mixture into gingersnap crust. Bake for 50–60 minutes or until cheesecake is set around edges but still soft in center. Remove from oven and place on wire rack; let cool for 1 hour. Cover and refrigerate until cold, at least 4 hours.

# Silken Chocolate Mousse

*This velvety-smooth and rich mousse has the best texture.*
*Top it with some fresh raspberries for the perfect finish.*

**Serves 6**

**Calories:** 219.73
**Fat:** 12.12 grams
**Saturated fat:** 7.86 grams
**Dietary fiber:** 2.13 grams
**Sodium:** 78.14 mg
**Cholesterol:** 11.62 mg

*2 (1-ounce) squares*
  *unsweetened chocolate*
*2 tablespoons butter*
*½ cup sugar*
*1 teaspoon vanilla*
*½ cup satin or silken soft tofu*
*1 cup chocolate frozen yogurt*
*1 cup frozen non-dairy*
  *whipped topping, thawed*

1. Chop chocolate and place in small microwave-safe bowl with the butter. Microwave on medium for 2–4 minutes, stirring twice during cooking time, until chocolate is melted and mixture is smooth. Stir in sugar until sugar dissolves.

2. In blender or food processor, place chocolate mixture and add vanilla and tofu. Blend or process until smooth. If necessary, let cool for 10–15 minutes or until lukewarm.

3. Then add the frozen yogurt and blend or process until smooth. Finally add the whipped topping and blend or process until just mixed. Spoon into serving glasses, cover, and chill for 4–6 hours before serving.

### Silken Tofu

*Make sure that you use silken tofu in this or any other mousse or pudding recipe. Do not use the block type that floats in water. Silken tofu may be packaged in aseptic packaging and stocked on the grocery shelves, not the dairy aisle. All tofu is made of the same ingredients; it's processed differently to make the different types.*

# Peach Granita with Raspberry Coulis

*Granita is made by freezing a liquid and periodically stirring it,
so it freezes in larger crystals and has a grainy texture.*

**Calories:** 162.59
**Fat:** 0.22 grams
**Saturated fat:** 0.02 grams
**Dietary fiber:** 2.49 grams
**Sodium:** 5.15 mg
**Cholesterol:** 0.0 mg

*½ cup orange juice*
*¼ plus ⅓ cup sugar, divided*
*2 peaches, peeled and sliced*
*1½ cups peach nectar*
*1 teaspoon vanilla*
*¼ cup lemon juice, divided*
*1 tablespoon corn syrup*
*1 (10-ounce) package frozen
    raspberries, thawed*
*1 teaspoon vanilla*
*2 tablespoons raspberry
    liqueur*

1. In small pan, combine orange juice and ⅓ cup sugar; bring to a simmer, stirring frequently, until sugar dissolves.

2. In blender or food processor, combine peach slices, nectar, vanilla, and 2 tablespoons lemon juice and corn syrup; blend or process until smooth. Add orange juice mixture; blend or process again until smooth.

3. Pour mixture into 9" square glass pan. Freeze for 1 hour, then remove from freezer and stir. Continue freezing for about 4 hours, stirring the mixture every 30 minutes, until a granular frozen texture forms.

4. In blender or food processor combine raspberries, ¼ cup sugar, remaining 2 tablespoons lemon juice, 1 teaspoon vanilla, and raspberry liqueur, and blend or process until smooth.

5. Stir granita and spoon into dessert cups or goblets. Pour raspberry coulis over and serve immediately.

# Apple-Date Turnovers

*Traditionally, turnovers are made of puff pastry, which is loaded with saturated fat. Using filo dough reduces the fat and increases the crispness.*

**Yields 12 turnovers**

**Calories:** 182.02
**Fat:** 9.01 grams
**Saturated fat:** 3.61 grams
**Dietary fiber:** 1.48 grams
**Sodium:** 99.11 mg
**Cholesterol:** 13.56 mg

*2 Granny Smith apples,
    peeled and chopped*
*½ cup finely chopped dates*
*1 teaspoon lemon juice*
*1 tablespoon flour*
*3 tablespoons brown sugar*
*1½ teaspoons cinnamon,
    divided*
*8 (14" × 18") sheets frozen filo
    dough, thawed*
*½ cup finely chopped walnuts*
*5 tablespoons sugar, divided*
*⅓ cup butter or margarine,
    melted*

1. In medium bowl, combine apples, dates, lemon juice, flour, brown sugar, and 1 teaspoon cinnamon, and mix well; set aside. Place thawed filo dough on work surface and cover with a damp kitchen towel to prevent drying. Work with one sheet at a time. In small bowl, combine walnuts and 3 tablespoons sugar.

2. Lay one sheet filo on work surface; brush with butter. Sprinkle with 2 tablespoons of the walnut mixture. Place another sheet of filo on top, brush with butter, and sprinkle with 1 tablespoon of the walnut mixture. Cut into three 4¾" × 18" strips.

3. Place 2 tablespoons of the apple filling at one end of dough strips. Fold a corner of the dough over the filling so edges match, then continue folding dough as you would fold a flag. Place on ungreased cookie sheets and brush with more butter. Repeat process with remaining strips.

4. Preheat oven to 375°F. In small bowl, combine remaining 2 tablespoons sugar and ½ teaspoon cinnamon and mix well. Sprinkle over turnovers. Bake for 20 to 30 minutes or until pastries are golden brown and crisp. Remove to wire racks to cool.

### Filo Dough

*Filo dough, also called fillo dough or phyllo dough, is paper-thin-layered dough used in Greek cooking. You can find it in the frozen foods aisle of the grocery store. Carefully follow the instructions for thawing and using on the box. The dough dries out in minutes, so be sure to keep it covered with a damp (not wet) towel while you're working with it.*

# Orange Chiffon Pie

*You must start this pie a day ahead of time so the yogurt has a chance to thicken. It's tart, smooth, and creamy.*

**Serves 8**

**Calories:** 322.70
**Fat:** 9.89 grams
**Saturated fat:** 3.20 grams
**Dietary fiber:** 1.38 grams
**Sodium:** 162.24 mg
**Cholesterol:** 3.62 mg

*2 cups vanilla yogurt*
*1 (3-ounce) package orange-flavored gelatin*
*¼ cup sugar*
*1 (15-ounce) can mandarin oranges*
*½ cup orange juice*
*1 cup nonfat frozen whipped topping, thawed*
*1 Loco Pie Crust (page 294), baked and cooled*
*3 tablespoons toasted coconut*

1. The day before, line a strainer with cheesecloth or a coffee filter. Place the strainer in a large bowl and add the yogurt. Cover and refrigerate overnight. The next day, place the thickened yogurt in a large bowl. Discard the liquid, or whey.

2. In medium bowl, combine gelatin and sugar. Drain oranges, reserving juice. In small pan, heat reserved juice over high heat until it boils. Pour over gelatin mixture; stir until gelatin and sugar are dissolved. Add orange juice and refrigerate for 30 minutes.

3. Beat the thickened yogurt and gradually add orange-juice mixture, beating until smooth. Add the drained oranges and fold in the whipped topping. Pour into pie crust and top with coconut. Cover and refrigerate for at least 4 hours before serving.

# Chocolate Granola Pie

*This fabulous and rich pie is packed full of fiber, but you'd never know it! Serve it at your next dinner party.*

1. Preheat oven to 350°F. In large saucepan, combine butter and chocolate. Melt over low heat, stirring frequently, until smooth. Remove from heat and add brown sugar, corn syrup, vanilla, egg, and egg whites and beat well until blended.

2. Stir in granola and pour into pie crust. Bake for 40–50 minutes or until filling is set and pie crust is deep golden brown. Let cool completely and serve.

### Dark Chocolate

*There is evidence that chocolate may be good for you, but dark chocolate only, please! Chocolate contains compounds called flavonoids which may help prevent cancer and heart disease. And the saturated fat in chocolate is stearic acid, a fatty acid which does not raise blood cholesterol levels. Chocolate contains a monounsaturated fat, oleic acid, which actually helps lower blood cholesterol levels.*

**Serves 12**

**Calories:** 384.56
**Fat:** 14.45 grams
**Saturated fat:** 4.65 grams
**Dietary fiber:** 3.56 grams
**Sodium:** 137.51 mg
**Cholesterol:** 25.70 mg

*3 tablespoons butter or margarine*
*2 (1-ounce) squares unsweetened chocolate, chopped*
*¾ cup brown sugar*
*½ cup dark corn syrup*
*2 teaspoons vanilla*
*1 egg*
*3 egg whites*
*2 cups Cinnamon Granola (page 24)*
*1 Loco Pie Crust (page 294), unbaked*

# Lemon Floating Island

*"Floating island" refers to the poached egg-white mixture that "floats" on the lemon mousse. This is a low-fat version of lemon meringue pie. Yum!*

**Serves 4**

**Calories:** 295.74
**Fat:** 0.80 grams
**Saturated fat:** 0.45 grams
**Dietary fiber:** 0.36 grams
**Sodium:** 190.06 mg
**Cholesterol:** 2.65 mg

*2 cups milk*
*6 egg whites*
*2 tablespoons lemon juice*
*½ cup sugar*
*Pinch salt*
*6 tablespoons crushed hard lemon candies, divided*
*1 recipe Lemon Mousse (page 286)*

1. Preheat oven to 275°F. In large skillet, place milk and bring to a simmer over medium heat. Reduce heat to low.

2. Meanwhile, in large bowl combine egg whites and lemon juice; beat until foamy. Gradually add sugar and salt, beating until very stiff peaks form. Fold in 3 tablespoons of the crushed candies.

3. With a large spoon, scoop out about ¼ cup of the egg white mixture and gently place in the simmering milk. Poach for 2 minutes, then carefully turn each meringue and poach for another 2 minutes. Remove from heat, drain briefly on kitchen towel, and place on Silpat-lined cookie sheets. Repeat with remaining egg white mixture.

4. Bake meringues for 12–16 minutes or until they puff slightly and start to turn light golden brown. Remove and refrigerate, uncovered, for 1–2 hours before serving.

5. When you prepare the Lemon Mousse, spoon the mousse into individual custard cups; chill until firm. Top each with a poached meringue, sprinkle with remaining 3 tablespoons crushed candies, and serve immediately.

# Whole-Wheat Chocolate Chip Cookies

*Fill your cookie jar with these excellent cookies! They're high in fiber yet studded with delicious dark-chocolate nuggets.*

1. Preheat oven to 375°F. Line cookie sheets with parchment paper or Silpat silicone liners and set aside.

2. In large bowl, combine butter, brown sugar, and applesauce and beat well until smooth. Add vanilla, egg, and egg whites and beat until combined.

3. Add flour, oatmeal, baking soda, and salt and mix until a dough forms. Fold in chocolate chips and hazelnuts.

4. Drop dough by rounded teaspoons onto prepared cookie sheets. Bake for 7–10 minutes or until cookies are light golden brown and set. Let cool for 5 minutes before removing from cookie sheet to wire rack to cool.

### Whole-Wheat Pastry Flour

*Whole-wheat pastry flour isn't the same as whole-wheat flour; it's slightly lighter and finer for baking. You can find it in specialty stores and online. You can substitute plain whole-wheat flour if you can't find the pastry flour, but use 2 tablespoons less per cup. With plain flour, the product will be denser, with a stronger flavor.*

**Yields 48 cookies**

**Calories:** 114.86
**Fat:** 4.89 grams
**Saturated fat:** 2.04 grams
**Dietary fiber:** 1.62 grams
**Sodium:** 26.49 mg
**Cholesterol:** 6.95 mg

¼ cup butter or plant sterol margarine, softened
1½ cups brown sugar
½ cup applesauce
1 tablespoon vanilla
1 egg
2 egg whites
2½ cups whole-wheat pastry flour
½ cup ground oatmeal
1 teaspoon baking soda
¼ teaspoon salt
2 cups special dark chocolate chips
1 cup chopped hazelnuts

# Oatmeal Brownies

*Ground oatmeal, prune puree, and finely chopped dates add
great chewy texture (and fiber) to these easy brownies.*

**Yields 16 brownies**

**Calories:** 153.83
**Fat:** 4.88 grams
**Saturated fat:** 2.63 grams
**Dietary fiber:** 2.54 grams
**Sodium:** 63.58 mg
**Cholesterol:** 17.39 mg

¼ cup prune puree
¼ cup finely chopped dates
½ cup all-purpose flour
½ cup ground oatmeal
½ cup cocoa powder
½ teaspoon baking soda
½ cup brown sugar
¼ cup sugar
1 egg
1 egg white
¼ cup chocolate yogurt
2 teaspoons vanilla
2 tablespoons butter or plant
    sterol margarine, melted
½ cup dark-chocolate chips

1. Preheat oven to 350°F. Spray an 8" square baking pan with nonstick cooking spray containing flour and set aside.

2. In small bowl, combine prune puree and dates; mix well and set aside. In large bowl, combine flour, oatmeal, cocoa, baking soda, brown sugar, and sugar, and mix well.

3. Add egg, egg white, yogurt, vanilla, and butter to prune mixture and mix well. Add to flour mixture and stir just until blended. Spoon into prepared pan and smooth top. Bake for 22–30 minutes or until edges are set but the center is still slightly soft. Remove from oven and place on wire rack.

4. In microwave-safe bowl, place chocolate chips. Microwave on 50 percent power for 1 minute, then remove and stir. Microwave for 30 seconds longer, then stir. If necessary, repeat microwave process until chips are melted. Pour over warm brownies and gently spread to cover. Let cool completely and cut into bars.

# Butterscotch Meringues

*The candies have to be very finely crushed for best results.*
*This simple little cookie is loaded with flavor.*

**Yields 30 cookies**

**Calories:** 29.39
**Fat:** 0.06 grams
**Saturated fat:** 0.04 grams
**Dietary fiber:** 0.0 grams
**Sodium:** 17.97 mg
**Cholesterol:** 0.16 mg

*3 egg whites*
*Pinch of salt*
*¼ teaspoon cream of tartar*
*⅔ cup sugar*
*2 tablespoons brown sugar*
*10 round hard butterscotch*
    *candies, finely crushed*

1. Preheat oven to 250°F. In large bowl, beat egg whites with salt and cream of tartar until foamy. Gradually beat in sugar and brown sugar until stiff peaks form and sugar is dissolved. Fold in the finely crushed candies.

2. Drop by teaspoonfuls onto a baking sheet lined with aluminum foil or Silpat liners. Bake for 50–60 minutes or until meringues are set and crisp and very light golden brown. Cool on the cookie sheets for 3 minutes, then carefully peel off the foil and place on wire racks to cool.

## Meringues

*Meringues can be flavored in many ways. If you have a favorite hard candy, use that to make these little treats. Just change the other ingredients slightly to enhance that flavor. For instance, if you want to make peppermint meringues, use all granulated sugar and add a drop of peppermint extract.*

# Blueberry-Hazelnut Crisp

*Blueberries are so good for you; enjoy them warm*
*in this crisp with some vanilla frozen yogurt.*

**Serves 8**

**Calories:** 373.56
**Fat:** 14.57 grams
**Saturated fat:** 5.59 grams
**Dietary fiber:** 6.04 grams
**Sodium:** 61.35 mg
**Cholesterol:** 20.34 mg

*3 cups blueberries*
*¼ cup sugar*
*1 teaspoon cinnamon*
*½ teaspoon nutmeg*
*1½ cups quick-cooking*
 *oatmeal*
*½ cup flour*
*¼ cup whole-wheat flour*
*½ cup brown sugar*
*½ cup chopped hazelnuts*
*⅓ cup butter or margarine,*
 *melted*

1. Preheat oven to 350°F. Spray a 9" round cake pan with nonstick cooking spray and set aside.

2. Combine blueberries in medium bowl with sugar, cinnamon, and nutmeg. Spoon into prepared pan.

3. In same bowl, combine oatmeal, flour, whole-wheat flour, brown sugar, and hazelnuts and mix well. Add melted butter and mix until crumbly. Sprinkle over fruit in dish.

4. Bake for 35–45 minutes or until fruit bubbles and topping is browned and crisp. Let cool for 15 minutes before serving.

# Appendix A
# Glossary

### Amino acid
The molecules that make up proteins. There are 20 amino acids the body needs; most are provided by food in various combinations.

### Antioxidants
Molecules that prevent oxidation, or the removal of an electron by an oxidizing agent. Antioxidants include vitamins C, A, and E.

### Atherosclerosis
From the Greek roots *athero,* meaning paste, and *sclerosis,* meaning hardness; signifies the formation of plaque on artery walls and hardening of the arteries.

### Bake
To cook in an oven using dry heat. Baked goods include bread, casseroles, pastries, cookies, and cakes.

### Beat
To mix vigorously to help incorporate air into a mixture.

### Bile salts
Steroids made from cholesterol, which aid in fat digestions. They are produced in the liver and stored in the gall bladder until they are needed in the intestines after a meal.

### Blood
A liquid, known as plasma, that carries cells like white blood cells, red blood cells, and platelets. Blood is drawn and tested to measure cholesterol levels and ratios.

### Blood cholesterol
The amount of cholesterol in your blood. Doctors measure the total blood cholesterol amounts, HDL levels, LDL levels, and the ratio between them.

### Blood clot
Clumps of material that occur when blood coagulates, or changes from a liquid to a solid. They can form in response to an injury in a blood vessel, inflammation, or from plaque.

### Calories
A measure of energy. One calorie is the amount of energy needed to raise the temperature of a kilogram of water by 1 degree Celsius. The number of calories in a food indicate the amount of energy needed to burn it off.

### Carbohydrates
Strings of simple sugars. Starch, glycogen, and cellulose are made of a string of six or

more simple sugars, or monosaccharides. A carbohydrate provides 4 calories per gram.

## Cholesterol
A combination of alcohol and sterol molecules that is necessary to life. The liver produces cholesterol, which is used to make steroids and bile salts.

## Dietary cholesterol
The cholesterol found in food. Since cholesterol is made in the liver, only animals and animal products contain cholesterol.

## Fat
A compound found in animal and vegetable products. It provides 9 calories per gram. Fat includes essential fatty acids, compounds necessary to life that the body does not produce.

## Fiber
Fiber is found in plants. Your body can't digest fiber; it's used to increase satiety and help regularity. It can also help remove cholesterol from the intestines.

## Flavonoid
Molecules found in fruits, vegetables, soy, and tea that have antioxidant benefits. They include isoflavones, anthocyanidins, and flavonols.

## Folate
The natural form of folic acid, found in leafy green vegetables, wheat germ, and beans. It lowers levels of homocysteine in the blood, which lowers the risk of heart disease.

## Free radical
Formed when molecules with weak bonds split unevenly, leaving an unpaired electron. These unstable molecules react with other compounds, attacking stable molecules. This disrupts cell function.

## Homocysteine
An amino acid attached to a sulfur molecule that occurs in the blood. A high level of homocysteine (about 100 micromoles per liter) is considered severe and a high risk for heart disease.

## Hypertension
Also called high blood pressure, a condition in which the pressure of the blood flowing through arteries is elevated. It is a risk factor for stroke and heart disease.

## Inflammation
Now thought to be a contributor to heart disease. Inflammation is the body's response to an injury. In arterial walls, inflammation can lead to the formation of plaque and blood clots.

## Lignan
A phytoestrogen, found in flaxseed, soybeans, and broccoli. It acts like an antioxidant in the body, reducing the risk of heart disease.

## Lipid

A class of hydrocarbon molecules that are used to store energy in the body. Fat is a subgroup of lipids.

## Liver

An organ in the body that controls waste and aids digestion. The liver removes toxins and waste products from the body and sends them to the intestines for excretion. The liver also manufactures cholesterol.

## Lp(a)

A genetic version of LDL cholesterol that is very prone to oxidation and may increase fatty deposits on artery walls.

## Mediterranean diet

A diet common in the countries surrounding the Mediterranean Sea. This diet is rich in fruits, vegetables, whole grains, olive oil, nuts, and pasta, and is considered one of the healthiest in the world.

## Monounsaturated fats

A fat that is missing one hydrogen molecule, resulting in one double bond between carbon atoms. This fat is usually liquid, and is found in nuts and oils.

## Nutrients

A molecule or compound used by the body for growth, repair, and development. Nutrients include vitamins, minerals, protein, carbohydrates, and fat.

## Omega-3 fatty acids

An essential fatty acid that must be obtained from food. *Omega-3* refers to the position of the double bonds, on the third carbon bond. May reduce the risk of coronary heart disease.

## Omega-6 fatty acids

Another essential fatty acid obtained from food. The double bond is on the sixth carbon molecule. Too much of this fatty acid can increase the risk of disease. Omega-6 fatty acids are very common in foods.

## Plant sterols

Present in fruits, nuts, seeds, and legumes, these compounds resemble cholesterol in structure. Plant sterols help reduce blood cholesterol levels, but there isn't enough in food to have significant effect. Modified forms are included in fatty foods like margarine.

## Plaque

An accumulation of substances, usually cholesterol and other fats, on the inner walls of blood vessels. Too much plaque can narrow the artery, leading to a heart attack, or break off to form a blood clot.

## Polyunsaturated fat

A fat that is liquid at room temperature. This fat is missing some hydrogen atoms, creating double bonds between some carbon atoms.

### Protein

The building block of life. Proteins are large compounds made up of amino acids. Found in all living organisms, protein provides 4 calories per gram.

### Risk factor

A variable that increases the probability of disease. Risk factors for heart disease include high blood pressure, obesity, age, smoking, high cholesterol levels, and high LDL cholesterol levels.

### Saturated fat

A fat that is solid at room temperature. All of the carbon molecules in the fat have hydrogen molecules attached, with no double bonds.

### Side effects

Physical effects that can occur with treatment for diseases, especially with prescription drugs. Usually an undesirable effect.

### Sodium

A chemical element essential to life found in most foods. Too much sodium can increase the risk of hypertension and heart disease.

### Soluble fiber

Dietary fiber that is soluble in water and forms a gel when combined with water. Soluble fiber can help reduce cholesterol levels by removing LDL cholesterol from the intestines.

### Statins

Drugs that reduce blood cholesterol levels by inhibiting an enzyme used in their production. They have some significant side effects.

### Trans fat

A fat produced by ruminant animals, also made artificially by bubbling hydrogen through unsaturated fats. The position of the hydrogen molecules is on opposite sides of the carbon chain, which straightens the chain and makes the fat solid at room temperature.

### Triglycerides

The form fat takes in the body as it moves in the blood and from cell to cell. They are made from excess calories.

### Vitamins

Molecules that act as catalysts in metabolic reactions in the body necessary for growth, repair, and development. There are fat-soluble and water-soluble vitamins, all necessary for health.

# Appendix B
# Resources

## Books

**Betty Crocker Healthy Heart Cookbook,** *by Betty Crocker (Betty Crocker Books)*
The home economists at General Mills partnered with the Johns Hopkins Ciccarone Center for the Prevention of Heart Disease to create delicious and healthy recipes for your heart.

**The Diabetes and Healthy Heart Cookbook,** *by the American Heart Association (McGraw-Hill)*
The American Heart Association and American Diabetes Association joined forces to create this book especially for diabetics at risk for heart disease.

**The American Heart Association Low-Fat, Low-Cholesterol Cookbook,** *by the American Heart Association (Clarkson Potter)*
Updated health information with fifty recipes to help you control your cholesterol levels.

**The American Heart Association Meals in Minutes Cookbook** *(Clarkson Potter)*
This book offers more than 200 low-cholesterol, low-fat recipes that are quick to make.

**The New Mayo Clinic Cookbook—Eating Well for Better Health,** *by Cheryl Forberg, Maureen Calahan Donald, M.D., et al. (Oxmoor Press)*
Winner of the 2005 Health category award from the James Beard Foundation, this book offers eating and dieting strategies, shopping, menu advice, and recipes.

# Web Sites

### Ediets.com
✎ *www.ediets.com*

This is an online weight-loss community that helps with personalized diet plans, meal planning, lots of recipes, and support.

### American Heart Association
✎ *www.americanheart.org*

This site has lots of information about heart disease diagnosis and prevention, including diet and exercise advice.

### Go Red For Women
✎ *www.goredforwomen.org*

This site is dedicated women's heart health.

### Cholesterol About.com
✎ *http://cholesterol.about.com*

This site provides basic information about cholesterol, what it does in the body and how to lower cholesterol counts and improve HDL/LDL ratios.

### Low-Fat Cooking About.com
✎ *http://lowfatcooking.about.com*

Site provides information about healthy fats and low-fat cooking along with many recipes.

# Magazines and Newsletters

### *Harvard's Women's Health Newsletter (Harvard University Press)*

This publication provides reports on many diet/nutritional studies related to women's health.

### *Wellness Letter (University of California, Berkeley)*

Both online and by subscription, this provides the latest in health news, including all of the nutritional studies worth reporting.

### *Cooking Light* Magazine

This magazine provides low-fat recipes with a nutritional analysis per serving.

### *Men's Health* Magazine

Available at news stand and by subscription, this magazine carries four to five feature stories a month on nutrition.

# Appendix C
# Menus

Menu planning can be a lot of fun as long as you consider color, taste, temperature, and flavor. All should be balanced. Make your plates as colorful as possible for the best nutrition. And when planning a menu for guests, be sure to ask about food preferences and allergies.

### Dinner for the Boss

Roasted Garlic Bread

Citrus-Blueberry Fish en Papillote

Oat-Bran Dinner Rolls

Red-Lettuce Jicama Salad

Snow Peas with Shallots

Strawberry-Mango Meringue Pie

### Breakfast on the Run

Apple-Cinnamon Smoothie

Good-Morning Muffins

Cranberry-Cornmeal Muffins

### Lunch on the Porch

Spring Asparagus Soup

Savory Zucchini Muffins

Crab Edamame Salad

Chocolate Granola Pie

### Christmas Eve Dinner

Fig Crostini with Prosciutto

Five-Onion Soup

Light Yeast Rolls

Filet Mignon with Capers

Citrus Shimmer

Roasted-Garlic Corn

Fennel-and-Orange Salad

Lite Creamy Cheesecake

### Simple Entertaining

Fresh Creamy Fruit Dip

Almond Snapper with
  Shrimp Sauce

Arugula Salad with
  Marinated Mushrooms

Sesame-Roasted Vegetables

Silken Chocolate Mousse

## Dessert Party

Peach Melba Parfait

Butterscotch Meringues

Strawberry-Rhubarb Parfaits

Crepes with Poached Pears

Blueberry Cloud

Apple-Date Turnovers

## Appetizer Buffet

Hawaiian Chicken Skewers

Greek Quesadillas

Salmon Pâté

Creamy Garlic Hummus

Super Spicy Salsa

High-Fiber Guacamole

Yogurt Cheese Balls

Lemon Floating Island

## Birthday Dinner

Flank Steak with Mango Salsa

Seeded Breadsticks

Cucumber-Mango Salad

Sautéed Fennel with Lemon

Mango Walnut Upside-Down Cake

## Memorial Day Cookout

Asian Beef Kabobs

Pasta Salad with Crunchy Vegetables

Green Grapes with Lemon Sorbet

## Picnic in the Park

New-Potato Salad

Waldorf-Salad Sandwiches

Oatmeal Brownies

## Cozy Dinner at Home

Lemon Bruschetta with Chopped Olives

Dark Dinner Rolls

Chicken Paillards with Mushrooms

Fennel-and-Orange Salad

Gingered Sugar-Snap Peas

Apple Pear-Nut Crisp

## Brown Bag Lunch

Turkey-Tomato Hoagie Sandwiches

Wheat-Berry Salad

Whole-Wheat Chocolate Chip Cookies

## Christmas Morning Breakfast

Chocolate Pancakes

Spicy Raspberry Spread

Prosciutto Fruit Omelet

Whole-Wheat Cinnamon Platters

# Index

# THE EVERYTHING SERIES!

## BUSINESS & PERSONAL FINANCE

Everything® Accounting Book
Everything® Budgeting Book
Everything® Business Planning Book
**Everything® Coaching and Mentoring Book, 2nd Ed.**
Everything® Fundraising Book
Everything® Get Out of Debt Book
Everything® Grant Writing Book
**Everything® Guide to Foreclosures**
Everything® Guide to Personal Finance for Single Mothers
Everything® Home-Based Business Book, 2nd Ed.
Everything® Homebuying Book, 2nd Ed.
Everything® Homeselling Book, 2nd Ed.
Everything® Improve Your Credit Book
Everything® Investing Book, 2nd Ed.
Everything® Landlording Book
Everything® Leadership Book
Everything® Managing People Book, 2nd Ed.
Everything® Negotiating Book
Everything® Online Auctions Book
Everything® Online Business Book
Everything® Personal Finance Book
Everything® Personal Finance in Your 20s and 30s Book
Everything® Project Management Book
Everything® Real Estate Investing Book
Everything® Retirement Planning Book
Everything® Robert's Rules Book, $7.95
Everything® Selling Book
Everything® Start Your Own Business Book, 2nd Ed.
Everything® Wills & Estate Planning Book

## COOKING

Everything® Barbecue Cookbook
**Everything® Bartender's Book, 2nd Ed., $9.95**
**Everything® Calorie Counting Cookbook**
Everything® Cheese Book
Everything® Chinese Cookbook
Everything® Classic Recipes Book
Everything® Cocktail Parties & Drinks Book
Everything® College Cookbook
Everything® Cooking for Baby and Toddler Book
Everything® Cooking for Two Cookbook
Everything® Diabetes Cookbook
Everything® Easy Gourmet Cookbook
Everything® Fondue Cookbook
Everything® Fondue Party Book
Everything® Gluten-Free Cookbook
Everything® Glycemic Index Cookbook
Everything® Grilling Cookbook
Everything® Healthy Meals in Minutes Cookbook
Everything® Holiday Cookbook

Everything® Indian Cookbook
Everything® Italian Cookbook
Everything® Low-Carb Cookbook
**Everything® Low-Cholesterol Cookbook**
Everything® Low-Fat High-Flavor Cookbook
Everything® Low-Salt Cookbook
Everything® Meals for a Month Cookbook
Everything® Mediterranean Cookbook
Everything® Mexican Cookbook
Everything® No Trans Fat Cookbook
Everything® One-Pot Cookbook
Everything® Pizza Cookbook
Everything® Quick and Easy 30-Minute,
    5-Ingredient Cookbook
Everything® Quick Meals Cookbook
Everything® Slow Cooker Cookbook
Everything® Slow Cooking for a Crowd Cookbook
Everything® Soup Cookbook
Everything® Stir-Fry Cookbook
**Everything® Sugar-Free Cookbook**
**Everything® Tapas and Small Plates Cookbook**
Everything® Tex-Mex Cookbook
Everything® Thai Cookbook
Everything® Vegetarian Cookbook
Everything® Wild Game Cookbook
Everything® Wine Book, 2nd Ed.

## GAMES

Everything® 15-Minute Sudoku Book, $9.95
Everything® 30-Minute Sudoku Book, $9.95
**Everything® Bible Crosswords Book, $9.95**
Everything® Blackjack Strategy Book
Everything® Brain Strain Book, $9.95
Everything® Bridge Book
Everything® Card Games Book
Everything® Card Tricks Book, $9.95
Everything® Casino Gambling Book, 2nd Ed.
Everything® Chess Basics Book
Everything® Craps Strategy Book
Everything® Crossword and Puzzle Book
Everything® Crossword Challenge Book
Everything® Crosswords for the Beach Book, $9.95
**Everything® Cryptic Crosswords Book, $9.95**
Everything® Cryptograms Book, $9.95
Everything® Easy Crosswords Book
Everything® Easy Kakuro Book, $9.95
Everything® Easy Large-Print Crosswords Book
Everything® Games Book, 2nd Ed.
Everything® Giant Sudoku Book, $9.95
Everything® Kakuro Challenge Book, $9.95
Everything® Large-Print Crossword Challenge Book
Everything® Large-Print Crosswords Book
Everything® Lateral Thinking Puzzles Book, $9.95

Everything® Literary Crosswords Book, $9.95
Everything® Mazes Book
**Everything® Memory Booster Puzzles Book, $9.95**
Everything® Movie Crosswords Book, $9.95
**Everything® Music Crosswords Book, $9.95**
Everything® Online Poker Book, $12.95
Everything® Pencil Puzzles Book, $9.95
Everything® Poker Strategy Book
Everything® Pool & Billiards Book
**Everything® Puzzles for Commuters Book, $9.95**
Everything® Sports Crosswords Book, $9.95
Everything® Test Your IQ Book, $9.95
Everything® Texas Hold 'Em Book, $9.95
Everything® Travel Crosswords Book, $9.95
**Everything® TV Crosswords Book, $9.95**
Everything® Word Games Challenge Book
Everything® Word Scramble Book
Everything® Word Search Book

## HEALTH

Everything® Alzheimer's Book
Everything® Diabetes Book
Everything® Health Guide to Adult Bipolar Disorder
**Everything® Health Guide to Arthritis**
Everything® Health Guide to Controlling Anxiety
Everything® Health Guide to Fibromyalgia
**Everything® Health Guide to Menopause**
**Everything® Health Guide to OCD**
**Everything® Health Guide to PMS**
Everything® Health Guide to Postpartum Care
Everything® Health Guide to Thyroid Disease
Everything® Hypnosis Book
Everything® Low Cholesterol Book
Everything® Nutrition Book
Everything® Reflexology Book
Everything® Stress Management Book

## HISTORY

Everything® American Government Book
Everything® American History Book, 2nd Ed.
Everything® Civil War Book
Everything® Freemasons Book
Everything® Irish History & Heritage Book
Everything® Middle East Book
Everything® World War II Book, 2nd Ed.

## HOBBIES

Everything® Candlemaking Book
Everything® Cartooning Book
Everything® Coin Collecting Book
Everything® Drawing Book

Everything® Family Tree Book, 2nd Ed.
Everything® Knitting Book
Everything® Knots Book
Everything® Photography Book
Everything® Quilting Book
Everything® Sewing Book
Everything® Soapmaking Book, 2nd Ed.
Everything® Woodworking Book

## HOME IMPROVEMENT

Everything® Feng Shui Book
Everything® Feng Shui Decluttering Book, $9.95
Everything® Fix-It Book
**Everything® Green Living Book**
Everything® Home Decorating Book
Everything® Home Storage Solutions Book
Everything® Homebuilding Book
**Everything® Organize Your Home Book, 2nd Ed.**

## KIDS' BOOKS

All titles are $7.95
Everything® Kids' Animal Puzzle & Activity Book
Everything® Kids' Baseball Book, 4th Ed.
Everything® Kids' Bible Trivia Book
Everything® Kids' Bugs Book
Everything® Kids' Cars and Trucks Puzzle and Activity Book
Everything® Kids' Christmas Puzzle & Activity Book
Everything® Kids' Cookbook
Everything® Kids' Crazy Puzzles Book
Everything® Kids' Dinosaurs Book
**Everything® Kids' Environment Book**
**Everything® Kids' Fairies Puzzle and Activity Book**
Everything® Kids' First Spanish Puzzle and Activity Book
Everything® Kids' Gross Cookbook
Everything® Kids' Gross Hidden Pictures Book
Everything® Kids' Gross Jokes Book
Everything® Kids' Gross Mazes Book
Everything® Kids' Gross Puzzle & Activity Book
Everything® Kids' Halloween Puzzle & Activity Book
Everything® Kids' Hidden Pictures Book
Everything® Kids' Horses Book
Everything® Kids' Joke Book
Everything® Kids' Knock Knock Book
Everything® Kids' Learning Spanish Book
**Everything® Kids' Magical Science Experiments Book**
Everything® Kids' Math Puzzles Book
Everything® Kids' Mazes Book
Everything® Kids' Money Book
Everything® Kids' Nature Book
Everything® Kids' Pirates Puzzle and Activity Book
Everything® Kids' Presidents Book
Everything® Kids' Princess Puzzle and Activity Book
Everything® Kids' Puzzle Book
**Everything® Kids' Racecars Puzzle and Activity Book**
Everything® Kids' Riddles & Brain Teasers Book
Everything® Kids' Science Experiments Book
Everything® Kids' Sharks Book

Everything® Kids' Soccer Book
**Everything® Kids' Spies Puzzle and Activity Book**
Everything® Kids' States Book
Everything® Kids' Travel Activity Book

## KIDS' STORY BOOKS

Everything® Fairy Tales Book

## LANGUAGE

Everything® Conversational Japanese Book with CD, $19.95
Everything® French Grammar Book
Everything® French Phrase Book, $9.95
Everything® French Verb Book, $9.95
Everything® German Practice Book with CD, $19.95
Everything® Inglés Book
Everything® Intermediate Spanish Book with CD, $19.95
**Everything® Italian Practice Book with CD, $19.95**
Everything® Learning Brazilian Portuguese Book with CD, $19.95
**Everything® Learning French Book with CD, 2nd Ed., $19.95**
Everything® Learning German Book
Everything® Learning Italian Book
Everything® Learning Latin Book
**Everything® Learning Russian Book with CD, $19.95**
Everything® Learning Spanish Book with CD, 2nd Ed., $19.95
Everything® Russian Practice Book with CD, $19.95
Everything® Sign Language Book
Everything® Spanish Grammar Book
Everything® Spanish Phrase Book, $9.95
Everything® Spanish Practice Book with CD, $19.95
Everything® Spanish Verb Book, $9.95
Everything® Speaking Mandarin Chinese Book with CD, $19.95

## MUSIC

Everything® Drums Book with CD, $19.95
Everything® Guitar Book with CD, 2nd Ed., $19.95
Everything® Guitar Chords Book with CD, $19.95
Everything® Home Recording Book
Everything® Music Theory Book with CD, $19.95
Everything® Reading Music Book with CD, $19.95
Everything® Rock & Blues Guitar Book with CD, $19.95
Everything® Rock and Blues Piano Book with CD, $19.95
Everything® Songwriting Book

## NEW AGE

Everything® Astrology Book, 2nd Ed.
Everything® Birthday Personology Book
Everything® Dreams Book, 2nd Ed.
Everything® Love Signs Book, $9.95
**Everything® Love Spells Book, $9.95**
Everything® Numerology Book
Everything® Paganism Book
Everything® Palmistry Book
Everything® Psychic Book
Everything® Reiki Book
Everything® Sex Signs Book, $9.95

**Everything® Spells & Charms Book, 2nd Ed.**
Everything® Tarot Book, 2nd Ed.
Everything® Toltec Wisdom Book
Everything® Wicca and Witchcraft Book

## PARENTING

Everything® Baby Names Book, 2nd Ed.
**Everything® Baby Shower Book, 2nd Ed.**
Everything® Baby's First Year Book
Everything® Birthing Book
Everything® Breastfeeding Book
Everything® Father-to-Be Book
Everything® Father's First Year Book
**Everything® Get Ready for Baby Book, 2nd Ed.**
Everything® Get Your Baby to Sleep Book, $9.95
Everything® Getting Pregnant Book
**Everything® Guide to Pregnancy Over 35**
Everything® Guide to Raising a One-Year-Old
Everything® Guide to Raising a Two-Year-Old
**Everything® Guide to Raising Adolescent Boys**
**Everything® Guide to Raising Adolescent Girls**
Everything® Homeschooling Book
Everything® Mother's First Year Book
Everything® Parent's Guide to Childhood Illnesses
Everything® Parent's Guide to Children and Divorce
Everything® Parent's Guide to Children with ADD/ADHD
Everything® Parent's Guide to Children with Asperger's Syndrome
Everything® Parent's Guide to Children with Autism
Everything® Parent's Guide to Children with Bipolar Disorder
Everything® Parent's Guide to Children with Depression
Everything® Parent's Guide to Children with Dyslexia
Everything® Parent's Guide to Children with Juvenile Diabetes
Everything® Parent's Guide to Positive Discipline
Everything® Parent's Guide to Raising a Successful Child
Everything® Parent's Guide to Raising Boys
Everything® Parent's Guide to Raising Girls
Everything® Parent's Guide to Raising Siblings
Everything® Parent's Guide to Sensory Integration Disorder
Everything® Parent's Guide to Tantrums
Everything® Parent's Guide to the Strong-Willed Child
Everything® Parenting a Teenager Book
Everything® Potty Training Book, $9.95
Everything® Pregnancy Book, 3rd Ed.
Everything® Pregnancy Fitness Book
Everything® Pregnancy Nutrition Book
Everything® Pregnancy Organizer, 2nd Ed., $16.95
Everything® Toddler Activities Book
Everything® Toddler Book
Everything® Tween Book
Everything® Twins, Triplets, and More Book

## PETS

Everything® Aquarium Book
Everything® Boxer Book
Everything® Cat Book, 2nd Ed.
Everything® Chihuahua Book

Everything® **Cooking for Dogs Book**
Everything® Dachshund Book
Everything® Dog Book
Everything® Dog Health Book
Everything® Dog Obedience Book
Everything® Dog Owner's Organizer, $16.95
Everything® Dog Training and Tricks Book
Everything® German Shepherd Book
Everything® Golden Retriever Book
Everything® Horse-Book
Everything® Horse Care Book
Everything® Horseback Riding Book
Everything® Labrador Retriever Book
Everything® Poodle Book
Everything® Pug Book
Everything® Puppy Book
Everything® Rottweiler Book
Everything® Small Dogs Book
Everything® Tropical Fish Book
Everything® Yorkshire Terrier Book

## REFERENCE

Everything® American Presidents Book
Everything® Blogging Book
Everything® Build Your Vocabulary Book
Everything® Car Care Book
Everything® Classical Mythology Book
Everything® Da Vinci Book
Everything® Divorce Book
Everything® Einstein Book
Everything® Enneagram Book
Everything® Etiquette Book, 2nd Ed.
Everything® **Guide to Edgar Allan Poe**
Everything® Inventions and Patents Book
Everything® Mafia Book
Everything® **Martin Luther King Jr. Book**
Everything® Philosophy Book
Everything® Pirates Book
Everything® Psychology Book

## RELIGION

Everything® Angels Book
Everything® Bible Book
Everything® **Bible Study Book with CD, $19.95**
Everything® Buddhism Book
Everything® Catholicism Book
Everything® Christianity Book
Everything® Gnostic Gospels Book
Everything® History of the Bible Book
Everything® Jesus Book
Everything® Jewish History & Heritage Book
Everything® Judaism Book
Everything® Kabbalah Book
Everything® Koran Book

Everything® Mary Book
Everything® Mary Magdalene Book
Everything® Prayer Book
Everything® Saints Book, 2nd Ed.
Everything® Torah Book
Everything® Understanding Islam Book
Everything® **Women of the Bible Book**
Everything® World's Religions Book
Everything® Zen Book

## SCHOOL & CAREERS

Everything® Alternative Careers Book
Everything® Career Tests Book
Everything® College Major Test Book
Everything® College Survival Book, 2nd Ed.
Everything® Cover Letter Book, 2nd Ed.
Everything® Filmmaking Book
Everything® Get-a-Job Book, 2nd Ed.
Everything® Guide to Being a Paralegal
Everything® Guide to Being a Personal Trainer
Everything® Guide to Being a Real Estate Agent
Everything® Guide to Being a Sales Rep
Everything® **Guide to Being an Event Planner**
Everything® Guide to Careers in Health Care
Everything® Guide to Careers in Law Enforcement
Everything® Guide to Government Jobs
Everything® **Guide to Starting and Running a Catering Business**
Everything® Guide to Starting and Running a Restaurant
Everything® Job Interview Book
Everything® New Nurse Book
Everything® New Teacher Book
Everything® Paying for College Book
Everything® Practice Interview Book
Everything® Resume Book, 2nd Ed.
Everything® Study Book

## SELF-HELP

Everything® **Body Language Book**
Everything® Dating Book, 2nd Ed.
Everything® Great Sex Book
Everything® Self-Esteem Book
Everything® Tantric Sex Book

## SPORTS & FITNESS

Everything® Easy Fitness Book
Everything® **Krav Maga for Fitness Book**
Everything® Running Book

## TRAVEL

Everything® **Family Guide to Coastal Florida**
Everything® Family Guide to Cruise Vacations
Everything® Family Guide to Hawaii
Everything® Family Guide to Las Vegas, 2nd Ed.
Everything® Family Guide to Mexico
Everything® Family Guide to New York City, 2nd Ed.
Everything® Family Guide to RV Travel & Campgrounds
Everything® Family Guide to the Caribbean
Everything® **Family Guide to the Disneyland® Resort, California Adventure®, Universal Studios®, and the Anaheim Area, 2nd Ed.**
Everything® **Family Guide to the Walt Disney World Resort®, Universal Studios®, and Greater Orlando, 5th Ed.**
Everything® Family Guide to Timeshares
Everything® Family Guide to Washington D.C., 2nd Ed.

## WEDDINGS

Everything® Bachelorette Party Book, $9.95
Everything® Bridesmaid Book, $9.95
Everything® Destination Wedding Book
Everything® Elopement Book, $9.95
Everything® Father of the Bride Book, $9.95
Everything® Groom Book, $9.95
Everything® Mother of the Bride Book, $9.95
Everything® Outdoor Wedding Book
Everything® Wedding Book, 3rd Ed.
Everything® Wedding Checklist, $9.95
Everything® Wedding Etiquette Book, $9.95
Everything® Wedding Organizer, 2nd Ed., $16.95
Everything® Wedding Shower Book, $9.95
Everything® Wedding Vows Book, $9.95
Everything® Wedding Workout Book
Everything® **Weddings on a Budget Book, 2nd Ed., $9.95**

## WRITING

Everything® Creative Writing Book
Everything® Get Published Book, 2nd Ed.
Everything® Grammar and Style Book
Everything® Guide to Magazine Writing
Everything® Guide to Writing a Book Proposal
Everything® Guide to Writing a Novel
Everything® Guide to Writing Children's Books
Everything® Guide to Writing Copy
Everything® **Guide to Writing Graphic Novels**
Everything® Guide to Writing Research Papers
Everything® Screenwriting Book
Everything® Writing Poetry Book
Everything® Writing Well Book